WAR WITHOUT QUARTER

Colombia and International Humanitarian Law

Human Rights Watch
New York · Washington · London · Brussels

ISBN: 1-56432-187-8
Library of Congress Catalog Card Number: 98-88045

Cover photograph: A woman mourns family members killed in a paramilitary massacre in Barrancabermeja, Santander in 1998. © Agencia Toma

Addresses for Human Rights Watch
350 Fifth Avenue, 34th Floor, New York, NY 10118-3299
Tel: (212) 290-4700, Fax: (212) 736-1300, E-mail: hrwnyc@hrw.org

1522 K Street, N.W., #910, Washington, DC 20005-1202
Tel: (202) 371-6592, Fax: (202) 371-0124, E-mail: hrwdc@hrw.org

33 Islington High Street, N1 9LH London, UK
Tel: (171) 713-1995, Fax: (171) 713-1800, E-mail: hrwatchuk@gn.apc.org

15 Rue Van Campenhout, 1000 Brussels, Belgium
Tel: (2) 732-2009, Fax: (2) 732-0471, E-mail:hrwatcheu@skynet.be

Web Site Address: http://www.hrw.org

Listserv address: To subscribe to the list, send an e-mail message to majordomo@igc.apc.org with "subscribe hrw-news" in the body of the message (leave the subject line blank).

Human Rights Watch is dedicated to
protecting the human rights of people around the world.

We stand with victims and activists to prevent
discrimination, to uphold political freedom, to protect people from inhumane
conduct in wartime, and to bring offenders to justice.

We investigate and expose
human rights violations and hold abusers accountable.

We challenge governments and those who hold power to end abusive practices
and respect international human rights law.

We enlist the public and the international
community to support the cause of human rights for all.

HUMAN RIGHTS WATCH

Human Rights Watch conducts regular, systematic investigations of human rights abuses in some seventy countries around the world. Our reputation for timely, reliable disclosures has made us an essential source of information for those concerned with human rights. We address the human rights practices of governments of all political stripes, of all geopolitical alignments, and of all ethnic and religious persuasions. Human Rights Watch defends freedom of thought and expression, due process and equal protection of the law, and a vigorous civil society; we document and denounce murders, disappearances, torture, arbitrary imprisonment, discrimination, and other abuses of internationally recognized human rights. Our goal is to hold governments accountable if they transgress the rights of their people.

Human Rights Watch began in 1978 with the founding of its Europe and Central Asia division (then known as Helsinki Watch). Today, it also includes divisions covering Africa, the Americas, Asia, and the Middle East. In addition, it includes three thematic divisions on arms, children's rights, and women's rights. It maintains offices in New York, Washington, Los Angeles, London, Brussels, Moscow, Dushanbe, Rio de Janeiro, and Hong Kong. Human Rights Watch is an independent, nongovernmental organization, supported by contributions from private individuals and foundations worldwide. It accepts no government funds, directly or indirectly.

The staff includes Kenneth Roth, executive director; Michele Alexander, development director; Reed Brody, advocacy director; Carroll Bogert, communications director; Cynthia Brown,program director; Barbara Guglielmo, finance and administration director; Jeri Laber special advisor; Lotte Leicht, Brussels office director; Patrick Minges, publications director; Susan Osnos, associate director; Jemera Rone, counsel; Wilder Tayler, general counsel; and Joanna Weschler, United Nations representative. Jonathan Fanton is the chair of the board. Robert L. Bernstein is the founding chair.

The regional directors of Human Rights Watch are Peter Takirambudde, Africa; José Miguel Vivanco, Americas; Sidney Jones, Asia; Holly Cartner, Europe and Central Asia; and Hanny Megally, Middle East and North Africa. The thematic division directors are Joost R. Hiltermann, arms; Lois Whitman, children's; and Regan Ralph, women's.

The members of the board of directors are Jonathan Fanton, chair; Lisa Anderson, Robert L. Bernstein, William Carmichael, Dorothy Cullman, Gina Despres, Irene Diamond, Adrian W. DeWind, Fiona Druckenmiller, Edith Everett, James C. Goodale, Vartan Gregorian, Alice H. Henkin, Stephen L. Kass, Marina Pinto Kaufman, Bruce Klatsky, Harold Hongju Koh, Alexander MacGregor, Josh Mailman, Samuel K. Murumba, Andrew Nathan, Jane Olson, Peter Osnos, Kathleen Peratis, Bruce Rabb, Sigrid Rausing, Anita Roddick, Orville Schell, Sid Sheinberg, Gary G. Sick, Malcolm Smith, Domna Stanton, and Maya Wiley. Robert L. Bernstein is the founding chair of Human Rights Watch.

CONTENTS

ACKNOWLEDGMENTS

We would like to thank the many organizations, governmental offices, and individuals who contributed time, energy, and information to Human Rights Watch during the research and editing of this report. For security reasons, we have chosen not to identify them by name. Without their courage and tenacity, this report could not have been written.

Since 1997, twenty human rights defenders have been murdered in Colombia, among them lawyers, students, writers, human rights researchers, and judicial investigators. Some of them were well known while others had less reknown. But they faced the same danger. Their deaths show that there is no safe place in Colombia so long as atrocity and impunity rule.

We dedicate this report to the memory of two brave and committed Colombians who assisted us in the preparation of this report and risked their lives to defend the rights of all Colombians. Josué Giraldo, co-founder of the Meta Civic Committee for Human Rights, was murdered by an unidentified gunman on October 13, 1996, as we began research for this report. With his colleagues, Giraldo documented dozens of cases involving human rights and international humanitarian law violations in Meta. Jesús María Valle, president of the "Héctor Abad Gómez" Permanent Human Rights Committee of Antioquia, was murdered on February 27, 1998, beside the desk where he had served us coffee weeks earlier. At the time, we were concluding this report. Valle helped document many of the Antioquia cases included in these pages, in particular the ones that took place in and near Ituango, where he had served on the town council.

Giraldo and Valle were valued and dear colleagues and we mourn them.Yet their example and their work convinces us that we should keep fighting for the respect of fundamental values; something that shouldn't be so difficult to achieve.

This report was made available in Spanish with the support of the Kaplan fund and was translated by Juan Luis Guillén and edited by José Miguel Vivanco.

At Human Rights Watch, special thanks are due to Megan Himan and Jessica Galeria for research and production assistance.

GLOSSARY

ACCU- *Autodefensas Campesinas de Córdoba and Urabá*; the Peasant Self-Defense Group of Córdoba and Urabá, a paramilitary group led by the Castaño family in northern Colombia.

AUC- *Autodefensas Unidas de Colombia*; United Self -Defense Groups of Colombia.

auxiliador/a de guerrilla - guerrilla supporter.

CCJ - *Comisión Colombiana de Juristas*; Colombian Commission of Jurists.

CCN - *Comisión de Conciliación Nacional*; National Conciliation Commission.

CIME - *Centro de Inteligencia Militar*; Military Intelligence Center, which centralizes the intelligence services of the Colombian military.

CINEP- *Centro de Investigación y Educación Popular*; Popular Research and Education Center, a Colombian human rights group based in Santafé de Bogotá.

CODHES- *Consultoría para los Derechos Humanos y el Desplazamiento*; Consultancy for Human Rights and the Displaced.

CONVIVIR - *Servicios de Vigilancia y Seguridad Privada*; Special Vigilance and Private Security Services.

CREDHOS - *Comité Regional para la defensa de los Derechos Humanos*; Regional Committee for the Defense of Human Rights, a Colombian human group that covers the Middle Magdalena region and is based in Barrancabermeja, in the department of Santander.

CTI - *Cuerpo Técnico de Investigación*; Technical Investigation Unit, investigators who work for the attorney general's office.

DAS - *Departamento Administrativo de Seguridad*; Administrative Security Department. An investigative police force that operates without uniforms and is administered by Colombia's executive branch. All other police units are administered by the Interior Ministry.

Data Bank - the Data Bank on Political Violence (*Banco de Datos de Violencia Política*) is run by the Intercongregational Commission for Justice and Peace and the Popular Research and Education Center. It compiles information on human rights and international humanitarian law violations.

Defensoría - Public Advocate's Office, the government's public advocate, responsible for protecting the citizenry against abuses of their constitutional rights. The advocate oversees regional and local offices as well as Colombia's corps of public defenders.

DIJIN - *Dirección Nacional de Policía Judicial e Investigación*; Intelligence and Judicial Investigations Bureau of the Police.

ELN- *Ejército de Liberacíon Nacional*; the National Liberation Army.

EPL - *Ejército Popular de Liberación*; Popular Liberation Army.

Esperanza - *Esperanza, Paz y Libertad*; Hope, Peace and Liberty party.

GAD - *Grupo de Apoyo a Desplazados*; Forcibly Displaced Persons Support Group.

FARC - *Fuerzas Armadas Revolucionarias de Colombia*; Revolutionary Armed Forces of Colombia, Colombia's largest insurgency.

FMLN- *Frente Farabundo Martí para la Liberación Nacional*; Farabundo Martí National Liberation Front.

FUNPAZCOR- *Fundación por la Paz de Córdoba*; Foundation for the Peace of Córdoba, a civilian organization with charitable goals founded in 1991 by the family of Carlos Castaño.

ICRC - International Committee of the Red Cross.

IHL - International Humanitarian Law.

JAC - *Junta de Acción Comunal*; Neighborhood Action Committee.

Justice and Peace - *Comisión Intercongregacional de Justicia y Paz*; Intercongregational Commission for Justice and Peace.

MAS - *Muerte a Secuestradores*; Death to Kidnappers. MAS was formed by drug traffickers in 1981. The name was also adopted by army-organized paramilitaries in the Middle Magdalena region, some of which later allied with drug traffickers. The name is now generic and is used throughout Colombia by some paramilitary groups.

Mine Ban Treaty - Convention on the Use, Stockpiling, Production, and Transfer of Anti-Personnel Mines and On their Destruction.

MINGA - *Asociación para la Promoción Social Alternativa*; Association for Alternative Social Development, Colombian human rights group. *Minga* is a Quechua term meaning collective work.

OAS - Organization of American States.

OIA - *Organización Indígena de Antioquia*; Antioquia Indigenous Organization.

personeros - municipal officials charged with receiving complaints about rights abuses from the citizenry.

polacheras - name used for girls who flirt with or date local soldiers and police officers.

Procuraduría - Internal Affairs, the government agency responsible for investigating reports of crimes by government employees and recommending administrative punishment like suspensions, fines and dismissals. Within the agency, specific divisions are responsible for investigating the abuses of various branches of government. They include the Delegate for the Armed Forces and the Delegate for the Police Forces. The Delegate for Human Rights investigates reports linking state agents to forced disappearance, torture, and massacres, defined as the killing of four or more people by the same individuals and at the same time. However, Internal Affairs can only recommend administrative, not criminal sanctions.

retenido - retained.

SIJIN - *Seccional de Policía Judicial*; Sectional Judicial Police.

toma/s - indiscriminate attacks, including temporary seizure of towns.

tomberas - see *polacheras*.

Twentieth Brigade - unit of the Colombian Army which centralized military intelligence.

UC-ELN - *Unión Camilista-Ejército de Liberación Nacional*; Camilista Union National Liberation Army.

Caribbean
Sea

La Guajira

Atlántico

Magdalena

Cesar

Gulf of
Urabá

PANAMA

Córdoba

Turbo

Sucre

Bolívar

Norte
de
Santander

VENEZUELA

Cúcuta

Caracas

Pacific

Ocean

Antioquia

Dabeiba

Barrancabermeja

Bucaramanga

Arauca

Medellín

Chocó

Rionegro

Santander

Puerto Carreño

Caldas

Risaralda

Manizales

Boyacá

Cundinamarca

Casanare

Vichada

Quindío

Bogotá

L L A N O S

Valle del
Cauca

Cali

Tolima

Distrito
Especial

Meta

Guainía

Huila

Cauca

San Jose
del Guaviare

Guaviare

Nariño

Florencia

Miraflores

Vaupés

Quito

Putumayo

Caquetá

ECUADOR

Amazonas

BRAZIL

PERU

| miles | |
| 0 | 250 |

| kilometers | |
| 0 | 250 |

NORTH

COLOMBIA

©1998 Michael S. Miller

I. SUMMARY AND RECOMMENDATIONS

Violations of international humanitarian law —the laws of war— are not abstract concepts in Colombia, but the grim material of everyday life. War bursts into the daily activities of a farm, a village, a public bus, or a school with the speed of armed fighters arriving down a path or in four-wheel drive vehicles. Sometimes, armed men carefully choose their victims from lists. Other times, they simply kill those nearby, to spread fear. Indeed, a willingness to commit atrocities is among the most striking features of Colombia's war.

The inauguration of a new president and the growth of a broad-based civic movement that has called for a just and fair peace have given Colombians new hope for an end to political violence. Indeed, civilians lead the effort to convince the parties to respect the laws of war and negotiate an end to the conflict.

Some communities thrust into the conflict have attempted to negotiate local accords with combatants as a way of protecting their civilian populations. Nevertheless, none of the parties to the conflict have fully respected these decisions. Indeed, negotiations have been doomed in large part by the failure to address fundamental issues, including impunity for violations of human rights and international humanitarian law.

Just as Colombia's war has no set battlefields, so does it lack safe haven. In traditional wars, civilians can flee the front lines in the hopes of saving their lives and the lives of their loved ones. But Colombia's war has no quarter, which in the strict definition means mercy or shelter.

That must change. Human Rights Watch holds all parties to the conflict in Colombia responsible for upholding the laws of war, which seek to protect human life in the midst of armed conflict. In doing so, we imply no political recognition, status, or approval for any armed group. Our goal is to promote these international standards as a way of saving lives and minimizing human suffering even in the midst of war.

The laws of war applicable to the armed conflict in Colombia are: Common Article 3 of the Geneva Conventions of 1949, which addresses armed confrontations between relatively organized armed forces or armed groups occurring exclusively within the territory of a particular state; Protocol II Additional to the Geneva Conventions, which applies to non-international armed conflict where insurgent forces are highly organized and is meant to protect civilians and captured combatants; and customary international law, which results from a general and consistent practice of states followed by a sense of legal obligation. Where necessary, we refer to other legal instruments, like Protocol I,

1

and relevant commentaries for authoritative guidance on terms or situations left unexplained by these central texts. Although Protocol I was drawn up to apply to international armed conflicts, many of its detailed norms have acquired the status of customary international law. We include Common Article 3 and Protocol II in Appendix I.

Few seriously question that Colombia's war satisfies the conditions for the application of the laws of war. In interviews with Human Rights Watch, all of the parties to the conflict agreed in principle that the laws of war should be observed in Colombia.

Yet the distance between words and deeds is vast. All parties actively manipulate the concept of international humanitarian law for perceived political and tactical gain. There is also deep disagreement about the terms used in the laws of war to identify non-combatants and military targets. While some disagreement may be the subject of honest debate, much of the opposition to the full compliance with laws of war in Colombia is a cynical justification for continued, deliberate, and atrocious violations of the minimum standards necessary to protect human life.

This report is divided by party to the conflict, beginning with the Colombian army, National Police, and "Special Vigilance and Private Security Services" (Servicios de Vigilancia y Seguridad Privada, or CONVIVIR); paramilitaries allied as the United Self-Defense Group of Colombia (Autodefensas Unidas de Colombia, AUC); and Colombia's three largest guerrilla groups, the Revolutionary Armed Forces of Colombia (Fuerzas Armadas Revolucionarias de Colombia, FARC), the National Liberation Army (Unión Camilista-Ejército de Liberación Nacional, UC-ELN), and the Popular Liberation Army (Ejército Popular de Liberación, EPL).

The Colombian army teaches its officers the basics of international humanitarian law and makes instructional material available to officers, professional soldiers, and recruits. Some commanders emphasize the importance of human rights and international humanitarian law to field officers and their men. Nevertheless, after examining hundreds of cases and interviewing many officers, government investigators, and civilians who have witnessed violations, Human Rights Watch concludes that the army continues to engage in serious violations of the laws of war, with little apparent will to investigate or punish those responsible. At the root of these violations is the Colombian army's consistent and profound failure or refusal to properly distinguish civilians from combatants.

Types of army violations vary according to region and unit. In eastern Colombia, where paramilitaries are weak or have yet to fully penetrate, the army is directly implicated in the killing of non-combatants and fighters who have surrendered or been taken prisoner (defined by the Geneva Conventions as *hors de combat)*, torture, and threats. In the rest of the country, where paramilitaries have a pronounced presence, the army fails to move against them and tolerates their activity, including egregious violations of international humanitarian law; provides some paramilitary groups with intelligence used to carry out operations; and in other cases actively promotes and coordinates with paramilitary units, including joint maneuvers in which atrocities are the frequent result.

The National Police has also incorporated the language of human rights and international humanitarian law in its official discourse and conducts regular training on international standards for its agents. In general, police commanders are more responsive than their military counterparts to reports of violations by their members and act more readily to investigate abuses.

Nevertheless, police agents continue to be implicated in violations. Most frequent are cases where officers capture suspects and execute them. In areas where paramilitaries are present, some police officers have been directly implicated in joint army-paramilitary actions or have supplied information to paramilitaries for their death lists. Police have also stood by while paramilitaries selected and killed their victims.

On many occasions, police have publicly described whole communities as guerrillas or sympathetic to them and have withdrawn police protection, a violation of their responsibility under Colombian law to protect civilians from harm. Instead of reinforcing the police after guerrilla attacks, police commanders have withdrawn officers, thus encouraging or allowing paramilitaries to move in unimpeded and kill civilians.

We conclude the section on state violations with CONVIVIRs. CONVIVIRs are licensed by the government and led by civilians who are supposed to engage in self-defense and as a rapid-response network against guerrilla attacks. Several CONVIVIRs have taken a direct role in hostilities, attacking guerrillas and closely coordinating with the army and police in operations.

Human Rights Watch believes CONVIVIRs dangerously blur the distinction between civilians and combatants, putting all civilians at risk of attack. In addition, the government has failed to effectively supervise and control CONVIVIRs, and some have murdered civilians and threatened them with death. In some cases described in this report, CONVIVIRs have used government-supplied weapons to commit these violations. Like other perpetrators of political violence in Colombia, most CONVIVIR members implicated in abuses have largely gone uninvestigated and unpunished.

At the time of this writing, there are at least seven paramilitary groups allied under the name AUC: the Peasant Self-Defense Group of Córdoba and Urabá (Autodefensas Campesinas de Córdoba and Urabá, ACCU), the largest and most public group; the Eastern Plains Self-Defense Group (Autodefensas de los Llanos Orientales, also known as Los Carranceros, after their leader, Víctor Carranza); the Cesar Self-Defense Group (Autodefensas del Cesar); the Middle Magdalena Self-Defense Group (Autodefensas del Magdalena Medio), the group with the longest history; the Santander and Southern Cesar Self-Defense Group (Autodefensas de Santander y el sur del Cesar); the Casanare Self-Defense Group (Autodefensas del Casanare); and the Cundinamarca Self-Defense Group (Autodefensas de Cundinamarca).

Although AUC units operate frequently in direct coordination with the Colombian security forces, the AUC also acts independently and has a separate command structure, source of weapons and supplies, and operations planning. When paramilitaries commit violations in coordination with state agents, like the army, we hold both the state agent and paramilitaries responsible for the violation.

The AUC leader, Carlos Castaño, has repeatedly stated a willingness to pledge his forces to respect the laws of war, which, if put into practice, would be an advance in protecting human life. However, Castaño has also argued that the nature of Colombia's war — with many combatants out of uniform and without any identification — makes strict standards difficult if not impossible to apply. Instead, he has advocated a "creole" version of international humanitarian law that contradicts a central principle of the laws of war: the protection of fighters who have surrendered, been captured, or otherwise been rendered defenseless.

After a detailed review of cases and on-site interviews, including one with Carlos Castaño, Human Rights Watch has concluded that far from attempting to respect the laws of war, the AUC depends on the explicit, deliberate, and systematic violation of these standards in order to wage war. Government investigators, church officials, humanitarian aid groups, and victims of AUC attacks also agree that the AUC pays only lip service to the protections contained in Common Article 3 and Protocol II. The AUC repeatedly and unequivocally flouts international standards by committing massacres, killing civilians and combatants *hors de combat*, and engaging in torture, the mutilation of corpses, death threats, forced displacement, hostage-taking, arbitrary detention, and looting, among other violations.

During our investigation, Human Rights Watch found no evidence that the FARC, Colombia's largest guerrilla group, has made an attempt to conform its methods to international standards. When the FARC perceives a political advantage, it showcases observance of international humanitarian law. However, in dozens of other cases where no political advantage is apparent, the FARC flagrantly violates the laws of war. Among the violations we document here are massacres and targeted killings of civilians, the killing of combatants *hors de combat*, torture, hostage-taking, looting, and attacks on non-military targets like ambulances. Repeatedly, the FARC denies involvement in violations even when evidence of their responsibility is overwhelming.

For their part, the UC-ELN was among the first insurgent groups in Colombia to begin an internal discussion of international humanitarian law. Even as Colombia refused to adopt Protocol II, the UC-ELN called for negotiations aimed at "humanizing" political conflict. However, this openness to negotiation as yet is not reflected in behavior in the field. Indeed, the UC-ELN strongly disputes the terms of international humanitarian law, at times to justify tactics that are clear violations, and openly flouts these standards in the field. In this report, we document the targeted killing of civilians, the killing of combatants *hors de combat*, torture, the executions of patients in hospitals, hostage-taking, and indiscriminate attacks, including attacks on civilian homes, hospitals, and public buses, and the use of land mines. In addition, the UC-ELN violates the ban on attacking non-military targets by systematically bombing Colombia's oil pipelines in order to extort money from oil companies and press a political point.

The EPL told Human Rights Watch that it respects international humanitarian law, with certain exceptions. For instance, the EPL allows its forces to execute people for participation in paramilitary groups. Such exceptions confirm that in fact, the EPL engages in political killings dressed up as some form of justice. Human Rights Watch also documents EPL violations like the killing of family members of guerrilla deserters and combatants *hors de combat*, hostage-taking, and attacks on non-military targets, like public buses.

We close the report with two types of violations committed by all sides in the conflict: the recruitment of children under fifteen years of age and forced displacement, both prohibited by the laws of war.

Article 4 (3) (c) of Protocol II prohibits the recruitment of children under the age of fifteen or allowing them to take part in hostilities. In addition to domestic legislation protecting the rights of children, Colombia has ratified the Convention on the Rights of the Child, which fixes a minimum recruitment age of fifteen.

Human Rights Watch fully supports the adoption of an optional protocol to the United Nations Convention on the Rights of the Child to raise the minimum age for recruitment and participation in hostilities from fifteen to eighteen. Persons under the age of eighteen have not reached physical or psychological maturity and are ill-prepared to face the harsh conditions of warfare. Many who have volunteered or who have been forced to serve emerge at the end of hostilities physically and psychologically scarred by their experience and unprepared to live in and contribute to a peaceful society. Even more than their adult counterparts, these children require extensive social and psychological rehabilitation after involvement in hostilities.

Moreover, the indirect participation of children in hostilities should also be outlawed. Children who serve in support functions for armed groups are often subsequently drawn into direct participation. This is particularly true in the case of conflicts like Colombia's.

Forced displacement of the civilian population is expressly prohibited by Article 17 of Protocol II. Unless civilians must move for their own security or a clear military imperative, the text states, combatants cannot order or force them to move. Nevertheless, in Colombia, all forces provoke displacements without any regard for international humanitarian law. Currently, over one million Colombians have reportedly been displaced by violence. Chief among the causes of forced displacement are violations of human rights and the laws of war. Forced displacement often results from indiscriminate attacks, the terror caused by massacres, selective killings, torture, and threats.

Recommendations

To all of the parties

- All parties should immediately instruct their combatants to strictly adhere to Common Article 3 of the Geneva Conventions and Protocol II. These minimum standards apply automatically to all groups engaged in Colombia's armed conflict; no negotiation is necessary to apply them. The following recommendations based on these standards reflect the type of violations all of the parties to the conflict are engaged in. Other recommendations pertinent to some, but not all, of the groups are included in separate recommendations made to each party. Specifically we recommend:

  - an end to the killing of non-combatants, regardless of the imposition of purported "death sentences." Protected are not only civilians who take no direct role in hostilities, but also civilians whose political opinions may be partisan;

  - an end to the killing of combatants *hors de combat*;

  - an end to torture;

- an end to the mutilation of cadavers;

- an end to death threats against civilians, including the threat to consider civilians a "military target";

- an end to attacks on religious and health personnel carrying out duties protected by the laws of war;

- respect for structures or vehicles marked with the red cross;

■ All forces should cease using, importing, producing, and stockpiling land mines, by definition indiscriminate weapons outlawed by the laws of war.

■ Human Rights Watch supports the adoption of an optional protocol to the United Nations Convention on the Rights of the Child to raise the minimum age for recruitment and participation in hostilities from fifteen to eighteen, and calls on the parties to the conflict to immediately take all appropriate measures to prevent recruitment of persons under the age of eighteen.

■ The prohibition on children's participation in hostilities should not be narrowly focused on "direct" participation, but should include children's participation in support services, since children who serve in this capacity are often subsequently drawn into direct participation.

■ All sides should eliminate practices that provoke forced displacement should instruct their combatants to avoid such practices.

■ All sides should adopt clear rules for mounting roadblocks to avoid civilian casualties. Combatants should be clearly instructed that on-the-spot executions at roadblocks are prohibited in all cases.

■ Attacks against democratically-elected officials, election candidates, and others for voicing a political opinion must be stopped. We call on all parties to the conflict to cease targeting civilians simply because they have voiced a controversial or partisan opinion.

■   The parties to the conflict should negotiate the following points as priorities:

- a mechanism to improve the location and identification of persons reported "disappeared," wounded, or killed in action, and assist in efforts to evacuate protected individuals from combat areas;

- a mechanism to establish demilitarized zones in combat areas for the protection of civilians and the treatment of the wounded;

- a mechanism to properly identify and mark health and religious buildings, historical and cultural monuments, and areas of dangerous forces such as dams or nuclear electrical generating stations since, according to Article 15 of Protocol II, these areas are protected from attack. Combatants should be instructed to refrain from attacking these installations. The education of the population about the meaning of these international symbols should go on at the same time.

■   All parties should formally invite the International Fact-Finding Commission established by the Geneva Conventions to come to Colombia to begin investigating reports of laws of war violations.

■   All parties should adopt clear rules of engagement that reflect the laws of war. Commanders should be required to assess planned attacks in light of the laws of war and demonstrate to their superiors that there will be no excessive damage to civilians. If evidence emerges showing that a violation has occurred, we encourage the parties to immediately share evidence with the International Fact-finding Commission.

To the Colombian government

■   The Colombian government must end the tolerance on the part of the security forces for paramilitaries and end any sharing of intelligence or logistical support for them. Officers who promote or coordinate with paramilitaries and go on joint maneuvers with them should be prosecuted and punished by civilian courts.

- Human rights defenders are among those most at risk in Colombia. We call on the Colombian government to take immediate steps to protect the lives of human rights defenders, conducting thorough and credible investigations into links between the army's Twentieth Brigade and the killings of Eduardo Umaña and Jesús María Valle. Also, the government should open security force intelligence files to outside and independent review, to ensure that reports that criminalize legitimate human rights work are removed.

- Armed forces officers against whom there are credible accusations of human rights and laws of war violations should be suspended immediately pending a serious and credible investigation. Should merit be found to the accusations, these officers should be tried in civilian courts, not military tribunals, in accordance with a 1997 Constitutional Court ruling.

- Important cases involving officers accused of serious human rights and laws of war violations have never been properly investigated or prosecuted in Colombia in part because the statute of limitations governing internal investigations by the executive branch's Internal Affairs Division (Procuraduría) has precluded action. The government should repeal all statutes of limitations on these serious crimes for both administrative and criminal proceedings.

- The Colombian government should actively promote the enactment of legislation that fully addresses continuing impunity in Colombia, including a military penal code reform, legislation making the act of forcibly disappearing someone a crime, legislation severely penalizing torture, and legislation that formally recognizes the office of the Human Rights Unit within the Attorney General's Office and allocates to that office sufficient funding to aggressively identify and investigate cases involving human rights and laws of war violations.

- The Colombian government should propose, strongly support, fully implement, and vigorously uphold legislation that makes violations of international humanitarian law punishable in Colombia.

- The administration of President Andrés Pastrana should immediately repeal legislation that violates Colombia's obligations under the laws of war, including the legislation establishing regional courts, which fail to ensure the due process guarantees required by Article 6 of Protocol II and human rights treaties ratified by Colombia such as the American Convention on Human Rights and the International Covenant on Civil and Political Rights. No new cases should be sent to regional courts. The government should appoint an independent commission chaired by the attorney general to review existing convictions. If due process violations are found after extensive review, mistrials should be declared and the cases should be retried in proceedings where due process is guaranteed.

- The government-sponsored CONVIVIRs dangerously blur the line between civilian and combatant and have committed serious and repeated human rights and laws of war violations. So far, reforms have not addressed the fundamental problems of control and accountability. Therefore, all such groups should be disbanded and their government-supplied weapons seized.

- We call on President Pastrana to make clear his unequivocal support for civil authority in Colombia. In particular, elected governors, mayors, town council members, and civic leaders should not be made the targets of military surveillance unless an independent judicial authority has confirmed that there is convincing evidence of a crime having been committed.

- Human Rights Watch calls on Colombia to ratify the Convention on the Prohibition of the Use, Stockpiling, Production, and Transfer of Anti-Personnel Mines and on Their Destruction (hereinafter Mine Ban Treaty) as soon as possible and to abide by the treaty until ratification. In the interim, Colombia should begin destruction of its stockpiled antipersonnel mines and should begin the process of identifying, marking, monitoring, and clearing its mined areas.

- Colombia should reform the laws governing military recruitment and bring them into accord with the emerging international consensus on banning the recruitment of children under eighteen. In addition, the government should repeal Law 81, which allows guerrillas, including children, to turn themselves in and serve their sentences in military barracks instead of in prisons. Often, this results in forced recruitment of the children into military service; these individuals, also called "guides," have been repeatedly coerced into or forced to take part in military and joint military-paramilitary operations.

■   The Colombian security forces must be professionalized. Success of this endeavor should be measured by a significant decrease in international humanitarian law violations, such as killing of civilians and combatants *hors de combat*, torture of detainees, and death threats. Moreover, any measure of success must include severing all military ties with paramilitaries and aggressive efforts to apprehend those wanted for these criminal activities. In addition to the reform of the military penal code, we believe the following measures are crucial for the professionalization of the security forces:

- the government should commission an independent study to determine to what degree troops now in the field understand their responsibilities under Common Article 3 and Protocol II. This study should include visits to military installations, on-site evaluation of operations, and interviews with officers and troops in conditions that favor a candid conversation. Informants should be asked to respond to hypothetical questions typical of the Colombian conflict to assess their ability to understand the complexities of the application of the laws of war. If it is found, as we suspect, that officers and soldiers are not aware of their responsibilities, the government should immediately implement training in coordination with the International Committee of the Red Cross (ICRC) to fully acquaint soldiers with their responsibilities. A priority should be made for commanders and field-grade officers who operate in high conflict areas;

- all manuals used to teach war tactics should be opened to review to insure that the laws of war are properly taught. Much of the material distributed by the government and armed forces simply repeats Common Article 3 and Protocol II, without giving case examples specific to Colombia that would allow security force officers and government officials to accurately describe and characterize violations. Many of those who need education in the laws of war are not legal professionals and need real-life examples in order to put the principles to the test. The review committee should be an independent one chaired by the

Attorney General's Office and including representatives from the Public Advocate's Office, the ICRC, the office of the U.N. High Commissioner for Human Rights, and human rights groups as well as internationally recognized experts;

- to advance their careers, officers must be required to pass a test in the laws of war to demonstrate their understanding of the principles and their practical application. In addition, their record in the field of observing the laws of war should be another important element in considering promotion.

■ The UC-ELN frequently attacks Colombia's oil pipeline to extort money and make a political point about its opposition to the way Colombia deals with the multinational corporations. Often, the government alleges that the oil spills that result do lasting damage to the water and soil that farmers depend on for their survival which, if true, would also violate Article 14 of Protocol II. However, there is little information about the environmental effect of oil spills caused by attacks on the oil pipeline. Human Rights Watch urges the government to commission a scientific study of the environmental and health damage of oil spills to better understand their effect on the civilian population.

■ The government should take immediate steps to fully implement Law 387, which provides for protection and assistance to the forcibly displaced. The protection of human rights and the observance of the laws of war are essential components of any acceptable and long-term solution to the problem of displacement, and all future legislation to address forced displacement should fully incorporate these principles.

■ The government should support the return of the forcibly displaced to their homes only when the safety of these civilians is fully assured and they return voluntarily.

■ The Colombian government should implement United Nations and Inter-American Commission on Human Rights recommendations regarding the continuing high level of human rights and laws of war violations.

To the AUC, the FARC, the UC-ELN, and the EPL

■   The AUC and guerrillas have failed to respect the most fundamental principles that characterize an independent and impartial tribunal, in accordance with Article 6 of Protocol II. Therefore, these groups should stop the practice of carrying out "sentences" based on these illegal and abhorrent procedures.

■   These parties to the conflict should negotiate a mechanism to safely release combatants taken *hors de combat.*

■   The AUC and guerrillas should unilaterally and unconditionally end the practice of hostage-taking.

■   All parties should declare publicly their intent to abide by the terms of the Mine Ban Treaty and to cease the use, stockpiling, production, and transfer of anti-personnel mines, and destroy their remaining supplies.

To the international community

■   We urge the office of the United Nations High Commissioner for Human Rights to continue its important work documenting reports of human rights and laws of war violations in Colombia.

■   We encourage Francis Deng, the special representative of the United Nations Secretary General on Forced Displacement, to return to Colombia for a follow-up visit.

To the government of Panama

■   We call on the government of Panama to abide by its commitments under the Convention on the Status of Refugees and cease forcibly deporting Colombian refugees.

To the European Union

■   The European Union has a moral as well as a formal obligation under the terms of its cooperation agreement with Colombia to continue pressing the authorities and all parties to the conflict to stop the abuse of civilians in Colombia and to insist on accountability for abuses.

- The European Union should increase funding to the European Community Humanitarian Office (ECHO) to assist forcibly displaced communities in Colombia. In addition, the European Commission should increase funds to non-governmental human rights organizations and allocate funds to the Human Rights Unit of the Attorney General's Office to strengthen their work in documenting human rights and laws of war violations in Colombia.

To the United States

- The United States has a special role to play in Colombia because of its close ties with and aid to the security forces. Upholding respect for human rights and the laws of war should be a central part of U.S. policy in Colombia.

- The U.S. government should continue enforcing Section 570 of the Foreign Operations Appropriations Act, the so-called Leahy amendment, and should strengthen its monitoring of military units that receive U.S. military aid. The Leahy amendment prohibits funds from being provided to any unit of the security forces of a foreign country if the secretary of state has credible evidence that such unit has committed gross violations of human rights, unless the secretary determines and reports to the congressional committees on appropriations that the government involved is taking effective measures to bring the responsible members of the security forces unit to justice. In an important and welcome move, the State Department has chosen to apply the spirit of the Leahy amendment broadly, to include all types of aid, including presidential drawdowns. These conditions have played an important role in sending a strong message to the Colombian security forces that the United States considers respect for human rights a key part of bilateral relations. That message needs to be strengthened by aggressive U.S. monitoring of units that receive aid, including ensuring that soldiers accused of committing abuses are fully investigated and, if believed responsible, prosecuted by an independent and competent court. The procedures used to monitor these units must not be kept secret; transparency is a key part of any mechanism meant to monitor the compliance of an institution, like the Colombian military, that has amassed such a horrifying human rights record.

■   The U.S. Defense Department's training and equipping of Colombian security force units should be cleared through the procedures established for the Leahy amendment. At present, such procedures are not applied by the Defense Department for these activities. Human Rights Watch believes that U.S. policy must be consistent in its support for human rights and international humanitarian law, and that all U.S. security assistance, including training, should be subject to the Leahy amendment.

■   To strengthen the rule of law and promote human rights, we encourage the United States to publicly support the Human Rights Unit of the Attorney General's Office, and in addition, allocate funds to support their work.

■   The United States should reform its drug certification process and ensure that it continues to allow and fund courses on human rights and international humanitarian law even when a country is decertified.

II. COLOMBIA AND INTERNATIONAL HUMANITARIAN LAW

The local priest was first to challenge the darkness in Guintar by stringing Christmas lights from the church steeple. Then someone hung lights above a nearby door and window. On the December 1997 day Human Rights Watch visited this village of 2,000 in central Colombia, Robert Jaramillo (not his real name) opened his coffee shop for the first time in four months, and light from this single door spilled onto a lovely, deserted, and dark central square.

Several months earlier, armed men had seized Guintar and accused its residents of supporting leftist insurgents. The men forced everyone from their homes, residents told us, then chose one local man and cut off his nose. One of the men told Jaramillo and other store owners that if they opened again, he would return, cut them open alive, and string their entrails from the manicured bushes in the square. The reason? Store owners were suspected of having sold food and medicine to the leftist insurgents who have operated in these dry mountains for decades.

Weeks later, guerrillas entered Guintar and vowed that their enemies would never win. To underscore their power, they killed the mayor, a town councilman, and a resident of the nearby town of Anzá, accused of supporting their enemies. Seven families left Guintar the next day, joining the thousands forced to flee their homes because of political violence in Colombia.

Jaramillo, though, holds on. He says he has no choice. "I have eleven people in my family, so how are we supposed to live?" Jaramillo asked Human Rights Watch near his store. The only one to reopen since August, Jaramillo knew he was risking his life and the lives of his family to reprisals. A mixture of fury, fear, and humiliation twisted his boyish features. "The minute we see them coming again, we are going to run for our lives."

The drama of Guintar is repeated throughout Colombia, where war is not fought primarily between armed and uniformed combatants on battlefields, but against the civilian population and in their homes, farms, and towns. Many of the victims of Colombia's war wear no uniform, hold no gun, and profess no allegiance to any armed group. Indeed, battles between armed opponents are the exception.

16

Instead, combatants deliberately and implacably target and kill the civilians they believe support their enemies, whether or not the civilians are even aware that they are in peril.

It is store owners like Jaramillo, truck drivers, farmers, teachers, doctors, community leaders, food vendors, and washerwomen who run the highest risks in today's Colombia.[1]

As much as a battle for control over territory, Colombia's conflict is one waged on the hearts and minds of its people, a cruel inversion of the Vietnam War-era strategy of winning the population's support. In Colombia, there is often no attempt to win allegiance, only punish it as it is perceived by men with guns.

In some wars, civilians can flee the front lines in the hopes of saving their lives and the lives of their loved ones. But there are no front lines in Colombia. According to the office of the Colombian High Commissioner for Peace, which represents the executive in peace negotiations with guerrillas and paramilitaries, Colombia's three guerrilla groups and paramilitaries are present in over half of Colombia's 1,067 municipalities.[2] Colombia's war has no quarter, which in the strict definition means mercy or safe haven.

In the words of former Apartadó mayor Gloria Cuartas, "This war is total... unofficial and waged in disguise."

Witnesses may later describe assailants as uniformed, which can identify any combatant, since all can wear military-style uniforms. In other cases, however, those same combatants wear civilian clothing. Occasionally, investigators examine the type of atrocity itself to determine probable responsibilities, since some armed groups have a reputation for particular horrors. Yet Human Rights Watch has also

---

[1]In this report, we use the terms "civilian" and "non-combatant" interchangeably to mean an individual who does not participate directly in hostilities. For other examples of where and how Human Rights Watch has applied the laws of war, see Robert Kogod Goldman, "International Humanitarian Law: Americas Watch's Experience in Monitoring Internal Armed Conflicts," *The American University Journal of International Law and Policy*, Vol. 9, No. 1, Fall 1993, pp. 56-65. See also Human Rights Watch, *Civilian Pawns: Laws of War Violations and the Use of Weapons on the Israel-Lebanon Border* (New York: Human Rights Watch, May 1996) and *Weapons transfers and Violations of the Laws of War in Turkey* (New York: Human Rights Watch, November 1995).

[2]"Violencia política," *Semana*, April 1, 1997.

received credible reports that parties to the conflict have committed unusual atrocities deliberately, to implicate their enemies.[3]

Indeed, the use of extreme means and a willingness to deliberate atrocity to send a swift message are among the most striking features of Colombia's war. Combatants speak to their enemies and the population at large in a language made up entirely of bodies, not sounds.

Despite increased attention to human rights and the laws of war, the toll of Colombia's war on the civilian population intensified in 1997. According to the Colombian Commission of Jurists (Comisión Colombiana de Juristas, CCJ), a human rights group that compiles information on human rights and international humanitarian law violations, 2,183 people were killed for political reasons in Colombia that year.[4]

Killings peak around political events, like elections. In the months preceding the October 1997 municipal elections, for example, 110 mayors, town council members, and candidates were killed for political reasons.[5] According to the Colombian Federation of Municipalities, at least forty-five mayors were kidnapped in 1997, most by guerrillas who threatened them in exchange for political concessions or to force them to resign.[6]

"The death penalty does not exist in Colombia, but more people are executed here than in the United States, except without a trial," one massacre survivor told Human Rights Watch. "The reason is that people have different ideas, nothing more. For that reason, you are given a sentence of death."[7]

In cases where a perpetrator is known, 67 percent of these killings in 1997 were attributed by the CCJ to paramilitaries, 20 percent were attributed to

---

[3]Human Rights Watch interviews with humanitarian aid workers, Apartadó, Antioquia, July 5-7, 1996.

[4]This figure does not include combatants killed in combat, recorded at 1,250 for 1997. This a low estimate since many guerrillas and paramilitaries killed in combat are never reported. CCJ, statistical summary, 1997.

[5]Héctor Torres, "Apuntes sobre las elecciones," *Utopías*, Año V, No. 50, November-December 1997, pp. 8-10.

[6]Letter to Human Rights Watch from Gilberto Toro Giraldo, Colombian Federation of Municipalities, February 5, 1998.

[7]Human Rights Watch interview with El Tomate survivors, Montería, Córdoba, October 16, 1992.

guerrillas, and 3 percent to state agents. Many of the paramilitary killings, however, were carried out with the tolerance or active participation of the security forces, particularly the army.[8]

Most victims of political killings are men. Women and children dominate the ranks of the forcibly displaced. Guerrillas, state agents, and paramilitaries have on occasion killed women because they were family members of a perceived enemy or because they investigated the death of a relative or colleague.[9]

"One woman whose husband had been taken by paramilitaries received a visit five days later, from the same men," one humanitarian aid worker told us. "They asked why she was still living in the house. That day, she abandoned it along with her five children."[10]

Combatants also target civilians because of their occupation. The most dangerous professions are often the most quotidian, like store owner, bus driver, street vendor, or teacher. What is key is that the occupation brings or appears to bring the civilian in contact with an adversary. For example, Jesús María Barrenechea Zuleta, an elementary school teacher who worked near Chigorodó, Antioquia, was seized from his home by ACCU members on February 3, 1996, and reportedly threatened for "recruiting boys for the guerrillas." After his release, he refused to leave his home. Three days later, residents discovered his mutilated corpse in a pasture outside town.[11]

Defending human rights is also a dangerous profession. In 1997, fifteen human rights defenders were murdered, among them *personeros*, the municipal officials charged with receiving complaints about rights abuses from the citizenry. Among the most dangerous departments for human rights work is Antioquia.[12]

---

[8]These statistics reflect only reported cases with a presumed responsible party. An estimated 19 percent of reported cases are without an alleged perpetrator. CCJ, statistical summary, 1997.

[9]Human Rights Watch interviews in Antioquia, June 1-6, 1996.

[10]Human Rights Watch interview with humanitarian aid worker, Apartadó, Antioquia, July 6, 1996.

[11]CCJ, *Colombia, Derechos Humanos y Derecho Humanitario: 1996* (Santafé de Bogotá: Colombian Commission of Jurists, 1997), pp. 28-29.

[12]The list was compiled by the CCJ in March 1998.

The killings continued as this report went to press. On February 27, 1998, three assassins gunned down human rights lawyer Jesús María Valle, president of the "Héctor Abad Gómez" Permanent Committee for Human Rights in Antioquia, in his Medellín office. He was the fourth president of the committee killed since 1987. Less that two months later, three assassins killed human rights lawyer Eduardo Umaña in his Bogotá apartment.[13] Government investigators believe both killings may be the work of the Colombian army's Twentieth Brigade, recently disbanded because of human rights violations.[14]

Location can also condemn civilians. One government investigator termed it the "McCarthyization" of entire towns.[15] For instance, a 1997 government intelligence report Human Rights Watch reviewed identified all of the residents of Recetor, Casanare, as guerrillas or their collaborators, simply because they lived in an area where guerrillas operate.[16]

"Entire towns have been written off as belonging to one side or another, putting them at risk of attack," according to Álvaro Gómez, the former Antioquia public advocate (Defensoría).[17]

Even the most ordinary civilian chore can suddenly turn deadly. Boarding a bus, buying beef, or sharing a meal can compromise civilians in the eyes of combatants. At a routine army roadblock in the department of Arauca on July 20, 1996, for example, soldiers informed the driver of an interstate bus carrying twenty-six passengers that guerrillas were in the area. Despite the obvious risk to

---

[13]Human Rights Watch telephone interview with "Héctor Abad Gómez" Permanent Committee for Human Rights in Antioquia, February 27, 1998; and Public Declaration, Corporación Colectivo de Abogados "José Alvear Restrepo," April 18, 1998.

[14]Human Rights Watch interviews with government investigators, Santafé de Bogotá, May 7-8, 1998.

[15]Human Rights Watch interview with government authority, Medellín, Antioquia, July 2, 1996.

[16]The report was filed by the Administrative Security Department (Departamento Administrativo de Seguridad, DAS), attached to the executive branch of Colombia's government and similar to the American Federal Bureau of Investigation (FBI). Oficio No. 2090, signed by Marco Andronio Girón Zorrilla, Intelligence Chief Coordinator, DAS, Seccional Casanare, May 2, 1996; and Human Rights Watch interviews in Yopal, Casanare, February 7, 1997.

[17]Human Rights Watch interview with Álvaro Gómez, Medellín, Antioquia, July 2, 1996.

civilian passengers, the army commander ordered the driver to carry six soldiers to a point further along the highway, so they could mount a new roadblock. There, the soldiers left the bus and it continued its regular route. Minutes later, guerrillas opened fire on the bus, apparently believing that soldiers remained on board. Guerrillas killed the driver, his assistant, and a nurse's aide, who was a passenger. Five other passengers were wounded, including a four-year-old boy.[18]

In a communiqué circulated in Arauca soon after the attack, guerrillas tried to justify their behavior by claiming that soldiers had gotten off unobserved by guerrilla lookouts. For its part, the army has no pending investigation of the commander.[19] In this case, both sides violated Article 13 of Protocol II, which requires combatants to protect civilians from the "dangers" of military operations.

The laws of war and Colombia

The laws of war have a long and complex history rooted in humankind's attempt to limit the damage caused by war to civilians and combatants who have been wounded or captured. In modern times, nations codified the laws of war into the Hague Regulations of 1899 and 1907 and the Geneva Conventions of 1949, which deal primarily with conflicts between states.[20]

Article 3 common to the four Geneva Conventions is virtually a convention within a convention. It is the only provision of the Geneva Conventions that directly applies to internal (as opposed to international) armed conflicts.[21]

Common Article 3, section 1, states:

> In the case of armed conflict not of an international character occurring in the territory of one of the High Contracting Parties, each Party to the conflict shall be bound to apply, as a minimum, the following provisions:

---

[18]We have received numerous reports of the army forcing civilian vehicles like buses to board armed soldiers. Human Rights Watch interview with a government investigator, Medellín, Antioquia, July 2, 1996; and "Farc hicieron más de mil tiros al bus," *El Tiempo*, July 22, 1996.

[19]"Caen más civiles en medio del conflicto," *El Corredor* (Arauca), August 3-16, 1996; Human Rights Watch interview with María Victoria Uribe de Guzmán, Human Rights Office, Defense Ministry, Santafé de Bogotá, January 29, 1997.

[20]Colombia ratified the Geneva Conventions in 1963.

[21]See Appendix I for the full text of Common Article 3.

(1)   Persons taking no active part in the hostilities, including members of armed forces who had laid down their arms and those placed *hors de combat* by sickness, wounds, detention, or any other cause, shall in all circumstances be treated humanely, without any adverse distinction founded on race, colour, religion or faith, sex, birth or wealth, or any other similar criteria.

To this end the following acts are and shall remain prohibited at any time and in any place whatsoever with respect to the above-mentioned persons:

(a)   violence to life and person, in particular murder of all kinds, mutilation, cruel treatment and torture;

(b)   taking of hostages;

(c)   outrages upon personal dignity, in particular humiliating and degrading treatment;

(d)   the passing of sentences and the carrying out of executions without previous judgment pronounced by a regularly constituted court, affording all the judicial guarantees which are recognized as indispensable by civilized peoples.

Common Article 3 thus imposes fixed legal obligations on the parties to an internal conflict to ensure humane treatment of persons not or no longer taking an active role in the hostilities.

Common Article 3 applies when a situation of internal armed conflict objectively exists in the territory of a State Party. It expressly binds all parties to the internal conflict including insurgents, although they do not have the legal capacity to sign the Geneva Conventions.[22]

The obligation to apply Common Article 3 is absolute for all parties to the conflict and independent of the obligation of the other parties. That means that the Colombian government cannot excuse itself from complying on the grounds that the other parties to the conflict are violating Common Article 3 and vice versa.

Application of Common Article 3 by the government cannot be legally construed as recognition of an insurgent party's belligerence, from which recognition of additional legal obligations beyond Common Article 3 would flow. Nor is it necessary for any government to recognize a party's belligerent status for article 3 to apply.

---

[22]As private individuals within the national territory of a State Party, certain obligations are imposed on them. ICRC, *Commentary on the Additional Protocols*, p. 1345.

Unlike international conflicts, the law governing internal armed conflicts does not recognize the combatant's privilege and therefore does not provide any special status for combatants even when captured.[23] Thus, the Colombian government is not obliged to grant captured members of non-state groups prisoner of war status. Similarly, government combatants who are captured by parties to the conflict need not be accorded this status. Any party can agree to treat its captives as prisoners of war, however.

Since World War II, most conflicts have taken place within states: wars of self-determination, wars of liberation, and internal armed conflicts. A new Diplomatic Conference was called to draft agreements to cover these radically different circumstances. The result – Protocols I and II Additional to the Geneva Conventions, adopted in 1977 – offer more precise and detailed standards for the protection of civilians and combatants rendered *hors de combat* by their capture or wounding. Protocol I addresses mainly international armed conflicts while Protocol II addresses the new circumstances of internal armed conflict.[24]

After initially refusing to consider the new protocols in the 1980s, Colombia adopted Protocols I and II without reservation in the 1990s.[25] Among those who aggressively supported the adoption of Protocol II was Colombia's first

---

[23]The combatant's privilege is a license to kill or capture enemy troops, destroy military objectives and cause unavoidable civilian casualties. This privilege immunizes members of armed forces or rebels from criminal prosecution by their captors for their violent acts that do not violate the laws of war but would otherwise be crimes under domestic law. Prisoner of war status depends on and flows from this privilege. *See* Solf, "The Status of Combatants in Non-International Armed Conflicts Under Domestic Law and Transnational Practice," *American University Law Review* 33 (1953): p. 59.

[24]For a history of the Geneva Conventions and the two Additional Protocols, see Sylvie Junod, "Additional Protocol II: History and Scope," *American University Law Review*, Vol. 33: 29, 1983, pp. 29-40.

[25]Although Colombia took part in the drafting of the protocols, the delegation initially objected, arguing that states should have the power to invoke the protocols instead of having them apply once the objective criteria exist for their application. Subsequently, however, Colombia adopted the protocols: Protocol I came into effect on March 1, 1994, and Protocol II came into effect on February 15, 1996. Human Rights Watch interview with Interior Minister Horacio Serpa, Santafé de Bogotá, June 25, 1996; República de Colombia, "Actividades del Gobierno de Colombia relativas a la aplicación del Derecho Internacional Humanitario," Santafé de Bogotá, December 1, 1995; and Alejandro Valencia Villa, *Humanización de la Guerra*, pp. 55-69.

public advocate, who sponsored the first government report on international humanitarian law violations in 1993.[26]

In interviews with Human Rights Watch, all groups engaged in the conflict said they support some form of enforcement of minimum humanitarian standards. In 1997, each submitted to the National Conciliation Commission (Comisión de Conciliación Nacional, CCN), a coalition of civic groups led by the Catholic Church, peace proposals and comments on the laws of war.[27] In some regions, parties to the conflict have established temporary agreements on standards, and have exchanged prisoners or suspended fighting to care for the wounded, demonstrating that it has been possible on occasion to agree on conduct in observance of the laws of war.[28]

In 1995, Colombia sought to implement the protocols with public education and security force training.[29] With the assistance of the ICRC, a government commission has been preparing legislation that would typify Protocol II violations as crimes in Colombia's penal code and has launched humanitarian aid programs to attend the forcibly displaced, discussed later in this report.[30]

A notable advance was the agreement that allowed the United Nations High Commissioner for Human Rights to set up a permanent office in Colombia,

---

[26]Jaime Córdoba Triviño, *Informe sobre infracciones del Derecho Internacional Humanitario en 1992* (Santafé de Bogotá: Defensoría del Pueblo, August 1993).

[27]CCN, *La Paz sobre la Mesa* (Santafé de Bogotá: CCN, International Committee of the Red Cross, and *Cambio 16*, 1997).

[28]Human Rights Watch interview with Carlos Castaño, July 9, 1996; and "Eln y autodefensas canjean secuestrados," *El Tiempo*, February 4, 1997.

[29]Among the texts we were provided with during our research was *Derecho Internacional Humanitario: Manual Básico para Personerías y Fuerzas Armadas de Colombia*, published by the Defense Ministry, Public Ministry, and Colombian Red Cross in 1995. Although valuable and necessary, the manual fails to make any explicit link between international documents and the Colombian situation, making it of only limited utility.

[30]Currently, only Colombia's military penal code directly addresses the laws of war. Article 169 expressly prohibits the mistreatment of prisoners of war, the looting of the dead on the field of battle, the improper use of the red cross or other internationally protected emblems, and the use of weapons prohibited by international law. Alejandro Valencia Villa, *Derecho Humanitario para Colombia* (Santafé de Bogotá: Defensoría del Pueblo, 1994), pp. 213-214.

with part of its mandate dedicated to reporting on international humanitarian law violations.[31] In May 1998, President Ernesto Samper signed a law to punish individuals who misuse the emblem of the red cross and guarantee protection for the work of the ICRC.[32]

As we demonstrate in this report, however, there continues to be, at best, a profound lack of understanding of the laws of war among combatants. At worst, as one European humanitarian group concluded after visiting the Urabá region of Antioquia, "the actors involved in the conflict [have no] willingness to respect international humanitarian law, a theme all invoke lightly solely for political benefit."[33]

This manipulation of the laws of war is frequent and ubiquitous. For instance, the Colombian security forces characterize almost all guerrilla activities as violations of the laws of war, in an apparent attempt to damage them in public opinion and gain sympathy. Yet they consistently fail to supply the evidence necessary to show how these actions violate the laws of war.

In a similar vein, guerrillas argued in repeated interviews with Human Rights Watch that although they support humanitarian standards in theory, they do not accept Protocol II since it was not negotiated directly with them. In fact, the international community made a determined effort to include non-state groups in the conference that led to the protocols. All told, eleven such groups, including the Palestinian Liberation Organization (PLO) and the Southwest African Peoples Organization (SWAPO), took part.[34] During the conflict in El Salvador, the Farabundo Martí National Liberation Front (Frente Farabundo Martí para la Liberación Nacional, FMLN) publicly announced its decision to abide by both

---

[31]Accord between Colombia and the U.N. High Commissioner for Human Rights, November 29, 1996.

[32]Press release, "Presidente Samper Pizano defiende misión de la Cruz Roja Internacional en Colombia," Office of the President, May 8, 1998.

[33]Press release from Pax Christi, November 7, 1995.

[34]Michael Bothe, Karl Josef Partsch, and Waldemar A. Solf, *New Rules for Victims of Armed Conflicts: Commentary on the Two 1977 Protocols Additional to the Geneva Conventions of 1949* (The Hague/Boston/London: Martinus Nijhoff Publishers, 1982), p. 8.

Common Article 3 and Protocol II, which the government had refused to apply but had ratified.[35]

For his part, AUC leader Carlos Castaño has repeatedly stated a willingness to pledge his forces to respect the laws of war, but qualifies that support by claiming that Colombia needs a "creole" version of international humanitarian law, adapted to Colombia's irregular warfare and specifically allowing the execution of combatants *hors de combat*.

The application of laws of war does not depend on the discretion of any one of the parties to the conflict. Common Article 3 of the Geneva Conventions applies automatically once a situation of armed conflict exists objectively. Protocol II is applicable when opposing forces in an internal conflict are under a responsible command, exercise enough control over territory to mount sustained and coordinated military operations, and are able to implement Protocol II, all of which Colombia clearly satisfies.[36]

Although the Colombian government has expressed its willingness to invite the International Fact-finding Commission, established by Article 90 of Protocol I, to Colombia to investigate reports of laws of war abuses, none of the other parties to the conflict have invited the commission to come to Colombia, a necessary step.[37]

Colombia is one of 126 governments that has signed the Convention on the Use, Stockpiling, Production and Transfer of Anti-Personnel Mines and On

---

[35]When a government ratifies a convention, it does so on behalf of all its nationals, including those who may revolt against it. Charles Lysaght, "The Scope of Protocol II and its relation to Common Article 3 of the Geneva Conventions of 1949 and other human rights instruments," *American University Law Review*, Vol. 33: 9, pp. 9-27.

[36]The Colombian state is also bound by many international treaties, including the American Convention on Human Rights and the International Covenant on Civil and Political Rights. On October 28, 1997, Colombia signed the Inter-American Convention to Prevent and Punish Torture, which is awaiting ratification. Articles 12, 18, 24, and 28 of the Colombian Constitution also prohibit summary execution and torture, the death penalty, forced disappearance, and cruel, inhumane, or degrading treatment. It also guarantees freedom of expression, thought, movement, and due process.

[37]Gustavo Gallón, "Derecho Internacional Humanitario en Colombia," in Álvaro Villarraga Sarmiento, editor, *Derecho Internacional Humanitario Aplicado: Los casos de Colombia, Guatemala, El Salvador, Yugoslavia y Ruanda* (Santafé de Bogotá: ICRC, Office of the Colombian High Commissioner for Peace, Pontífica Universidad Javeriana, Fundación Konrad Adenauer, 1998), pp. 319-329.

their Destruction since December 1997 (referred to as the Mine Ban Treaty). This comprehensive treaty prohibits in all circumstances any use of antipersonnel land mines. It also requires that stockpiles be destroyed within four years of the treaty's entry into force and that mines already in the ground be removed and destroyed within ten years.[38]

The use of antipersonnel land mines by all parties to the conflict is already banned under the provisions of international humanitarian law that protect civilians from indiscriminate attack and that mandate that parties to a conflict refrain from using weapons that exact a disproportionate toll on civilians. Because the Mine Ban Treaty has been signed by two-thirds of the governments of the world, it has established an emerging global consensus against antipersonnel mines.

In Colombia, there are mechanisms in place to encourage compliance with the laws of war. For instance, Common Article 3 states that humanitarian organizations such as the ICRC may provide humanitarian services during armed conflict if invited to do so. In Colombia, the ICRC has advised the government since 1969. Two days after Protocol II went into effect in 1996, the ICRC and the Colombian government signed a new agreement that allows the ICRC to move freely within Colombia and maintain contacts with all armed groups.

Although clearly limited given the magnitude of violations, the ICRC's role is crucial. Representatives visit hostages and the detained, oversee their release when invited to do so, provide the parties with information and training about the laws of war, assist civilian victims and the wounded, and, when appropriate, present the government with cases of alleged violations.[39]

In the future, stronger mechanisms to punish serious violations of the laws of war may be available through the International Criminal Court (ICC).[40] Already, individuals charged with violating Common Article 3 are being tried by the International Criminal Tribunal for the former Yugoslavia. As the Yugoslav

---

[38]Colombia signed on December 3, 1997. For a detailed legal analysis of the use of antipersonnel land mines, see Human Rights Watch, *Land Mines: A Deadly Legacy* (New York: Human Rights Watch, 1993), pp. 261-318.

[39]ICRC, "Actividades en Colombia," May 1997.

[40]On July 17, 1998, more than 160 governments signed a treaty that provides the basis for establishing the ICC. The mission of the court is to prosecute individuals charged with crimes accountable under international law, including genocide, crimes against humanity, and war crimes. The final treaty formalizing the establishment of the court has yet to be ratified.

Tribunal has determined, "customary international law imposes individual criminal responsibility for serious violations of Common Article 3, as supplemented by other general principles and rules for the protection of victims of internal armed conflict, and for breaching certain fundamental principles and rules regarding means and methods of combat in civil strife."[41]

In a similar vein, the U.N. Security Council expressly empowered the International Criminal Tribunal for Rwanda to prosecute persons for crimes against humanity, including systematic murder and torture. Individual criminal responsibility under the statutes of both the Yugoslav and Rwanda Tribunals extends to a person who commits or orders serious crimes like massacres and hostage-taking.[42]

Types of Combatants and Targets

Any report on laws of war violations must first marshal the facts necessary to distinguish civilians and combatants *hors de combat* from those actively engaged in hostilities. This can be a difficult, though not impossible task in Colombia.

All parties to Colombia's conflict overtly and aggressively target civilians, yet claim that civilian casualties are in fact combatants in disguise. All sides also seek to draw civilians into direct participation in the war. The government did this by organizing civilians into paramilitary groups in the 1980s and CONVIVIRs in the 1990s.[43] The guerrillas create militias, whose tactic of forcibly recruiting children is discussed in a later section of this report. Paramilitaries routinely describe civilians as combatants simply because they cross paths with guerrillas, if only to share a dipper of water or witness the passing of an armed unit.

Similarly, all sides routinely attack civilian persons and objects, in clear violation of the laws of war. Yet rarely does anyone take responsibility for errors; instead, combatants find ever more cynical ways to justify or deny attacks that merit international condemnation.

---

[41]International Criminal Tribunal for the former Yugoslavia, Appeals Chamber decision on the Tadic Jurisdictional Motion, Case No. IT-94-1-AR72, Prosecutor vs. Dusko Tadic a/k/a "Dule," October 2, 1995, paragraph 134.

[42]Ibid., paragraph 133.

[43]Human Rights Watch reviewed the history of government support for paramilitaries in Human Rights Watch/Americas, *Colombia's Killer Networks: The Military-Paramilitary Partnership and the United States* (New York: Human Rights Watch, 1996), pp. 10-26.

In this, Colombia is not unique. Parties in many internal armed conflicts blur the distinction between civilians and combatants, who attempt to apply the narrowest definition possible of "civilian" to justify attacks against those they suspect of allegiance to their enemies.[44]

In this section, we discuss how Human Rights Watch has interpreted the laws of war, in particular the definition of civilian, combatant, and military target. We then apply these definitions to the cases we have documented on each of the parties to the conflict to show how the laws of war have been violated.

In this report we have chosen to highlight cases where eyewitness testimony and credible investigations point to a responsible party. Human Rights Watch traveled to conflict areas to interview witnesses, government investigators, security force personnel, guerrillas, and paramilitaries, and collected abundant documentary evidence to support each case. As part of the research for this report, we also met with Carlos Castaño, leader of the AUC, and guerrilla representatives, and submitted to each of the parties engaged in Colombia's internal conflict lists of violations attributed to their forces for comment or additional information.

The Colombian army, National Police, and the AUC responded in written and verbal form. The UC-ELN and EPL promised to respond in repeated interviews, but did not. The FARC failed to respond to repeated requests. In our interview with a FARC representative, he had no information on the cases we presented, although he denied categorically that his organization committed violations.

To define civilian, we have relied on the laws of war as well as the body of theoretical and practical commentary published since Protocol II was adopted. In *New Rules for Victims of Armed Conflicts: Commentary on the Two 1977 Protocols Additional to the Geneva Conventions of 1949* (hereafter *New Rules*), an authoritative commentary on the laws of war, a civilian is defined as someone who does not actively participate in hostilities by intending to cause physical harm to enemy personnel or objects.[45]

---

[44]Roman Jasica, "Civilian Population," in *Guerilla* (sic) *and International Humanitarian Law: International Symposium of the Red Cross, Antwerp, February 2 and 3 1984* (Brussels: Belgian Red Cross, 1984), p. 77.

[45]The authors were members of the West German and American delegations at the Diplomatic Conference that led to the drafting of Protocol II. Michael Bothe, Karl Josef Partsch, and Waldemar A. Solf, *New Rules for Victims of Armed Conflicts: Commentary on the Two 1977 Protocols Additional to the Geneva Conventions of 1949* (The Hague/Boston/London: Martinus Nijhoff Publishers, 1982), pp. 293-296.

It is crucial to underscore that simply feeding a combatant, providing information outside the immediate battle zone, disseminating propaganda, or engaging in political activities in support of an armed group does not convert a civilian into a combatant. Both direct participation and the intent to cause physical harm to a combatant must be present in order for a civilian to lose his or her protected status. If there is any doubt about an individual's status, combatants should presume that the individual is a civilian unless there is clear proof that the individual meets the criteria for being a combatant.[46]

The issue of intelligence gathering is particularly important. While Protocol II was being negotiated, conference participants agreed that residents of territories where combatants are present necessarily come across information of use to the parties to a conflict and may, either knowingly or unknowingly, transmit it, a common occurrence in Colombia. However, this does not make them combatants. Essential to the definition of a combatant who is a spy or intelligence agent is that the person use disguise to gain access to information, acquire it under false pretenses or deliberately clandestine acts, or knowingly supply information that is of direct and immediate use in launching an attack.[47]

In addition, as the *New Rules* stress, the mere presence of combatants, off-duty combatants, or persons doing business with parties to the conflict within a civilian population does not rob it of its civilian character.[48]

A civilian can also be someone who has previously taken part in hostilities, but has ceased to play a role. In Colombia, all men are required to complete between twelve to twenty-four months of obligatory military duty. While in the military, these individuals are combatants. Once they cease taking part in hostilities, however, they are civilians and are protected by the laws of war.[49] Also protected as civilians are the civilian employees of a group of combatants, such as mechanics, and the crews of civil aircraft who transport military personnel, material, and supplies.[50]

---

[46]Ibid., p. 296.

[47]Ibid., pp. 123-128, 148-150.

[48]Ibid., p. 296.

[49]Former combatants may be subject to prosecution for acts committed while they were combatants. Ibid., pp. 293-296.

[50]Ibid., pp. 293-296.

"There should be a clear distinction between direct participation in hostilities and participation in the war effort," the ICRC noted in its *Commentary on the Additional Protocols*. "The latter is often required from the population as a whole to various degrees."[51]

As the ICRC Commentary notes, wars like Colombia's make the determination of who is a civilian "more difficult... but not to the point of becoming impossible." Ultimately, there must be "a direct causal relationship between the activity engaged in and the harm done to the enemy at the time and the place where the activity takes place."[52]

To define a military target, we have used as a starting point Article 52 (2) of Protocol I, which says a military target by its nature, location, purpose, or use, must make an effective contribution to military action. Although Protocol I applies only to international armed conflicts, it provides useful guidance because of the precision with which it has developed concepts contained in other instruments. The total or partial destruction, capture, or neutralization of the military target in the circumstances ruling at the time must offer a definite military advantage. Both conditions must be present in order for an object to be a military target.

The element of time is crucial. An object that serves a civilian use may at a given moment provide one of the parties with a distinct military advantage and may at that moment satisfy the conditions defining a military target. For instance, if paramilitaries detect a guerrilla column using a bridge to transport supplies or as a regular transit point and there are no civilians present, the bridge may be a military target, since its destruction would serve a definite military advantage. However, the bridge may not qualify as a military target the next day, when farmers are using it to carry goods to market. In that case, there is no definite military advantage at that moment and its destruction would be a violation.[53]

As the *New Rules* note, in the dynamic circumstances of armed conflict, "objects which may have been military objectives yesterday may no longer be such

---

[51]Yves Sandoz, Christophe Swinarski, and Bruno Zimmermann, eds, *Commentary on the Additional Protocols of 8 June 1977 to the Geneva Conventions of 12 August 1949* (Geneva: International Committee of the Red Cross, 1987), p. 619.

[52]Ibid., p. 516

[53]Michael Bothe, et. al., *New Rules for Victims of Armed Conflicts*, p. 326; and Fritz Kalshoven, *Reaffirmation and Development of International Humanitarian Law Applicable in Armed Conflicts: The Diplomatic Conference, Geneva, 1974-1977*, Neth. Y.B. International Law 107, 111 (1978).

today and vice versa. Thus, timely and reliable information of the military situation is an important element in the selection of targets for attack."[54]

A civilian object can forfeit its immunity from attack when it is occupied and used by military forces in an armed engagement. In all cases, however, the force launching an attack must not only determine that it can gain a direct military advantage in the circumstances ruling at the time, but also that an attack would not cause excessive harm to civilians.

As the *New Rules* elaborate, the rule of proportionality "clearly requires that those who plan or decide upon attack must take into account the effects of the attack on the civilian population in their pre-attack estimate." Just as the rules regarding objects that can have dual civilian-military functions demand that there be a direct military advantage evident in such deliberations, so too does the rule of proportionality require that the advantage be specific, not general, and perceptible to the senses.

"A remote advantage to be gained at some unknown time in the future would not be a proper consideration to weigh against civilian losses," the *New Rules* state.[55]

An influential manual used by the U.S. Air Force echoes the language of Protocol I, Article 57 in stating that "in conducting military operations, constant care must be taken to spare the civilian population... and civilian objects." In each attack, the manual stresses, officers in command must "take all feasible precautions in the choice of means and methods of attack with a view to avoiding, and in any event to minimizing, incidental loss of civilian life, injury to civilians, and damage to civilian objects." If it is impossible to minimize damage to civilians, "an attack must be canceled or suspended."[56]

Even when an objective is clearly military, however, the parties to the conflict do not have unlimited license to attack. For example, in Article 51(5) (b) of Protocol I, an indiscriminate or disproportionate attack is an attack that "may be expected to cause incidental loss of civilian life, injury to civilians, damage to civilian objects, or a combination thereof, which would be excessive in relation to the concrete and direct military advantage anticipated."

---

[54]Michael Bothe, et. al., *New Rules for Victims of Armed Conflicts*, p. 326.

[55]Ibid., pp. 310, 365.

[56]U. S. Department of the Air Force, "International Law - The Conduct of Armed Conflict and Air Operations," Air Force Pamphlet 100-31, November 19, 1976, p. 5-9.

Among other cases, the rule of proportionality applies to guerrilla attacks on towns where there are significant civilian casualties and damage to civilian objects, like stores, homes, and churches. In many instances, it is clear that guerrillas have taken few, if any, precautions to minimize excessive harm to civilians and often attack when there is little if any direct military advantage. Clearly, faulty intelligence and unforeseen circumstances can lead to unplanned damages. However, combatants cannot claim error if there is evidence that they omitted taking into account obvious risks to civilians or a reasonable estimate of potential damage.

It is important to note, however, that the rule of proportionality in no way justifies or ignores civilian casualties that may result from an attack. If a force suspects that civilians may suffer from an attack, the attack must be suspended or canceled until the commanders have taken specific measures to avoid or minimize civilian casualties.[57]

Just as combatants are required to consider an individual a civilian if there is any doubt about his or her status, so too must they refrain from attacking a normally civilian target if there is any doubt about the uses to which it is being put.[58]

The laws of war also protect civilians against indiscriminate attack. Although Protocol II does not define these terms, the *New Rules* infer a protection from Protocol I, which expressly forbids belligerents from attacking objectives without distinguishing between military targets and civilians and civilian objects. Article 51 (4) of Protocol I describes indiscriminate attacks as:

(a) those which are not directed at a specific military objective;
(b) those which employ a method or means of combat which cannot be directed at a specific military objective; or
(c) those which employ a method or means of combat the effects of which cannot be limited as required by this Protocol...

In Colombia, for instance, the army has reacted to guerrilla offensives by launching rocket attacks against areas where civilians live, violating the laws of war by treating the region as a single military objective and failing to properly separate out and identify the legitimate military targets within the area.

---

[57]Yves Sandoz, et. al., *Commentary on the Additional Protocols of 8 June 1977 to the Geneva Conventions of 12 August 1949*, p. 626.

[58]Michael Bothe, et. al., *New Rules for Victims of Armed Conflicts*, p. 326.

Article 51 (5) (a) of Protocol I considers a bombardment indiscriminate if it "treats as a single military objective a number of clearly separated and distinct military objectives located in a city, town, village, or other area containing a similar concentration of civilians or civilian objects."

A civilian object may forfeit protected status through use that only incidentally relates to combat action, but which effectively contributes to the military aspect of a party's general war effort. For instance, a power station providing electricity to a military base may qualify as a military target since it contributes directly to the combat capability of a party to the conflict.[59]

However, attacks on Colombia's oil pipeline are almost always violations, since its destruction serves no direct military advantage.[60] The UC-ELN itself has said that it targets the pipeline not for military reasons, but to protest Colombian economic policy. They argue that attacks are justified since oil provides the Colombian government with money used to fund the war effort. However, Human Rights Watch rejects this logic as dangerous and ungrounded in the laws of war, since it could be used to justify any attack on a source of government revenue, including tax-paying civilians.

Types of Violations

We have divided cases according to two criteria: by party to the conflict and, within each of those sections, by type of violation of the laws of war. In choosing cases to highlight, we have not attempted to include all violations reported nor necessarily the best-known ones. Instead, we have selected cases that either illustrate a common violation or stand out as particularly egregious or inhumane.

For each case described, there are perhaps dozens more that share similar horrors. We have established the facts to the best of our ability, despite the

---

[59]Yves Sandoz, et. al., *Commentary on the Additional Protocols of 8 June 1977 to the Geneva Conventions of 12 August 1949*, pp. 632-33.

[60]The ICRC Commentary names "installations providing energy *mainly* for national defense [sic], e.g., coal, other fuels, or atomic energy, and plants producing gas or electricity" (emphasis added) as military objectives, a criteria that Colombia's oil pipeline does not meet.
The Colombian government considers attacks on the oil pipeline a violation of Article 4 (d) of Protocol II, which prohibits acts of terrorism. Ibid., pp. 632-33; and "Denunciado terrorismo contra oleoductos y medio ambiente ante ONU," Office of the President, October 3, 1997.

tremendous difficulties due not only to the failure in many cases of the relevant government authorities or the party to the conflict implicated to carry out even a cursory investigation, but also to the high level of violence against those who dare report abuses, which has made many Colombians fearful of reporting or talking about cases.

Each section begins with the killings of civilians, led by massacres. Massacres constitute multiple violations of the most fundamental rights guaranteed in Common Article 3 and Protocol II and in many cases also constitute a "collective punishment" meant to threaten and terrorize. Both civilians and combatants placed *hors de combat* by sickness, wounds, detention, or any other cause are protected under international humanitarian law and as such cannot be subjected to murder, torture, or other ill-treatment.

In 1997, the Data Bank on Political Violence (Banco de Datos de Violencia Política), run by the Intercongregational Commission for Justice and Peace (Comisión Intercongregacional de Justicia y Paz, hereafter Justice and Peace) and the Popular Research and Education Center (Centro de Investigación y Educación Popular, CINEP), which compiles information on human rights and international humanitarian law violations, recorded 185 massacres in Colombia.[61]

Although massacres might appear to be the fruit of chaos and disorder, in fact they more often serve the closely weighed and measured purpose of promoting terror. In one blow, massacres eliminate those close or perceived to be close to an opposing side, punishing a family or population for the perceived action of one or a few of its members. The threat to those who survive or witness or hear of the massacre afterwards is clear. If you have had or may be seen to have had contact with the enemy, it is best to flee.

Often, combatants claim that they have killed individuals proven through trial to be guilty of certain crimes, like support for their enemies. Human Rights Watch found no evidence that either the AUC or guerrillas can guarantee the fair trial required by the laws of war. Indeed, none of these groups makes any serious attempt to argue that their trials satisfy these conditions.[62] In fact, these are

---

[61]Human Rights Watch and most Colombian human rights groups define massacres as the killing of four or more people in the same place, at the same time, and by the same force. CINEP and Justice and Peace, *Noche y Niebla: Balance Sheet 1997*, p. 6.

[62]During the Salvadoran conflict, the FMLN argued unconvincingly that its trial procedures satisfied Protocol II. For our analysis of their claim, see Americas Watch, "Violation of Fair Trial Guarantees by the FMLN's Ad Hoc Courts," *An Americas Watch Study* (New York: Human Rights Watch, May 1990).

summary executions dressed up as judicial procedures and are abhorrent violations of the laws of war.[63]

In addition, Human Rights Watch has serious reservations about the government's ability to carry out fair trials in the so-called regional court or public order system, which prosecutes individuals charged with rebellion, terrorism, and the formation of paramilitary groups. These courts have failed to provide the essential guarantees of independence and impartiality required by Article 6 (2) of Protocol II.[64]

These courts lack essential fair trial guarantees, among them access to a proper defense, restrictions on the defense's ability to fully review evidence brought before the court or question secret witnesses presented by the prosecution, and a reliance on evidence brought by the military, which on some occasions has presented deeply flawed or illegally obtained material. In some cases, prosecutors who present evidence are strongly biased in favor of the military, particularly prosecutors who do business from military barracks.[65]

In previous reports, we have called on the government to reform this system in accord with its obligations to ensure for all of those accused of crimes a fair and impartial trial. Colombia had determined that these courts will be dissolved as of June 30, 1999. This is a first step. However, given the deeply flawed nature of these courts, we call on the government to abolish these courts immediately. In addition, Colombia should establish an independent commission to review cases of individuals convicted by regional courts and rectify injustices done.

---

[63]To qualify as fair according to Article 6 of Protocol II, these trials must guarantee due process rights, including ensuring that the accused is informed of the charge against him or her as well as the trial procedure; allowing the accused a proper defense, including competent counsel; charging defendants based only on individual responsibility for a crime, not group responsibility; affording the accused the presumption of innocence; and avoiding *in absentia* trials. Moreover, Protocol II requires a clear appeals process. If these guarantees are not assured, no sentence may be carried out.

[64]The right to a fair trial is also guaranteed by treaties ratified by Colombia, including Articles 14 and 15 of the International Covenant on Civil and Political Rights and Article 8 of the American Convention of Human Rights.

[65]Human Rights Watch interview with government investigators, Santafé de Bogotá, December 4, 1997; and Lawyers Committee for Human Rights, *Comments Relating to the Fourth Periodic Report on Colombia before the U.N. Human Rights Committee* (New York: Lawyers Committee for Human Rights, 1997).

We follow with cases involving murder and torture, expressly banned by the laws of war. These cases include non-combatants, elected and government officials, and combatants *hors de combat*.

The Data Bank recorded 150 cases of torture in 1997, all but nine attributed to paramilitary groups. Often, victims are tortured before being summarily executed.[66] As the Office of the High Commissioner for Human Rights noted in its 1998 report, torture is severely under-reported in Colombia. "Many of the persons tortured only appear in the lists of victims of enforced disappearance or extrajudicial execution." State agents, the report notes, often threaten their victims to force them to declare in writing that they were well treated or risk reprisals.[67]

The mutilation of bodies is also expressly banned by the laws of war. Both torture and mutilation are often used to threaten survivors, also a violation of the ban on acts of terror and threats of violence against civilians.

Often, forced disappearances are carried out by state agents or their paramilitary allies in the course of other violations, like the killing of non-combatants. A forced disappearance occurs when state agents or their allies conceal the fate or whereabouts and deny custody of persons who have been deprived of their liberty. Clearly, forced disappearances are a violation of Colombia's responsibilities under human rights treaties. At the same time, forced disappearances violate the ban contained in Article 4 of Protocol II against violence to the life, health, and physical or mental well-being of persons, in particular murder as well as cruel treatment.[68]

Currently, the United Nations Working Group on Enforced or Involuntary Disappearances has registered 1,006 cases of forced disappearance in Colombia

---

[66]CINEP and Justice and Peace, *Noche y Niebla: Balance Sheet 1997*, pp. 4-5; and Commission on Human Rights, "Report by the United Nations High Commissioner for Human Rights," 54th Session, E/CN.4/1998/16, March 1, 1998.

[67]Commission on Human Rights, "Report by the United Nations High Commissioner for Human Rights," 54th Session, E/CN.4/1998/16, March 1, 1998.

[68]In 1992, the United Nations make an explicit link between the Geneva Conventions and forced disappearances and determined that this practice was a violation of international law. Declaration on the Protection of All Persons from Enforced Disappearances, General Assembly resolution 47/133, December 18, 1992.

since 1981, most carried out by paramilitary groups acting with the complicity of the armed forces. In 1997 alone, the Working Group received sixteen new cases.[69]

We also include cases of arbitrary detention, when a force engaged in the conflict detains individuals without explanation. Like forced disappearances, arbitrary detentions can end with executions and the secret disposal of bodies, meaning that people are never seen or heard from again. Often in Colombia, the bodies of individuals who have been arbitrarily detained are mutilated in a variety of ways meant to maximize terror: with machetes, chain saws, acid, and even surgical instruments. Often, paramilitaries eviscerate the bodies of the dead to ensure that the bodies will not float and be found after they are thrown into a river.

Cases involving hostage-taking follow. According to the ICRC, hostages are "persons who find themselves, willingly or unwillingly, in the power of the enemy and who answer with their freedom or their life for compliance with [the enemy's] orders."[70]

Although the international press has paid most attention to non-Colombians who have been taken hostage, by far the largest number of victims are Colombian nationals. According to País Libre, a non-governmental organization that studies the phenomenon, known popularly as kidnapping to extort money or political concessions, at least 1,693 people were taken in 1997, over half by guerrillas. In the same time period, paramilitaries were considered responsible for twenty-six kidnappings.[71] In only the first three months of 1998, 509 people were reported kidnapped, an increase of 25 percent over the same period in 1997.[72]

Most hostages are taken by guerrillas, who deny that they engage in hostage-taking. The UC-ELN, for instance, claims that victims are "retained" (*retenido*) and that these acts are not violations, since any ransom or political concessions gained for release do not benefit individual guerrillas, but the group as a whole.

---

[69]Report of the United Nations Working Group on Enforced or Involuntary Disappearances, E/CN.4/1998/43, January 12, 1998.

[70]Yves Sandoz, et. al., *Commentary on the Additional Protocols of 8 June 1977 to the Geneva Conventions of 12 August 1949*, p. 874.

[71]Letter to Human Rights Watch from Francisco Santos, País Libre, July 3, 1998.

[72]Andrea Domínguez Duque, "Colombia, en la cima del secuestro," *El Colombiano*, April 15, 1998.

However, there is an international consensus that a hostage-taking occurs when something is demanded in exchange for release, whether it be money or political concessions. Hostage-taking is prohibited by Article 1(b) of Common Article 3 to the Geneva Conventions as well as Article 4 (2) (c) of Protocol II. According to the laws of war, hostage-takers seek to influence the behavior of third parties in some way by threatening a hostage with physical harm; the definition relies on the hostage's disempowerment in the hands of a party to the conflict and the possibility that the hostage will be exchanged for some concession made by a third party. Indeed, the ICRC definition differs little from ones we found in authoritative dictionaries, like Webster's, which defines a hostage as "a person kept as a pledge pending the fulfillment of an agreement."[73]

In all cases where an individual is either detained or taken hostage, combatants are required to treat captives humanely and, when a release is planned, guarantee their well-being during that release.

Attacks on medical workers and installations and lack of respect for the emblem of the red cross follow. Few prohibitions are as clear in the laws of war as the prohibition against harming medical facilities, medical vehicles, and medical professionals for the simple act of caring for the wounded, whether they be combatants or civilians. Ambulances and formal hospitals are not the only facilities protected; any structure or vehicle marked with the red cross and used exclusively at a given moment to treat the wounded is protected.

The next category of abuses are actions that harm or threaten the civilian population. We include in this category the use of land mines and the indiscriminate use of bombs; indiscriminate attacks; attacks that violate the rules of proportionality and cause excessive harm to the civilian population; attacks on essential civilian installations, like potable water; and pillage.

We follow with a section on land mines. The Mine Ban Treaty prohibits in all circumstances any use of antipersonnel land mines. As delayed action weapons, they are not meant for immediate effect, but rather are primed, concealed, and lie dormant until triggered. However, they are not triggered solely by combatants, but by anyone who happens to be the first to activate the mechanism. Therefore, they are by their nature indiscriminate weapons.[74]

---

[73]Webster's Seventh New Collegiate Dictionary, p. 402. See also CCJ, *Colombia, Derechos Humanos y Derecho Humanitario: 1996*, pp. 17-23.

[74]The Arms Project: A Division of Human Rights Watch/Physicians for Human Rights, *Land Mines: A Deadly Legacy* (New York: The Arms Project: A Division of Human Rights Watch/Physicians for Human Rights, 1993).

Often in Colombia, they are used around a perimeter to defend a base. But since bases are often within or close to civilian areas, civilians and their children are frequent victims. According to the Public Advocate's Office, in 1995 and 1996, forty-four children were killed by landmines in Colombia.[75] To our knowledge, all land mines used in Colombia are rudimentary and are not designed to self-destruct.

Booby traps would fall under a similar category when they are used indiscriminately. Also, when bombs are disguised as non-military objects, like books, or are placed in and around corpses, they may qualify as a violation of the ban against perfidy, a concept contained in customary international law and defined as inviting a person's confidence, betraying that confidence, and leading the adversary to believe that the perpetrator of a perfidious act is entitled to the protection of the laws of war.[76]

We also include other types of violations, such as the failure to take precautions in attacks to spare the civilian population and civilian objects. These kinds of violations sometimes occur during the temporary seizure of towns, called *tomas*. While *tomas* are not per se violations, since towns can contain military targets, such as security force bases, military vehicles, and troops, often the force involved fails to clearly identify these targets and determine if an attack may cause excessive harm to civilians and damage to civilian installations. Other atrocities during seizures — including the execution of police officers who are wounded or have surrendered, indiscriminate fire that kills or harms civilians, and looting — are clear violations.

Following the sections devoted to each of the forces engaged in combat, we have described two types of abuses that are endemic in Colombia: the forced recruitment of children and forced displacement, both expressly prohibited by the laws of war.

As we note, both guerrillas and paramilitaries forcibly recruit children or allow them to fight in their ranks, violating Article 4 (3) (c) of Protocol II, which forbids the recruitment of children under fifteen or their inclusion in hostilities. The Colombian state is also bound by the Convention on the Rights of the Child, which fixes the minimum recruitment age at fifteen.

Human Rights Watch fully supports the adoption of an optional protocol to the United Nations Convention on the Rights of the Child to raise the minimum

---

[75]Public Advocate's Office, *Cuarto Informe Anual del Defensor del Pueblo al Congreso de Colombia*, p. 42.

[76]Michael Bothe, et. al., *New Rules for Victims of Armed Conflicts: Commentary on the Two 1977 Protocols Additional to the Geneva Conventions of 1949*, pp. 204-205

age for recruitment and participation in hostilities from fifteen to eighteen. Persons under the age of eighteen have not reached physical or psychological maturity, and are ill-prepared to face the harsh conditions of warfare. Many who have volunteered or who have been forced to serve emerge at the end of hostilities physically and psychologically scarred by their experience, and unprepared to live in and contribute to a peaceful society. More than their adult counterparts, these children require extensive social and psychological rehabilitation after participation in hostilities.

Forced displacement is also prohibited, as laid out in Article 17 of Protocol II. Unless civilians are forced to move for safety reasons or a clear military imperative, any displacement for reason of conflict is a violation. In addition, forced displacement often occurs as the result of other violations, including indiscriminate attacks, the terror caused by massacres, selective killings, torture, and threats. In some cases we document, an armed force has used internally displaced civilians to shield or strategically favor military operations, a violation of the guarantee in Protocol II that protects civilians from the harm produced by military operations.

III. STATE VIOLATIONS OF INTERNATIONAL HUMANITARIAN LAW

In this section, we discuss laws of war violations by three state agents: the Colombian army, the National Police, and CONVIVIRs.

Numerous international organizations, including the United Nations and the Inter-American Commission on Human Rights, have repeatedly submitted to the Colombian government detailed recommendations to improve human rights protections and combat impunity. We fully support those recommendations, most of which have yet to be adopted and implemented.

It is appropriate here to include our concern about Colombia's failure to provide humane conditions in detention for many of the individuals charged and convicted of terrorism or rebellion. In general, conditions are grim, especially for individuals believed by the state to occupy middle to lower level positions within insurgent organizations. While leaders may be provided with virtual suites within maximum security facilities and access to foods and medicines of their choosing, rank-and-file prisoners live in severely overcrowded cell blocks where acts of violence are common along with chronic shortages of food, water, and medical care.[77] According to the National Penitentiary and Jail Institute, which runs Colombia's prisons, 49 percent of the prisoners are awaiting sentence for a crime. Although Colombia's prison are built to hold about 32,000 prisoners, the actual population is well over 41,000.[78]

---

[77]Public Advocate's Office, *Cuarto Informe Anual del Defensor del Pueblo al Congreso de Colombia*, p. 50-51.

[78]Press Bulletin No. 187, "Gobierno anuncia medidas de emergencia frente a crisis carcelaria," Office of the President, March 20, 1998; "Reyerta en La Picota: 15 muertos," *El Tiempo*, April 14, 1998; and "Renunció Director del Inpec," *El Colombiano*, April 15, 1998.

Army

> *I can't count the number of times I've been stopped at a joint*
> *army-paramilitary roadblock. The soldiers are there with their*
> *green uniforms and the paramilitaries with their blue uniforms.*
> *It's like different units of the same army.*

> *— Humanitarian aid worker, Antioquia*
> *May 1997*

The Colombian army had its beginnings in the country's fight for independence from Spain. Legally, all of Colombia's 121,000 soldiers, 18,000 Navy sailors, and 7,300 Air Force members are under the command of the president.[79] In practice, however, civilians have limited influence, and decisions are made by the armed forces commander and the commander of each branch.

The army is organized by task and has infantry, cavalry, artillery, mechanized units, military engineering, logistical and administrative corps, and military intelligence. The army's five divisions are arranged into a total of twenty-four brigades, themselves divided into 154 battalions, two regional "operative commands," and sixteen specialized anti-extortion units with a combined military-police staff. In addition, Colombia has three mobile brigades, specialized counterinsurgency units with up to 2,000 professional soldiers; military schools; and an aviation brigade.[80]

All Colombian males are required to serve a minimum of eighteen months in the armed forces, and most serve in the army.

The Colombian army and International Humanitarian Law

The army has taught its officers the basics of international humanitarian law and made instructional material available to officers, professional soldiers, and recruits. Officers who wish to advance must take laws of war courses. The army

---

[79]The International Institute for Strategic Studies, *The Military Balance 1997/98* (London: Oxford University Press, 1997), pp. 213-214.

[80]Unit names are available on the Internet at http://204.146.47.148/organiza. For more on Mobile Brigades, see Human Rights Watch/Americas, *State of War: Political Violence and Counterinsurgency in Colombia* (New York: Human Rights Watch/Americas, 1993), pp. 65-113.

also receives courses from ICRC instructors, and the ICRC told Human Rights Watch that Colombia's armed forces have incorporated their curricula in training.[81]

Some commanders make an effort to emphasize the importance of human rights and international humanitarian law to field officers and their men. In one 1992 memo circulated by Brig. Gen. Agustín Ardila Uribe, then commander of the Fifth Brigade, officers are told to make it clear to their men that they must observe "irreproachable conduct, respectful of human dignity and underscoring that no military procedure or operation can violate constitutional, legal, moral, or ethical boundaries."[82]

In 1997, the Colombian government forced the retirement of Gen. Harold Bedoya, whose hostility to human rights and career-long association with the dramatic increase in joint army-paramilitary operations is notorious. "We took Bedoya out because of human rights," President Ernesto Samper told Human Rights Watch in an interview.[83]

Despite these measures, the army continues to commit serious violations, with little apparent will to investigate or punish those responsible. At the root of many violations is the Colombian army's consistent and pervasive failure or unwillingness to distinguish civilians from combatants in accordance with the laws of war. As the Office of the U.N. High Commissioner for Human Rights noted in its 1998 report, the Colombian army has publicly stated that 85 per cent of the "subversives" they must attack are engaged in a "political war," not combat, and include some non-governmental organizations, trade unions, and political parties. Indeed, for the Colombian army, only 15 percent of so-called subversives even carry a weapon.[84]

---

[81]"Normas sobre derechos humanos," distributed by the army in 1996; sample agenda from the Fourth Brigade, June 26, 1996; Letter to all division and brigade commands from Gen. Harold Bedoya Pizarro, army commander, June 26, 1996; and Human Rights Watch interview with Col. Guillermo García, army human rights office, Santafé de Bogotá, June 24, 1996.

[82]Memo No. 010/BR5-CDO-ODH-743, from Brigadier General Ardila, Fifth Brigade, 1992.

[83]Human Rights Watch interview with President Ernesto Samper, Santafé de Bogotá, September 10, 1997.

[84]Commission on Human Rights, "Report by the United Nations High Commissioner for Human Rights," 54th Session, E/CN.4/1998/16, March 1, 1998.

In effect, this is a rejection of the most basic principle of the laws of war, the distinction between civilians and combatants. This attitude is not new or unusual. In a 1995 memo addressing army strategy in the Middle Magdalena region, then-Second Division Commander Gen. Manuel Bonett instructed his troops to focus intelligence-gathering on towns and strike civilian "support networks" since guerrillas "reclaim their sick and wounded there, their weapons caches, their tailors, their bank accounts, their businesses, and other types of logistical activities essential to subversive combat." Targeting civilians, Bonett stressed, would "noticeably weaken [the guerrillas'] capability."[85]

Nowhere in the letter does this officer, later promoted to the position of commander in chief of Colombia's armed forces, caution his men that these same tailors, bankers, and medical professionals are not themselves combatants and are therefore protected under the laws of war.

This attitude had led, among other things, to repeated threats and attacks against elected officials. For instance, after Gloria Cuartas courageously accepted the position of mayor of Apartadó, Antioquia, replacing a series of murdered mayors, local army commanders repeatedly described her as a "guerrilla supporter" ("*auxiliadora de la guerrilla*"), putting her life, in her words, in "imminent danger."[86]

After Cuartas told journalists that the armed forces favored paramilitary groups in her city — a conclusion shared by many national and international organizations, including Human Rights Watch — the commander of the Seventeenth Brigade brought charges of slander against Cuartas.[87] When she was deposed in the subsequent investigation, Cuartas noted that she had repeatedly warned the Seventeenth Brigade about paramilitary activity in the Pueblo Nuevo section of Apartadó. At the time, the ACCU was carrying out a coordinated

---

[85]Letter from Maj. Gen. Manuel José Bonett Locarno to Brigade and Battalion Commanders within the Second Division, No. 2554, July 24, 1995.

[86]Letter from Mayor Gloria Cuartas to President Ernesto Samper, August 28, 1996.

[87]Cuartas was interviewed by Nelson Freddy Padilla, who published a story on August 26, 1996, in the magazine *Cambio 16* under the title "La tierra donde decapitan niños." Letter to the regional office of the Attorney General from Gen. Rito Alejo del Río Rojas, August 28, 1996.

campaign to push the Fifth and Thirty-Fourth Fronts of the FARC south and out of Urabá. Apartadó, for decades a FARC stronghold, was among their objectives.[88]

Nevertheless, General Del Río did nothing to pursue paramilitaries. When Cuartas visited Pueblo Nuevo on August 21 and spoke before a hundred children gathered at an elementary school, she reported that suspected paramilitaries grabbed twelve-year-old César Augusto Romero from the school, killed him, and cut off his head.[89]

"To speak does not mean to take sides or negotiate or provide support," Cuartas noted in a letter to President Samper. "My obligation has been to ensure

---

[88]Human Rights Watch interviews in Apartadó, Antioquia, July 4-6, 1996.

[89]Nelson Freddy Padilla, "La tierra donde decapitan niños," *Cambio 16*, August 26, 1996 pp. 24-25.

Live ammunition training of soldiers from the 17th Brigade at the army base in Carepa, Antioquia.

that the civil population is respected as such, whether or not they have political sympathies with one or the other side in the conflict."[90]

Types of army violations vary according to region and unit. For instance, in eastern Colombia, where paramilitaries are weak or have yet to fully penetrate, the army is directly implicated in the killing of non-combatants and prisoners taken *hors de combat*, torture, and death threats. In the rest of the country, where paramilitaries have a pronounced presence, the army fails to move against them and tolerates their activity, including egregious violations of international humanitarian law; provides some paramilitary groups with intelligence and logistical support to carry out operations; and actively promotes and coordinates with paramilitaries and goes on joint maneuvers with them.

In 1997, of the 185 massacres recorded by human rights groups, four were committed by the Colombian army. Many of the paramilitary massacres, however,

[90]All charges against Cuartas were eventually dropped for lack of evidence. Letter from Mayor Gloria Cuartas to President Ernesto Samper, August 28, 1996.

were carried out with army tolerance or support. The army was also believed to be responsible for fifty-four selective killings.[91]

Although the government and Colombia's military leaders deny that they promote or even tolerate paramilitaries, abundant evidence— reflected in dozens of investigations carried out by the Colombian Attorney General's Office, the United Nations, the Organization of American States, Human Rights Watch, Amnesty International, and even the U.S. State Department— is consistent and terrifying. As the office of the High Commissioner for Human Rights noted in its March 1998 report, "Witnesses frequently state that [massacres] were perpetrated by members of the armed forces passing themselves off as paramilitaries, joint actions by members of the armed forces or police and paramilitaries, or actions by paramilitaries enjoying the complicity, support or acquiescence of the regular forces."[92]

The army's use and tolerance of paramilitaries has not reduced the overall number of violations recorded in Colombia or their effect; yet it has allowed high-ranking officers to claim that soldiers are directly implicated in fewer abuses than in years past. Overall, the army's willingness to talk about human rights and international humanitarian law while at the same time tolerating and promoting paramilitary activity in large parts of Colombia is striking.[93]

"The army tendency is to make this war increasingly clandestine and assign the dirty work to paramilitaries," one human rights investigator told Human Rights Watch.[94]

Fueling direct abuses by soldiers is the army's emphasis on body counts as a means of measuring the performance of officers eager for promotion. Officers who fail to amass lists of enemy casualties risk seeing their careers stalled and ended. As the cases below demonstrate, soldiers often execute detainees, then claim

---

[91]CINEP and Justice and Peace, *Noche y Niebla: Balance Sheet 1997*, pp. 2, 6.

[92]Commission on Human Rights, "Report by the United Nations High Commissioner for Human Rights," 54th Session, E/CN.4/1998/16, March 1, 1998.

[93]Human Rights Watch interview with human rights investigators, Santafé de Bogotá, December 1-3, 1997.

[94]Ibid.

the bodies as guerrillas killed in action as a way of boosting the body count for their superiors.[95]

"The commander would give the order, and says that he wanted results, casualties (*bajas*)," one former army officer told Human Rights Watch. "So anyone who came near our patrol would be killed." This officer also told us that soldiers would receive bonuses for a high number of casualties produced during operations, directly linked to how medals would be awarded.[96]

This practice continues despite assurances to the contrary. Less than a month after Armed Forces Commander General Bonett told Human Rights Watch that the army had revised the way it measured success and planned to put a black mark on an officer's record if massacres were registered in his jurisdiction, Gen. Iván Ramírez summarized the work of his First Division, responsible for much of northern Colombia, by releasing to the press long lists of people claimed killed in action by his troops. Absent from the review was any measure of the chaos and terror produced by the paramilitary groups that soldiers under Ramírez's direct command allowed and often helped massacre civilians.[97]

The Twentieth Brigade, which centralized military intelligence, was among the most feared in Colombia because of its record of targeted killings until it was formally disbanded on May 19, 1998, in part because of human rights violations.[98] Among others, the Twentieth Brigade is believed responsible for the 1995 murder of conservative political leader Álvaro Gómez Hurtado, in an apparent plot to destabilize Colombia's civilian leadership and provoke a military coup d'etat.

The U.S. State Department first reported on Twentieth Brigade death squads in its 1996 human rights report. Far from improving, the situation deteriorated the next year, when the State Department noted that authorities were

---

[95]Human Rights Watch interview with Col. (ret.) Carlos Velásquez, Santafé de Bogotá, May 12, 1997.

[96]Human Rights Watch interview with former army officer, Santafé de Bogotá, November 12, 1995.

[97]Tonny Pérez Mier, "Balance de I División del Ejército," *El Tiempo*, December 23, 1997; and Human Rights Watch interview with General Bonett, Santafé de Bogotá, December 12, 1997.

[98]Press Bulletin No 339, "Comandantes del Ejército ordenan desmonte de la Brigada XX," Office of the President, May 20, 1998.

investigating the brigade commander for the murder of several of the brigade's own informants.[99]

Government investigators believe that a group within the Twentieth Brigade calling itself "The Hunters" was implicated in the murders of these informers as well as cases of extortion and car theft.[100] According to press reports, one of the Hunters, former army Sgt. Omar de Jesús Berrío Loaiza, is believed by government investigators to have hired the gunmen who carried out the Gómez killing and is currently under arrest along with three other Twentieth Brigade members and three civilians.[101]

In November 1997, four Twentieth Brigade intelligence officers were passed over for promotion, effectively ending their careers, and the military retired a former brigade commander, apparently because of involvement with human rights crimes.[102] However, we are not aware of any investigations of Twentieth Brigade commanders who presided over the unit when it amassed its homicidal record or may have ordered killings. Former Twentieth Brigade commanders Gen. (ret.) Álvaro Velandia and Gen. Iván Ramírez have never been effectively investigated for their involvement in alleged human rights abuses.[103]

---

[99]U.S. State Department, "Colombia Report on Human Rights Practices for 1997," (Washington, D.C.: U.S. Government Printing Office, 1998), p. 454. The report is also available at http://www.state.gov/www/global/human_rights/ 1997_hrp_report/colombia.html; and "'Poda' en servicio de inteligencia," *El Tiempo*, November 21, 1997.

[100]The Gómez case remains complicated and may never be fully resolved. Investigations are on-going within the Attorney General's Office and Internal Affairs. Human Rights Watch interview with U.S. Embassy officials, Santafé de Bogotá, December 2, 1997; Human Rights Watch interview with Human Rights Unit, Attorney General's Office, Santafé de Bogotá, December 4, 1997; and "'Cazadores' de inteligencia," *El Tiempo*, November 2, 1997.

[101]Attorney General's Office press release, "Otros cinco acusados por crimen de Álvaro Gómez Hurtado," March 2, 1998; and "'El cazador'," *El Tiempo*, March 3, 1998

[102]Laura Brooks, "Army Unit Investigated In Colombia, *Washington Post*, May 10, 1998.

[103]Velandia was forced to retire in 1995 and Ramírez was forced to retire in 1998, both because of human rights problems. In May 1998, the U.S. revoked Ramírez' visa to the UnitedStates, allegedly because of his long-standing ties to drug trafficking, paramilitaries, and human rights violations. The *Washington Post* also reported that he had been a paid

The Twentieth Brigade is also implicated in the killing of human rights defenders, among them Jesús María Valle, president of the "Héctor Abad Gómez" Permanent Human Rights Committee of Antioquia, and Eduardo Umaña, a noted human rights lawyer.[104]

Twentieth Brigade threats against defenders continued until shortly before it was reorganized and renamed the Military Intelligence Center (Centro de Inteligencia Militar, CIME).[105] After a retired general and former defense minister was assassinated in Santafé de Bogotá on May 12, 1998, the Twentieth Brigade supplied fraudulent information to the Attorney General's Office linking the crime to Justice and Peace, a respected human rights group.[106] The following day, soldiers seized the offices. Soldiers concentrated their search on the office of "Nunca Más," a research project that is collecting information on crimes against humanity. Soldiers forced employees to kneel at gun point in order to take their pictures, a gesture apparently meant to evoke a summary execution. During the search, soldiers addressed employees as "guerrillas" and filmed them and documents in the office. At one point, soldiers told the employees that they wanted precise details of the office in order to later construct a scale model, apparently to plan further incursions. After human rights defenders gathered outside out of concern, soldiers set up a camera to film them, an act of intimidation. [107]

In addition to forming death squads like "The Hunters," the army directly promotes, supports, and takes part in paramilitary actions. Human Rights Watch has identified specific units with a pattern of this activity. They are the First, Second, and Fourth Divisions; the Fourth, Fifth, Seventh, Ninth, Fourteenth, and Seventeenth Brigades; Mobile Brigades One and Two; and the Barbacoas, Bárbula,

---

informant for the CIA, a charge he denied. Douglas Farah and Laura Brooks, "Colombian Army's Third in Command Allegedly Led Two Lives, General Reportedly Served as a Key CIA Informant While Maintaining Ties to Death Squads Financed by Drug Traffickers," *Washington Post,* August 11, 1998; and Douglas Farah, "Colombian Official Denies CIA Link, Resigning General Says He Was Not a Paid Informant," *Washington Post,* August 12, 1998.

[104]Human Rights Watch interview with Attorney General Alfonso Gómez Méndez, Santafé de Bogotá, May 7, 1998.

[105]"Revolcón militar," *Semana,* August 24, 1998.

[106]"A calificar servicios," *Semana,* May 25, 1998.

[107]Public Statement, Justice and Peace, May 19, 1998.

Batín No. 6, Bomboná, Cacique Nutibara, Caycedo de Chaparral #17, Héroes de Majagual, Joaquín París, La Popa, Los Guanes, Girardot, Palonegro #50, Rafael Reyes, Ricuarte, Rogelio Correa Campos, and Santander Battalions. These make up over 75 percent of the Colombian army.[108]

Though high-ranking officers deny that units under their command organize and promote paramilitary activities, the evidence is overwhelming that such activity is commonplace. Although in cases of joint army-paramilitary action, both share responsibility for violations of international humanitarian law, we believe the onus lies with the state force in these cases, pledged to protect the rights of citizens and uphold the law, not develop and support means to circumvent and violate it.

One army colonel in command of an important base told Human Rights Watch that there are army bases "clearly identified as paramilitary organization points, where officers know that there is support from certain civilians. Officers sent there have been clearly identified as supporting this type of work."[109]

A humanitarian aid worker who travels frequently in Urabá was as direct. "I can't count the number of times I've been stopped at a joint army-paramilitary roadblock," he said. "The soldiers are there with their green uniforms and the paramilitaries with their blue uniforms. It's like different units of the same army." Other times, witnesses have told us, the only way to tell the difference between camouflage-wearing men is that soldiers wear black army-issue boots while paramilitaries prefer "Brahma" brand boots, which are yellow.[110]

In the departments of Cesar and Norte de Santander, army commanders have openly organized and promoted paramilitary groups and shared intelligence with them. There, residents told us, they have seen paramilitary vehicles freely enter military bases and coordinate with military vehicles in joint operations.[111]

---

[108]This list is based on Human Rights Watch interviews throughout Colombia in 1995, 1996, and 1997. A list of Colombian military units is available through the Colombian Defense Ministry web page at http://www.mindefensa.gov.co/mdnffmm.htm.

[109]He spoke on condition of anonymity.

[110]Human Rights Watch interviews in Santafé de Bogotá and Antioquia, May 1-14, 1997.

[111]Human Rights Watch interviews with Aguachica and Ábrego residents, Cesar, April 14-15, 1995. For more, see Human Rights Watch/Americas, *Colombia's Killer Networks*, pp. 42-60.

In 1993, the U.S. Embassy reported that Gen. Carlos Gil Colorado, just given the command of the Fourth Division, not only supported the actions of paramilitary groups, but had admitted to providing them with army weapons. Colorado was never punished and died in what was reported to be a FARC ambush in 1994.[112] Human Rights Watch also received consistent reports throughout Colombia that soldiers patrol without any insignia identifying name, unit, or rank, thus adding to the confusion among forces.[113]

In the Urabá region, army commanders use informants who double as paramilitaries, as in the El Aracatazo case described below. In Colombia, it is common for former guerrillas who surrender to serve their prison sentences within military bases. In exchange for leniency in sentencing, former guerrillas inform on their former comrades. Also called "guides," these individuals have been implicated repeatedly in joint military-paramilitary operations.[114]

"Violations directly attributable to the army have decreased in this region, but reports of direct support for paramilitaries have increased," one government investigator from the Middle Magdalena region told Human Rights Watch. "The paramilitaries do the dirty work that the army wants done."[115]

Even high-ranking security force members outside the army agree that, at the very least, the military high command has a policy of tacitly accepting and

---

[112]Memorandum to Deputy Chief of Mission John B. Craig from Thomas Hamilton, Political Section, U.S. Embassy, Santafé de Bogotá, November 17, 1993.

[113]Human Rights Watch interviews with Calamar residents, San José del Guaviare, Guaviare, May 5, 1997; and Human Rights Watch interviews with social workers, Barrancabermeja, Santander, April 8, 1995.

[114]This is authorized by Law 81, passed in 1983, which allows the army to keep these individuals in barracks confinement. In February 1997, the magazine *Alternativa* published a letter from former FARC member Angel Augusto Trujillo Sogamoso claiming that after he surrendered to the army in 1994, soldiers sent him to work with paramilitaries in the departments of Cesar and Norte de Santander. Trujillo also claimed that while working with the army's Twentieth Brigade, he had taken part in the kidnapping of José Ricardo Sáenz, the brother of FARC commander Alfonso Cano. Trujillo later recanted in an army-sponsored press conference. Equipo de Alternativa, "'Ejército secuestró al hermano de Cano,'" *Alternativa*, No. 6, January-February, 1997, pp. 18-19; and "Pille el detalle," *Alternativa*, No. 7, February-March, 1997, pp. 14-15.

[115]Human Rights Watch interview with government investigator, Barrancabermeja, Santander, June 28, 1996.

protecting army-paramilitary links. "Their policy is not mine," said one well-known officer who requested anonymity. "They protect these bad elements within the institution."[116] A high-level government investigator, also speaking on condition of anonymity, echoed this statement. "The army does nothing against paramilitaries," he told Human Rights Watch.

While army support for paramilitary groups varies from region to region, the policy of tacit acceptance and the protection of officers who work with paramilitaries is nearly universal. Officers who dare question the army-paramilitary alliance are swiftly marginalized or dismissed from service.

This was made clear in 1996, when Col. Carlos Alfonso Velásquez, a highly decorated officer who had received praise for pursuing members of the Cali drug cartel, reported to his superiors that his commanding officer supported paramilitaries in Urabá. At the time, Velásquez was the chief of staff for Gen. Rito Alejo del Río, Seventeenth Brigade commander.

"At a minimum," Velásquez reported, "[Del Río] is not convinced that [paramilitaries are] also a dangerous factor of public disorder and violence in Urabá."[117]

Colonel Velásquez also reported that General Del Río maintained a relationship with a retired army major who worked with the ACCU.[118] This officer, Velásquez said, attended a party at the Seventeenth Brigade to celebrate General Del Río's promotion and repeatedly attempted to contact Velásquez personally, on one occasion inviting him to work with the ACCU.[119]

---

[116]Human Rights Watch interview with security force officer, Santafé de Bogotá, September 1997.

[117]Report to Gen. Manuel José Bonnet from Col. Carlos Alfonso Velásquez, Carepa, Antioquia, May 31, 1996.

[118]Maj. (ret.) Guillermo Visbal Lazcano was named on a 1983 list published by Internal Affairs of military officers who belonged to Death to Kidnappers (Muerte a Secuestradores, MAS), a paramilitary group that operated in the Middle Magdalena region. Internal Affairs considered Visbal, at the time a member of the Bomboná Battalion, the intellectual author of the murder of Jaime Nevado, a member of the Puerto Berrío, Antioquia town council on July 22, 1982. *El terrorismo del Estado en Colombia* (Brussels: Ediciones NCOS, 1992), p. 369.

[119]Report to Gen. Manuel José Bonnet from Col. Carlos Alfonso Velásquez, Carepa, Antioquia, May 31, 1996.

Colonel Velásquez verbally reported these incidents to his superiors. His written report was sent to the commander of the First Division, Gen. Iván Ramírez.[120] Instead of prompting a serious investigation into his charges of Seventeenth Brigade support for paramilitaries, however, the reports prompted the army to investigate Velásquez, in an apparent attempt to silence him. Even as General Del Río punished Velásquez by cutting him off from the day-to-day responsibilities of a chief of staff, an army investigation noted that Velásquez met with human rights groups, unions, members of the Patriotic Union party, and Apartadó Mayor Gloria Cuartas, behavior, it noted, that revealed mental problems and was "more than sufficient to [withdraw] confidence in an officer... who maintains a great friendship with people and institutions that have openly declared themselves enemies of the army."[121]

Nevertheless, the report noted that Velásquez had credible information about ties between soldiers and paramilitaries in Necoclí, another Urabá town. In that case — in which no high-ranking official was named — the army filed formal charges against the soldiers for "failing to act" to prevent paramilitary activity.[122]

The army concluded the inquiry by recommending punishment not for General Del Río, who was later promoted, but for Colonel Velásquez, for "insubordination, [acts] against duty and esprit de corps." Velásquez was forced to retire on January 1, 1997.[123]

Despite the international condemnation of the army-paramilitary link and its responsibility for the majority of human rights and international humanitarian law violations in Colombia, neither the military itself nor the government has taken the steps necessary to break this tie. As the U.S. State Department noted for 1997, "There was no credible evidence of any sustained military action to constrain the

---

[120]While he was attached to the Twentieth Brigade, General Ramírez was implicated in at least two extrajudicial executions, including the 1985 murder of Oscar William Calvo, secretary general of the Communist Party. The area under Ramírez's command as First Division chief became a paramilitary stronghold in the mid-1990s. Human Rights Watch interview with Col. (ret.) Carlos Velásquez, Santafé de Bogotá, May 12, 1997; and *El terrorismo del Estado en Colombia* (Brussels: Ediciones NCOS, 1992), pp. 269-270.

[121]Translation by Human Rights Watch. Nelson Freddy Padilla, "Enredo de Sables," *Cambio 16*, January 13, 1997, pp. 20-23.

[122]Ibid.

[123]Translation by Human Rights Watch. "'Hay omisión en lucha contra paramilitares,'" *El Tiempo*, January 10, 1997.

paramilitary groups. While the President announced on December 1 a series of measures to combat paramilitary forces, including a task force to hunt down their leaders, these measures had not been implemented by year's end."[124]

Stung by yet another series of massacres, the government vowed in 1998 to aggressively pursue paramilitaries, among them Víctor Carranza, a legendary emerald dealer, rancher, and paramilitary chieftain linked to hundreds of political killings in the department of Boyacá and Colombia's eastern plains. Carranza was arrested near midnight on February 24, 1998, and is being prosecuted for violating Decree 1194, which prohibits the formation of paramilitary groups.[125] Human Rights Watch has noted an increasing number of government attempts to confront and arrest paramilitary groups, usually led by the Attorney General's Technical Investigation Group (Cuerpo Técnico de Investigación, CTI), which captured Carranza, the National Police, and the DAS.[126]

The army also continues to be implicated in the torture of detainees, whether for political or common crimes. However, torture can be especially intense if a detainee is implicated in a soldier's death. Methods are crude: beatings and the "submarine," near suffocation in buckets of often filthy water, are most common.[127]

---

[124]U.S. State Department, "Colombia Report on Human Rights Practices for 1997," p. 453.

[125]According to press reports, the case against Carranza is based largely on the testimony of former gunmen who belong to the paramilitary groups he organized and led. U.S. officials also believe Carranza is directly involved in shipping cocaine into Europe and the United States. "Carranza, a responder por 'paras'," *El Tiempo*, February 20, 1998; "A rendir cuentas," *Semana*, March 2-9, 1998; and testimony of Amb. Rand Beers, International Narcotics Matters, Department of State, before the House International Relations Committee, Washington, D.C., February 27, 1998.

[126]For instance, in March, DAS agents shot and killed Jaime Matiz Benítez, known as "El 120," leader of the so-called Contraguerrilla Llanera. According to press reports, Matiz had left the AUC after being criticized for leading a deadly attack against a government judicial commission near San Carlos de Guaroa in October 1997. The commission had been seizing the assets of a convicted drug trafficker when they were attacked by over one hundred well-armed paramilitaries. Eleven of the commission members were killed. "La contabilidad secreta del abatido '120,'" *El Tiempo*, March 21, 1998.

[127]Human Rights Watch interview with humanitarian aid workers, Santafé de Bogotá, December 3, 1997.

Regardless of the violation, however, impunity remains the rule for officers who operate with or without paramilitaries. In general, the government has failed to exercise minimum control over its armed forces by properly investigating and punishing individuals who commit abuses.

Colombia's military argues that its courts are effective and cites high overall conviction rates. For instance, as commander of the armed forces, General Bedoya cited a 47 percent conviction rate for investigations carried out by military tribunals. However, he could not cite a single conviction for a human rights crime like extrajudicial execution. Indeed, most military tribunal convictions are for military offenses, like failing to follow an order. In cases of human rights and humanitarian law violations, allegations against officers are rarely investigated. Historically, the few officers who face a formal inquiry see the charges dropped or are acquitted.[128]

Typical is the case involving the Naval Intelligence Network No. 7 and its responsibility for the killings of dozens of people in and around the city of Barrancabermeja, Santander from 1991 through 1993. Despite overwhelming evidence showing that Lt. Col. Rodrigo Quiñones and seven other soldiers planned, ordered, and paid hit men to carry out these killings, all eight were acquitted by a military tribunal in 1994.[129]

The only people to be convicted for the crimes were two civilian employees of Naval Intelligence Network No. 7. In his ruling on the case, the civilian judge admitted that he was "perplexed" by the military tribunal's acquittals of the officers, since he considered the evidence against them "irrefutable." "With [this acquittal] all that [the military] does is justify crime, since the incidents and the people responsible for committing them are more than clear."[130]

As the U.S. State Department noted in its 1997 annual human rights report, "At year's end, the military exercised jurisdiction over many cases of

---

[128]Human Rights Watch interview with Gen. Harold Bedoya, Santafé de Bogotá, March 6, 1997; and "Defensa de la justicia penal militar," *El Tiempo*, February 25, 1997.

[129]Human Rights Watch/Americas, *Colombia's Killer Networks*, pp. 40-41.

[130] Translation by Human Rights Watch. Sentence of the Regional Court, No. 1953, Cúcuta, February 24, 1998.

military personnel accused of abuses, a system that has established an almost unbroken record of impunity."[131]

Although Colombia's Constitutional Court ruled on August 5, 1997 that cases involving members of the armed forces accused of human rights and international humanitarian law violations should be prosecuted in civilian courts, the Superior Judicial Council, the body charged with resolving jurisdictional disputes between civilian courts and military tribunals, continues to rule frequently in favor of the military.[132] Even though the Constitutional Court ruling clearly applies to pending cases that were sent to military tribunals, but are yet to conclude, the council has argued that unless new evidence is admitted, "no judicial authority can ignore [our jurisdictional ruling], modify it, or change it."[133]

The government has also failed to aggressively push for existing cases to be transferred, reflecting a long-standing passivity when faced with the military's determination to preserve impunity. "I would describe the government's role as absent in this effort to ensure accountability," one government investigator told Human Rights Watch.[134]

When Human Rights Watch asked General Bonett if officers who failed to act to prevent paramilitary massacres would be punished, he cited the case of Gen. Jaime Uscátegui, commander of the Seventh Brigade during a series of paramilitary massacres in his jurisdiction in 1997. In the Mapiripán massacre, detailed in the paramilitary section, General Uscátegui failed to act despite repeated requests for assistance from the Mapiripán judge and is currently under investigation by Internal Affairs (Procuraduría).[135]

For this "omission," General Bonett told us, General Uscátegui had been relieved of his command and would be called to retire. Nevertheless, we learned

---

[131] U.S. State Department, "Colombia Report on Human Rights Practices for 1997," p. 452.

[132]Constitutional Court ruling C-358/97.

[133]Consejo Superior de la Judicatura, Sala Jurisdiccional Disciplinaria, Santafé de Bogotá, December 4, 1997.

[134]Human Rights Watch interview with government investigators, Santafé de Bogotá, March 6, 1997.

[135]Human Rights Watch interview with Attorney General Alfonso Gómez Méndez, May 7, 1998.

later that not only was General Uscátegui still on active duty, but in 1998 he was chosen as second-in-command for an army offensive in the department of Caquetá.[136]

According to Internal Affairs, in the six months following the Constitutional Court ruling, the Superior Judicial Council sent 141 cases involving security force officers to civilian courts and thirty-three cases to military courts.[137] For its part, the Defense Ministry claimed that over the same time period, thirty-three other cases had been transferred from military tribunals to civilian courts. Most involved police officers, not soldiers, and none ranked above the level of major.[138]

However, Colombia's civil jurisdiction, known as the *contencioso administrativo*, has consistently found the armed forces and especially the army liable for damages resulting from violations. In one case settled in 1997, for instance, the Arauca Administrative Tribunal found the army liable for the 1991 deaths of a peasant couple near Tame, Arauca. Soldiers killed them as they ran in fear, the court concluded. As the court wrote in its judgment, the soldiers then lied about the presence of guerrillas in order to cover up their mistake.[139]

Civilian investigators who take on cases involving the military continue to be harassed and threatened, and some have been forced to leave their posts – or the country. "During my investigation, I was subjected to constant harassment and evasion, when the military would refuse to provide material I had requested or delay in locating an officer I wanted to question," one investigator from Internal Affairs told Human Rights Watch.[140] Another, from a different institution, echoed

---

[136]Human Rights Watch interview with General Bonett, Santafé de Bogotá, December 12, 1997; and Human Rights Watch interview with Alfonso Gómez Méndez, Attorney General, May 7, 1998.

[137]Comité de Seguimiento a las Recomendaciones del Comité de Impulso en los casos de Los Uvos, Caloto y Villatina, Santafé de Bogotá, February 12, 1998.

[138]Fuerzas Militares de Colombia, Tribunal Superior Militar, "Procesos enviados justicia ordinaria - observancia pronunciamiento Corte Constitucional," Santafé de Bogotá, January 28, 1998.

[139]The state was ordered to pay the families the equivalent of US $79,000 in gold. "Nación debe pagar US $79 milliones por dos muertes," *El Tiempo*, June 21, 1997.

[140]Human Rights Watch interview with government investigator, Santafé de Bogotá, June 25, 1996.

this opinion. "The doors are closed, and officers believe they are being persecuted by guerrilla sympathizers hidden within the government."[141]

Massacres

El Aracatazo: On August 12, 1995, a group calling itself the "People's Alternative Command" (Comando Alternativo Popular) carried out a massacre of eighteen people — including two children — at the El Aracatazo bar in the El Bosque neighborhood of Chigorodó, Antioquia. Armed gunmen surrounded the bar with its patrons inside, then systematically shot into the premises and executed some of the patrons at point blank range. Subsequent government investigations linked the "People's Alternative Command" to the army's Voltígeros Battalion, which shares a base with the Seventeenth Brigade and is under that unit's command, and amnestied EPL guerrillas with ties to the Hope, Peace, and Liberty party (Esperanza, Paz y Libertad, hereafter Esperanza), the political party they formed. An internal army investigation determined that Voltígeros soldiers had allowed at least two former guerrillas who were working as informants to leave the base two days before the El Aracatazo massacre.[142] One of them, Gerardo Antonio Palacios, was later convicted of having taken part in the massacre.[143] Another, José Luis Conrado Pérez, known as "Carevieja," was identified by eyewitnesses as also having taken part. Three months before the massacre, Carevieja had appeared in a photograph published in the magazine *Cambio 16*, uniformed, heavily armed, and speaking directly to then-Army Commander General Bonett.[144] A humanitarian aid worker told Human Rights Watch that it was well known that Carevieja worked for

---

[141]Human Rights Watch interview with government investigator, Santafé de Bogotá, December 1, 1997.

[142]Human Rights Watch interview with Human Rights Unit, Attorney General's Office, Santafé de Bogotá, July 11, 1996; and Report to Gen. Manuel José Bonett from Col. Carlos Alfonso Velásquez, Carepa, Antioquia, May 31, 1996.

[143]"Condenan a paramilitar," *El Tiempo*, March 4, 1997.

[144]In 1996, the Seventeenth Brigade provided Human Rights Watch with a briefing packet that identified Carevieja as a member of an "organized crime group (improperly called paramilitaries)." Human Rights Watch interview with Gen. Rito Alejo del Río Rojas, commander, Seventeenth Brigade, Carepa, Antioquia, July 6, 1996; and Nelson Freddy Padilla, "Enredo de Sables," *Cambio 16*, January 13, 1997, pp. 20-23.

the army and took part in joint army-paramilitary operations.[145] The Human Rights Unit of the Attorney General's Office is investigating the civilians believed responsible for the massacre, but the soldiers have gone unpunished.[146]

Segovia, Antioquia: The region around Segovia, called the "northeast," has been a battleground for over a decade, with joint army-paramilitary units and guerrillas targeting their suspected adversaries within the civilian population.[147] On April 22, 1996, a group of men, including six gunmen driven to Segovia by Bomboná Battalion Capt. Rodrigo Cañas, seized a bar in the El Tigrito neighborhood and executed four people. Continuing to the La Paz neighborhood, they killed five more people. By the time they left town, authorities registered fifteen dead, among them two children, and as many wounded. Although Segovia was heavily militarized, the gunmen passed three army bases and a police station with no trouble. Subsequently, the driver of a car commandeered to replace one of their vehicles and the driver's fifteen-year-old assistant were forcibly disappeared.[148] The massacre had been preceded by written and telephoned death threats to community leaders, creating an atmosphere of terror.[149] In an important decision on July 25, 1996, the case against Captain Cañas for arranging the massacre with paramilitaries was sent to a civilian court over the army's objections. The attorney general formally charged Cañas and his driver with homicide and the formation of

---

[145]Human Rights Watch interview with humanitarian aid worker, July 6, 1996.

[146]The army has denied involvement. Human Rights Watch interview with Human Rights Unit, Attorney General's Office, Santafé de Bogotá, July 11, 1996; and Human Rights Watch interview with Gen. Rito Alejo del Río Rojas, commander, Seventeenth Brigade, Carepa, Antioquia, July 6, 1996.

[147]Human Rights Watch has reported on Segovia numerous times, most recently in Human Rights Watch/Americas, *Colombia's Killer Networks,* pp. 70-73.

[148]Human Rights Watch interview with Human Rights Unit, Attorney General's Office, Santafé de Bogotá, July 11, 1996, and December 5, 1997; Urgent Action, "Otra masacre anunciada en Segovia," Corporación Jurídica Libertad, et al., April 23, 1996; Marisol Giraldo Gómez, "Masacre fue anunciada hace 15 días," *El Tiempo,* April 24, 1996; and "Colombia: Armed Groups Fuel Mistrust of Segovia People," *El Tiempo,* Foreign Broadcast Information Service (hereafter FBIS), Latin America, April 30, 1996.

[149]Public complaint, Corporación Jurídica Libertad, et al, May 1996.

paramilitary groups.[150] It is worth noting that in their 1996 summit conclusions, the paramilitary coalition known as the AUC singled out the Segovia massacre as an example of the difficulties involved in mounting joint operations with the army.[151] Military authorities allowed Human Rights Watch to interview Cañas on July 4, 1996, in the military police barracks where he was lodged. Despite the gravity of the case, Cañas was not confined and remained on active duty.[152] Within a month of our visit, a military court acquitted him of compromising "military honor" for the Segovia massacre and released him, despite the fact that he was still under arrest and formal investigation by the attorney general. In addition, government investigators believe he continued to coordinate paramilitary actions while in military confinement. While Human Rights Watch was in Medellín in December 1997, civilian authorities arrested Cañas as he did errands in the office building where the civilian prosecutors investigating his case work. In civilian custody, he was then sent to that city's Bellavista Prison to await the outcome of his trial in a civilian court.[153]

---

[150]Human Rights Watch interview with Human Rights Unit, Attorney General's Office, Santafé de Bogotá, July 11, 1996; and Letter to Human Rights Watch from the office of the presidential human rights counselor (Consejería presidencial para los derechos humanos), September 12, 1997.

[151]"III Cumbre Nacional," Movimiento Autodefensas de Colombia, 1996.

[152]Cañas was also implicated in a March 3, 1995, laws of war violation. According to a Public Advocate's investigation, Cañas ordered his troops to fake a guerrilla attack on Segovia, to distract attention from a UC-ELN dynamite heist earlier that day. During the exercise, soldiers extrajudicially executed two men and fired on the local school, putting the sixty-five students inside in serious danger. Human Rights Watch interview with regional Public Advocate's Office, Medellín, Antioquia, April 16, 1995; and Letter to Human Rights Watch from Alejandro Valencia Villa, national director, Office of Complaints, Public Advocate's Office, September 28, 1995.

[153]Cañas denied orchestrating the massacre. Previously, he had been accused of other violations, but has been repeatedly acquitted by military tribunals. Human Rights Watch interview with Capt. Rodrigo Cañas, Medellín, Antioquia, July 4, 1996; Human Rights Watch interview with government investigator, Medellín, Antioquia, December 10, 1997; and "Que justicia ordinaria juzgue militar vinculado en masacre," El Colombiano, July 5, 1996.

Tiquisio and Puerto Coca, Bolívar: Residents say that on March 28, 1997, a combined army-paramilitary force of 200 entered Tiquisio and seized two Franciscan priests, Friar Bernardo Villegas and Friar Diego García, imprisoning them in the parish house for twenty-four hours. Paramilitaries told Villegas that he would be killed and that others had eight days to leave the area. The armed men also said that they planned to kill Father Jesús Martínez, who was in another village at the time. The armed men also seized medical doctor Navarro Patrón, and told him that they had an order to execute him. Only after hours of interrogation were Villegas and Patrón allowed to live.[154] Witnesses later identified the men as ACCU members and soldiers from the Nariño Battalion, which had been patrolling the region the previous week.[155] The unit continued to Puerto Coca and assassinated four men — Robinson Acevedo Chamorro, Jairo Jaramillo Acosta, Wilson García Carrascal, and Wilson Simanca Acosta. During the maneuver, the ACCU distributed a death list with thirty-four names. When they left the area, they took 600 head of cattle, mechanical water pumps belonging to a community development project, money, medicines, and goods looted from local pharmacies and stores.[156] In addition to slaying civilians, the army violated Article 4 (g) and (h) which prohibit pillage and threats to commit murder, and Article 17, which prohibits the forced displacement of civilians except when necessary to protect their security or for "imperative military reasons," conditions that were clearly not satisfied in this case.

San José de Apartadó, Antioquia: During 1997, Human Rights Watch received numerous credible and consistent reports of army-paramilitary patrols around this town of 850. One paramilitary roadblock set in February was less than a mile from the army base in town. There, paramilitaries routinely stopped, searched, and occasionally killed and forcibly disappeared travelers for the next several months. Despite frequent and detailed reports from local authorities and residents, human

---

[154]Letter to Gustavo Castro Guerrero, Colombian ambassador to the United Nations, from John Quigley, OFM, Franciscans International, April 8, 1997.

[155]Acción Urgente, CREDHOS, April 1997.

[156]The ACCU accepted responsibility for killing four people, but denied threatening the local priest, looting, or stealing cattle. Letter to Human Rights Watch from the ACCU, July 27, 1997; Letter to Human Rights Watch from Franciscan order, April 8, 1997; and Human Rights Watch interview with the Asociación para la Promoción Social Alternativa, known as MINGA, Santafé de Bogotá, December 1, 1997.

rights groups, the church, and national and international humanitarian aid workers, the army did nothing to dismantle the patrols or arrest those responsible. Indeed, in one case, a humanitarian aid worker told Human Rights Watch that soldiers had told residents that unless they abandoned their houses, the "head cutters will come and eliminate you."[157] Yet when Human Rights Watch presented this case to Armed Forces Commander Gen. Manuel Bonett, he replied curtly: "These roadblocks don't exist."[158] The army is directly responsible not only for the killings in which soldiers took a direct role, but also for failing to act to prevent future killings by arresting the men who set up and staffed the roadblocks. The largest single massacre took place on March 29, 1997, only seven days after community leaders had declared the town a "Peace Community." That day, residents say the ACCU entered the village of Las Nieves. There, they seized and executed at least five people: brothers Elias and Heliodoro Zapata; Alberto Valle; his fourteen-year-old son, Félix; and Carlos Torres, a hired hand. According to human rights groups, the Zapata brothers had left their house that morning to purchase the family's breakfast. When they did not return, family members Valle and his son went to look for them. Finally, Torres left to check on all four, who had not returned. When the mother of the Zapata brothers left the house to find her sons, she was fired on, but managed to escape unharmed, She later found burned and bloody clothing and personal documents in the vicinity. Later, an army helicopter collected the bodies. Paramilitaries told villagers that they had five days to abandon their homes.[159] The Seventeenth Brigade continues to describe the four as guerrillas killed in combat.[160] Dozens of other residents were seized and killed at paramilitary roadblocks

---

[157]Human Rights Watch letter from humanitarian aid worker, June 1997; Human Rights Watch interviews with humanitarian aid workers, Santafé de Bogotá, May 8, 1997; and Letter to President Ernesto Samper from Father Javier Giraldo, Justice and Peace, July 22, 1997; and Amnesty International Urgent Action 393/97, December 16, 1997.

[158]Human Rights Watch interview with General Bonett, Santafé de Bogotá, September 11, 1997.

[159]The case is currently being investigated by the Internal Affairs Special Investigations Unit. Human Rights Watch interview with María Girlesa Villegas, regional Public Advocate's Office, Medellín, Antioquia, December 9, 1997; Letter to Human Rights Watch from San José de Apartadó leaders, June 1, 1997; and "'Comunidad de Paz' en la mira de los violentos," *Utopías,* Año V, No. 43, April 1997.

[160]Letter from Major General Velasco Chávez, inspector, Colombian armed forces, to Human Rights Watch, December 31, 1997.

tolerated by the army. Among them was Francisco Tabarquino, a local leader who supported the Peace Community. Tabarquino was forced from a public bus at a checkpoint on May 17, bound, and executed despite the pleas of fellow passengers and the Catholic priest who runs the diocese's regional human rights program.[161] Although the Attorney General's Office is investigating the killings that were reported, including that of Tabarquino, we are aware of no arrests to date.[162]

Nudo del Paramillo, Antioquia: On October 25, witnesses told Human Rights Watch that a joint army-ACCU force surrounded the village of El Aro and the 2,000 people who live in and around it. The operation was part of a region-wide offensive launched by the army and ACCU against the FARC and designed to force residents to abandon villages identified as providing the FARC with supplies and "conquer" the region, in the words of ACCU leader Castaño.[163] While soldiers maintained a perimeter around El Aro, an estimated twenty-five ACCU members entered the village, rounded up residents, and executed four people in the village plaza. Among the ACCU leaders were men who called themselves "Cobra" and "Junior." Store owner Aurelio Areiza and his family were told to slaughter a steer and prepare food from their shelves to feed the ACCU fighters on October 25 and 26, while the rest of Colombia voted in municipal elections. The next day, Areiza was taken to a nearby house, tied to a tree, tortured, and killed. Witnesses say the ACCU gouged out his eyes and cut off his tongue and testicles. One witness told journalists who visited El Aro soon afterwards that families who attempted to flee were turned back by soldiers camped on the outskirts of town. Over the five days they remained in El Aro, ACCU members executed at least eleven people, including three children, burned forty-seven of the sixty-eight houses, including a pharmacy, a church, and the telephone exchange, looted stores, destroyed the pipes that fed the homes potable water, and forced most of the residents to flee. When they left on October 30, the ACCU took with them over 1,000 head of cattle along

[161]Letter to Human Rights Watch from San José de Apartadó leaders, June 1, 1997; and Human Rights Watch interview with María Girlesa Villegas, Defensoría, Medellín, Antioquia, December 9, 1997.

[162]Colombian government's response to cases submitted to the office of the U.N. High Commissioner for Human Rights, January-June, 1997.

[163]This wasn't the first time the ACCU entered this area. In 1996, the group was implicated in the killings of three people in the hamlets of El Inglés and La Granja. Human Rights Watch interview with a government investigator, Medellín, Antioquia, July 2, 1996.

with goods looted from homes and stores.[164] Afterwards, thirty people were reported to be forcibly disappeared.[165] Carlos Castaño assumed responsibility for the El Aro killings but denied that the army took part in the operation. He claimed the victims were guerrillas, fugitives, or their supporters. He made one exception, saying that the execution of a fifteen-year-old boy was an "error."[166] By year's end, hundreds of displaced families were divided between shelters in Ituango, Puerto Valdivia, and Medellín.[167] Jesús Valle Jaramillo, a local town councilman and president of the "Héctor Abad Gómez" Permanent Human Rights Committee, helped document the massacre and was representing the families of victims when he was assassinated in his Medellín office on February 27, 1998. Members of the army's Twentieth Brigade are currently under investigation for his murder.[168] Because of its role facilitating every aspect of this paramilitary operation, we hold the army responsible for this egregious violation of the laws of war.

Murder and Torture

María Celsa Pernía and Bernardo Domicó: According to an investigation done by the Office of Special Investigations of Internal Affairs, eight FARC guerrillas came to the home of this couple near Dabeiba, Antioquia, on May 5, 1996, and

---

[164]Areiza's common-law wife was allowed to bury his body, but it was later moved. During these five days, the FARC apparently attacked the army perimeter and penetrated to the village outskirts, causing some paramilitary casualties. There are also reports of a helicopter retrieving paramilitary casualties, though it is unclear whether the vehicle belonged to the ACCU or the army. Human Rights Watch interviews with El Aro survivors, Medellín, Antioquia, December 11, 1997; Human Rights Watch interview with Jesús Valle, president, "Héctor Abad Gómez" Permanent Human Rights Committee, Medellín, Antioquia, December 11, 1997; and Javier Arboleda, "Cinco días de infierno en El Aro," *El Colombiano*, November 14, 1997.

[165]Amnesty International Urgent Action 01/97, January 3, 1997.

[166]He also challenged authorities to find Areiza's body to prove that he had been tortured. Family members told us that the ACCU told them they would be killed if they searched for it. "Autodefensas niegan barbarie en El Aro," *El Colombiano*, November 15, 1997.

[167]"Los desplazados no se veían en el norte de Antioquia," *El Tiempo*, November 6, 1997.

[168]Human Rights Watch telephone interview with "Héctor Abad Gómez" Permanent Human Rights Committee, February 27, 1998; and Human Rights Watch interview with Attorney General Alfonso Gómez Méndez, May 7, 1998.

demanded shelter. The next morning, the couple awoke to the sounds of an army attack on their home. Using grenades and automatic weapons, soldiers killed three of the guerrillas. Also killed were Pernía and Eduardo, her eight-year-old son. Two other children – an eleven-year-old and a six-year-old – were wounded. Although the army later claimed that the civilians had been killed in the crossfire, Internal Affairs concluded that they had been killed by the army at a distance of less than a meter, making it clear that soldiers could see they were firing on a woman and a child.[169] The use of the house by guerrillas is a violation of the laws of war, since it put civilians in danger. However, the army is responsible for a more serious violation, failing to properly identify a military target and weigh the potential damage to civilians in a pre-attack estimate.

Joaquín Bello and Luis Evelio Morales: These farmers were arbitrarily detained by an army patrol on September 8, 1996, near Caranal, Arauca. Bello, a peasant from Caranal, was the victim of an extrajudicial execution by soldiers on September 8, 1996.[170] On that date at about 2:45 a.m., soldiers came to his house looking for him by name. The soldiers were wearing ski masks and handkerchiefs to cover their faces. They handcuffed Bello, searched his house, and asked "Where are the arms?" When Bello asked why he was being handcuffed they responded that it was for security precautions. The soldiers accused Bello of collaborating with the guerrillas and took him away. When asked where he was being taken, the soldiers replied to the military base at Tame or the city of Arauca. Bello's wife was ordered not to leave her house until 7:00 a.m. Shortly afterwards, residents heard significant gunfire, so much that it sounded like a battle about one kilometer away. Residents found Bello corpse, apparently bearing signs of torture, on a bridge about one kilometer away from Caranal. Bello's widow went to military installations in Fortul to attempt to identify the soldiers responsible for her husband's detention. Over the course of half a day, approximately fifteen soldiers passed in front of her some half-dozen times. She did not recognize any of the soldiers.[171] Soldiers extrajudicially executed another man from Caranal, professional driver Luis Evelio

---

[169]Domicó is a common surname among the indigenous Emberá Katío people. Justice and Peace, *Boletín*, April-June 1996, p. 44.

[170]Human Rights Watch interview with witness, name withheld for security, Arauca, February 1997.

[171]Human Rights Watch interview with witnesses, Arauca, February 1997; and "Acusan el Ejército de dos asesinatos," *El Corredor*, September 14-27, 1996.

Morales, that same night. About five soldiers, faces uncovered, arrived at his house and informed family members that they were detaining Morales. They handcuffed him, telling his family to remain calm, that they were only taking care of an official act (*diligencia*), and that they had three more houses to search. Morales's family members asked why he was being detained, and where they could find him. The soldiers replied that they were taking him to either Tame or Yopal. After Morales's body was found, relatives lodged a complaint at the Fortul municipality and before military authorities. A community protest took place about a month after the killing.[172] Notice of his death aired publicly, together with that of Bello. Local press cited Operative Command No. 2 stating that soldiers of the Héroes of Pisba Counter-guerrilla Battalion No. 24 had engaged in armed combat with the UC-ELN.[173] The army continues to report the two as guerrillas killed in combat.[174]

Antonio Angarita and Carmen Angel Clavijo: These farmers were detained and executed by soldiers belonging to the Batalla de Palonegro Battalion No. 50, near San Calixto, Norte de Santander, on October 6, 1996. Angarita was president of the San Juan Neighborhood Action Committee. When the bodies were found four days later, authorities did an autopsy that revealed that Angarita had been tortured before being executed.[175] In the months following these killings, municipal officials were flooded with reports of joint army-paramilitary operations around San Calixto, Ábrego, and Ocaña.[176]

Jefferson Dario, González Oquendo, Oscar Orlando Bueno Bonnet, and Jhon Jairo Cabarique: These three young men were on a motorcycle in the 6 de Octubre

---

[172]Human Rights Watch interview with witness, name withheld for security reasons, Arauca, February 1997.

[173]*El Corredor*, "Acusan al Ejército de dos asesinatos," September 14-27, 1996.

[174]Letter from Major General Velasco Chávez, inspector, Colombian Armed Forces, to Human Rights Watch, December 31, 1997.

[175]CINEP and Justice and Peace, *Noche y Niebla*, No. 2, October-December, 1996, p. 89.

[176]Acción Urgente, Comisión para los Derechos Humanos, Comunidades eclesiales de base, Ocaña, Norte de Santander, April 11, 1997; Letter to Human Rights Watch from Francisco Antonio Coronel Julio, Personero Municipal, Ocaña, Norte de Santander, November 21, 1997; and Human Rights Watch interview with MINGA, December 1, 1997.

neighborhood of Saravena, Arauca, when soldiers belonging to the Rebeiz Pizarro Battalion detained them on January 10, 1997. Local human rights groups reported that a professional soldier known as "Careleche," in charge of an army patrol, fired on the three indiscriminately. Human Rights Watch also received reports that Bueno, a technician, was hit and took off his shirt to show his wounds, at which point Careleche beat and executed him. We also received reports that witnesses heard one of the men beg for mercy before soldiers killed him with four shots. González ran for three blocks before being shot down and killed. The army later presented all three bodies as guerrillas killed in combat. In the weeks surrounding this killing, the walls of Saravena were filled with graffiti signed by a group calling itself "The Black Hand," which government authorities and residents believed was made up of Rebeiz Pizarro soldiers.[177] Internal Affairs has opened a formal investigation against army soldiers.[178] The army continues to claim that the three were guerrillas killed in combat.[179] However, the evidence strongly suggests that this is a violation of the ban on killing civilians, since these young men were not combatants but were targeted because of their youth and the fact that they were in a neighborhood believed by the army to be under guerrilla control.

Miguel Angel Graciano: This young man was seized by an army unit patrolling with paramilitaries near his home in Salto de Apartadó, Antioquia on March 26, 1997. A brother-in-law later told authorities that he had been detained before Graciano, who came to his house to bring him some fish. An army officer asked the brother-in-law to identify Graciano, which he did. The two were taken to the El Trebol Ranch. Paramilitaries freed the brother-in-law, who was told to tell his neighbors that they had only eight days to abandon their homes and farms.[180]

---

[177]Human Rights Watch interview with Colombian government investigator, Santafé de Bogotá, January 30, 1997; Human Rights Watch interviews with human rights defenders and family members, Saravena, Arauca, February 4, 1997; and statement from Arauca residents to Human Rights Watch, June 1997.

[178]Letter to Human Rights Watch from Jesús Orlando Gómez López, Internal Affairs delegate for human rights, November 28, 1997.

[179]Letter from Major General Velasco Chávez, inspector, Colombian Armed Forces, to Human Rights Watch, December 31, 1997.

[180]Declaration of Bernardo Moreno Londoño to the regional Public Advocate's Office, Apartadó, Antioquia, April 7, 1997; and Human Rights Watch interview with María Girlesa Villegas, Public Advocate's Office, Medellín, Antioquia, December 9, 1997.

Neighbors found Graciano's body tied to a tree near the El Trebol Ranch, bound and garrotted. His eyes had been removed, his teeth shattered, his skin burned, and his throat slit.[181]

El Carmen del Cucú, Bolívar: After a clash between the UC-ELN and the army's Héroes de Majagual Battalion No. 45 on June 20, 1997 guerrillas asked townspeople for help in treating six wounded fighters. With no medical workers or Red Cross officials available, El Carmen del Cucú Police Inspector Edinson Canchila, a driver, and a local resident used a tractor to pick up the wounded guerrillas. With wounded fighters on board, the tractor was ambushed by soldiers, who killed Canchila and driver Ismael Guarín. The six wounded guerrillas were apparently executed on the spot. All eight, including Canchila and Guarín, were later presented to the press as guerrillas killed in combat.[182] The massacre of wounded combatants and townspeople who assisted them is an egregious violation of the laws of war.

Ortiz family: On November 11, 1997, brothers José Rosario and Jesús Salvador Ortiz and their nephew, sixteen-year-old Diomar Eli Ortiz, were on their way to make purchases at a store near Ábrego, Norte de Santander, when soldiers from the Santander Battalion began firing on them. The three first ran, then surrendered and were captured alive. However, soldiers delivered their cadavers to a local funeral home later that day. The bodies showed signs of torture. A Santander Battalion press release described the three as guerrillas killed in combat.[183]

---

[181]Declaration of José Isaias Graciano Moreno to the regional Public Advocate's Office, Apartadó, Antioquia, April 7, 1997; and Human Rights Watch interview with María Girlesa Villegas, regional Public Advocate's Office, Medellín, Antioquia, December 9, 1997.

[182]Human Rights Watch interview with MINGA, Santafé de Bogotá, December 1, 1997; and CINEP and Justice and Peace, Noche y Niebla, No. 4, April-June 1997, p. 54.

[183]A day earlier, the army reported combat with the UC-ELN nearby. Letter to Human Rights Watch from Francisco Antonio Coronel Julio, personero, Ocaña, Norte de Santander, November 21, 1997; and Letter from MINGA to Volmar Pérez, national director, Office of Complaints, Public Advocate's Office, November 21, 1997.

Attacks on medical workers, installations, and ambulances

Gaitania, Tolima: After a clash between soldiers and guerrillas in this mountainous area on January 13, 1997, medical workers from the Planadas Central Hospital sent an emergency medical team. Since their ambulance was not working, two nurses, a medical worker, and a driver traveled in a green vehicle. At the entrance to Gaitania, one of the nurses later told reporters, soldiers ordered them to stop, which they did. The soldiers, from the Caicedo Battalion and under the command of Sixth Brigade Col. Hernán Gutiérrez, fired on the vehicle even though the team identified itself and its mission. Apparently, soldiers believed there was an injured guerrilla in the vehicle. Miraculously, none of the passengers was hurt. However, the car behind the medical team was also fired on, killing Israel Tapiero, a civilian, and wounding three others, including a seven-year-old girl.[184]

Fredy Yessid Contreras Osorio: This Saravena, Arauca medical worker had reported threats from a professional soldier known as "Careleche" in 1997. On April 20, Careleche and several other soldiers reportedly broke into the Sarare Regional Hospital and executed Contreras. Contreras was also a member of a medical workers union. Soldiers again broke into the hospital to interrogate medical workers and patients on May 23.[185]

Ascanio family: Long a target of army and paramilitary threats, the Ascanio family had their home in Mesa Rica, Norte de Santander, seized by soldiers belonging to the Santander Battalion on July 20, 1997. Accompanied by known paramilitaries, soldiers interrogated Elizabeth Ascanio about the whereabouts of her father and husband, beating her. Although she was pregnant, soldiers jumped on her and put a knife to her neck. Several children were also beaten, and others in the household were pistol-whipped, one so severely that his skull was fractured. When Elizabeth

---

[184]"Denuncian disparos de soldados contra civiles," *El Tiempo*, January 14, 1997.

[185]According to the Colombian government, the case is under investigation by the Attorney General's Office. Statement from Arauca residents to Human Rights Watch, June 1997; CINEP and Justice and Peace, *Noche y Niebla*, No. 5, July-September 1997, p. 168; and Colombian government's response to cases submitted to the office of the U.N. High Commissioner for Human Rights, January-June, 1997.

Ascanio went via ambulance to the Hacarí hospital the next day, soldiers stopped the vehicle and again interrogated her.[186]

Threats

José Estanislao Amaya Páez: This San Calixto, Norte de Santander personero reported receiving death threats from soldiers of the Santander Battalion on July 13, 1997, apparently because he accepted written complaints by residents of army abuses. As Amaya was in his home with a friend, the friend saw a death threat slipped under the door. Rushing to investigate, Amaya discovered that the threat had been delivered by a group of soldiers wearing ski masks patrolling town. The threat read: "Personero: You have exactly eight days to abandon Norte de Santander and especially San Calixto. Auto Defenzas [sic] del Catatumbo. Death to those who aid or collaborate with guerrillas. After you, many more will follow." After reporting the threat to authorities, Amaya received continued threats, and reliable sources told him that soldiers had been given orders to kill him. Amaya was murdered on December 9, 1997, in circumstances that remain unclear.[187] We believe the army authored the death threat against Amaya.

Other acts that violate international humanitarian law

Army bases: Repeatedly, Human Rights Watch received credible information that army bases were located in or adjoining civilian structures, endangering non-combatants. Often, bases are surrounded by land mines, endangering the civilian population. Near Arauquita, Arauca, for example, the municipal education secretary requested that a military base be moved from a location adjoining a school attended by 180 students. Local authorities were concerned not only about a potential guerrilla attack; according to news reports, soldiers occasionally fired on the school, pockmarking its walls.[188] Another army base within the limits of Calamar, Guaviare has put the civilian population in repeated danger. Residents told Human Rights Watch that the location of the army's Joaquín París Battalion

---

[186]Human Rights Watch interview with Ascanio family, Mesa Rica, Norte de Santander, April 15, 1995; and CINEP and Justice and Peace, *Noche y Niebla*, No. 5, July-September, 1997, pp. 91-92.

[187]Formal complaint by José Estanislao Amaya Páez to the Cúcuta District Judge, July 16, 1997.

[188]"Piden trasladar base militar," *El Tiempo*, April 25, 1997; and CINEP and Justice and Peace, *Noche y Niebla*, No. 4, April-June, 1997, p. 101.

is dangerous not only for adjacent houses, but also to a school serving 500 students that shares a border with the base. During attacks, residents have taken shelter under furniture. Witnesses told us that it is common after attacks to find bullet casings on the streets and rooftops.[189] In Miraflores, Guaviare, the Anti-Narcotics Police, the army's Joaquín París Battalion, and Mobile Brigade Two have joined their bases and now completely surround the only Catholic Church and what was formerly the town's only playground.[190] The army should not use residential and protected areas to shield bases in war zones.

Operation Genesis: After the ACCU began a sweep into the department of Chocó in 1996, the army's Seventeenth Brigade followed in February 1997 with aerial attacks, some indiscriminate. Called Operation Genesis, the army operation prompted widespread and credible reports that soldiers coordinated openly with paramilitary groups and attacked civilian dwellings indiscriminately, provoking mass displacement and severe hardship to the civilian population in violation of Protocol II. Following army bombings and rocket attacks, ACCU paramilitaries repeatedly entered villages and ordered residents to leave. While in some places paramilitary threats were enough to convince people to flee, in others the paramilitaries executed village leaders or other residents to show that they meant business.[191] According to one survivor who fled from Riosucio with a family of eight and was later interviewed by Human Rights Watch,

> At around 6:15 a.m., the bombs began to fall. One bomb fell fifty meters from a house. In Caño Seco, Salaquí, a school was destroyed and in Tamboral and La Loma, three houses were destroyed. The paramilitaries threatened us that the bombing would continue so the communities began to flee in wave after wave. Some of us walked for twenty and thirty days. Two children died on the way and another woman and her baby died during childbirth. About sixty woman who were pregnant made

---

[189]Human Rights Watch interviews with Calamar residents and authorities, San José del Guaviare, Guaviare, May 5-6, 1997.

[190]Human Rights Watch interview with authorities, San José del Guaviare, Guaviare, May 5, 1997; and Human Rights Watch interview with Public Advocate's Office, Santafé de Bogotá, November 9, 1995.

[191]Human Rights Watch interviews with displaced, Santafé de Bogotá, July 22, 1997.

the journey. Four babies were born, but the mothers had to walk
again the next day. We had to keep moving because we were
afraid that our way would be blocked and it was the only way
out.[192]

Subsequently, in a public meeting with representatives of the displaced at
Pavarandó in June 1997, Gen. Rito Alejo Del Río, then-commander of the
Seventeenth Brigade responsible for Operation Genesis, claimed that army attacks
had been provoked by fire from the ground and said that no "decent people" (*gente
de bien*) had been harmed. Human Rights Watch rejects this notion entirely
because it ignores the most basic tenet of the laws of war — that combatants must
make careful distinctions between combatants and civilians regardless of whether
individuals may qualify for army officers as "decent people." The displaced who
had witnessed the attacks told humanitarian aid workers that military airplanes had
initiated many of the attacks when there was no ground fire or guerrillas present.[193]
In this case, the army treated this region as a target, harming the civilian population
and causing between 15,000 and 17,000 people to flee. In addition, we hold state
forces responsible for paramilitary killings and forced disappearances, which they
apparently promoted and certainly failed to prevent even though they had troops
in the area.

Operation Destructor II: According to Yaguará indigenous leaders, on September
4 and 5, 1997, on and near this indigenous reservation in the departments of
Caquetá, Meta, and Guaviare, 220 people were forced to flee because of
indiscriminate rocket attacks from five army helicopters and one army airplane. A
strong FARC contingent was reportedly in the area.[194] Nevertheless, these attacks
set some civilian homes on fire when there were no guerrillas present according to
a report by the Public Advocate's Office after an on-site visit. The Public
Advocate's Office also noted that army projectiles killed animals and seriously
damaged crops. Some families had dug holes in the dirt floors of their houses, to

---

[192]Ibid.

[193]Letter to Human Rights Watch from humanitarian aid worker, June 1997.

[194]"Pacto de guerra," *Semana*, September 22, 1997.

protect themselves from stray bullets as they slept at night.[195] Because of a motion filed by the Public Advocate's Office, the Administrative Tribunal of Cundinamarca ruled July 30, 1998 that the Colombian government and the Ministry of Defense must pay $24,000 (US) to residents of Yaguara II for damages suffered during the military operation.[196]

Roadblocks: Human Rights Watch has received numerous credible reports of civilians killed or seriously injured at army roadblocks. According to the army, there are two types of roadblocks: public ones, to provide security on highways, with soldiers identified by road signs and reflective jackets; and occasional ones, often hidden to travelers, to capture suspects.[197] This latter style has resulted in numerous civilian casualties, when soldiers open fire from hidden locations and without warning, harming non-combatants. For instance, on February 15, 1998, soldiers shot at a car that did not stop when they said they hailed it near Cúcuta, Norte de Santander, killing seventeen-year-old Carlos Eduardo Flórez Méndez.[198] Near midnight on January 25, 1998, soldiers from the Colombia Infantry Battalion 28 fired on civilian vehicles near Villeta, Cundinamarca, killing five people and wounding five. Survivors told reporters that the roadblock was poorly marked, and they didn't realize it was there until they heard shots. Apparently, soldiers believed a guerrilla caravan was near, but failed to check before attacking.[199] The army commander later admitted that the deaths "could have been avoided" and that there were "mistakes made in the planning, procedures, and execution of the military operation.[200] The case was closed to independent inquiry when it was passed to a

---

[195]The army denied destroying any civilian structure. Public Advocate's Office, "Informe Comisión a los Llanos del Yarí," September 25, 1997; CINEP and Justice and Peace, *Noche y Niebla*, No. 5, July-September, 1997, p. 135; and Orlando Restrepo and Jorge González, "'Destructor II, éxito estratégico': Galán," *El Tiempo*, October 20, 1997.

[196]"Minidefensa pagará errores de la operación 'Destructor II,'" *El Espectador*, September 4, 1998.

[197] "ABC de retenes," *El Tiempo*, January 27, 1998.

[198]CINEP and Justice and Peace, *Noche y Niebla*, No. 4, April-June, 1997, p. 156.

[199]"Extraña muerte de 5 personas en retén militar," *El Colombiano*, January 26, 1998; and "Muertos cinco civiles en retén militar en Villeta," *El Tiempo*, January 26, 1998.

[200]"Ejército admite fallas en retén militar," *El Tiempo*, January 27, 1998.

military tribunal on March 15, 1998.[201] During a similar roadblock set up a week later near Puerto Carreño, Vichada, the army fired on UC-ELN guerrillas traveling with five kidnapped shop owners, killing both guerrillas and their hostages, even though the army knew that guerrillas had the shop owners in their custody.[202]

Public buses: Repeatedly, Human Rights Watch has received credible information that the Colombian army has failed to remove civilian passengers before using public buses to transport troops during operations. This practice puts the civilian population at serious risk, and there have been numerous attacks by guerrillas against these vehicles. The army should not use these vehicles to transport troops when there are civilian passengers present. In one particularly egregious case, a combined army-paramilitary patrol forcibly boarded a public bus near Ituango, Antioquia, that was later attacked by the FARC. In the attack, the driver was reportedly paralyzed.[203]

National Police

> *If the civilian population fails to collaborate with us, well, we'll withdraw the police and let the guerrillas enter and finish them off.*
>
> *– Gen. Rosso José Serrano, Sucre*
> *March 13, 1996*

Colombia's National Police were formed in 1891 as a constabulary independent of the military. During the period of internal conflict known as La Violencia from 1948-1958, the police were incorporated into the armed forces and

---

[201]Guillermo Restrepo Gutiérrez, "Retenes, ¿Peligro o seguridad en la vía?" *El Colombiano*, February 15, 1998; and "Justicia militar sigue con el caso del retén de Villeta," *El Tiempo*, March 6, 1998.

[202]"Cinco muertos en otro 'reten'," *El Espectador*, February 3, 1998; and "Sabíamos que iban comerciantes," *El Tiempo*, February 14, 1998.

[203]Human Rights Watch interview with Jesús Valle Jaramillo, president, "Héctor Abad Gómez" Permanent Committee for Human Rights, Medellín, Antioquia, December 10, 1997; and Human Rights Watch interview with Antioquia businessman, Guarné, Antioquia, December 11, 1997.

remain under the direct command of the military officer in command of the armed forces. Police are responsible for keeping public order within towns where their stations are located and in the villages they visit. Colombia's 103,000 police officers are present in over 90 percent of Colombia's municipalities.[204]

The National Police is divided by task. Most agents work at either the metropolitan or departmental level. Colombia also has specialized units, including the Anti-Narcotics Police, responsible for pursuing traffickers and destroying laboratories and drug crops, and police intelligence. The Judicial Police (Dirección Nacional de Policía Judicial e Investigación, DIJIN) are responsible for investigating cases destined for a judge. This unit is divided at the departmental level into Sectional Judicial Police (Seccional de Policía Judicial, SIJIN). Police also join soldiers in the anti-kidnapping groups known as the GAULA and in Search Blocks, set up to investigate and capture well-known criminals.[205]

With the appointment of Gen. Rosso José Serrano as chief in 1994, the police began a improvement campaign, in part to instill a greater respect for human rights and recoup lost credibility among a populace that considered the institution corrupt and abusive. A new law, implemented in 1993, established the position of civilian commissioner to pursue complaints or evidence of human rights abuse. Although the commissioner's office has been hampered in its ability to oversee the police and abuses continue, human rights groups agree that the National Police have improved their record in the 1990s.

National Police and International Humanitarian Law

Like the military, the National Police have embraced the language of human rights and international humanitarian law and conduct regular training on these international standards. Various sources consulted by Human Rights Watch agreed that overall, Gen. José Rosso Serrano and the National Police are more responsive to reports of violations by their members than in previous years, when

---

[204]Human Rights Watch interview with Gen. Rosso José Serrano, Santafé de Bogotá, September 8, 1997; and Grupo de Estrategas para el Cambio, *Transformación Cultural y Mejoramiento Institucional* (Santafé de Bogotá: Policía Nacional, 1995), p. 48.

[205]SIJIN agents are often identified by civilians as F-2 agents, reflecting a former police structure that no longer exists. More information is available at http:// trauco.colomsat.net.co/ policia.co/.

officers were routinely linked to massacres, political killings, forced disappearances, and torture and little was done about it.[206]

For example, using Decree 573, passed in 1995, General Serrano can summarily fire officers accused of abuses if there is convincing evidence against them.[207]

"If they believe a report is credible, the officer is relieved of duty immediately and put at the disposition of government investigators," one government investigator told us.[208]

Nevertheless, police continue to be implicated in violations, as described below.[209] Most notorious are cases where officers belonging to the SIJIN capture and execute suspected guerrillas. In areas where paramilitaries are present, police

---

[206]Among the more well-known cases were the Trujillo, Valle del Cauca killings of over 100 people, most of which took place in 1990 and included the participation of the National Police; the Caloto, Cauca massacre of seventeen people on April 7, 1991, carried out by National Police and Anti-Narcotics Police officers working with paramilitaries; and the 1992 Villatina massacre, carried out by police intelligence agents in Medellín, Antioquia and resulting in the deaths of eight children. According to the Attorney General's Office, two National Police officers are currently being prosecuted by civilian courts for their alleged participation in the Villatina massacre. President Samper has acknowledged the state's responsibility for all three massacres. Centro de Información de Colombia, Press Bulletin No. 338, "Fiscalía entrega resultados de investigaciones sobre masacres," May 19, 1998; and Tim Johnson, "Samper apologizes for state killings," *Miami Herald*, July 30, 1998.

[207]According to the decree, a judge can request that a junior officer be suspended based on evidence he or she deems credible. The suspension becomes permanent if the judge does not revoke it within 180 days or convicts the junior officer. In the cases of officers with the rank of colonel or above, in addition the a judge's request for a suspension, a committee of officers evaluates the accusation and collects evidence from police, the attorney general, Internal Affairs, and non-governmental organizations. If credible evidence is found suggesting that an officer has committed a crime, including human rights abuses, the officer can be fired within twenty-four hours and the case forwarded to authorities for investigation and prosecution. Decree 573, April 4, 1995.

[208]Human Rights Watch interview with government investigator, Santafé de Bogotá, December 1, 1997.

[209]Also, police continue to be implicated in abuses related to public order, particularly the use of excessive force in evicting poor squatters from urban areas, and the arrest and treatment of common criminals. Human Rights Watch telephone interview with CCJ, August 26, 1998.

have been directly implicated in joint army-paramilitary actions and have sometimes organized paramilitaries and supplied information to them to assemble death lists. For instance, government investigators concluded in 1998 that police in La Ceja, Antioquia organized and deployed paramilitaries considered responsible for at least thirty killings in 1996 and 1997.[210]

Police have also stood by while paramilitaries select and kill their victims. Over a four-day period in October 1997, for instance, the Anti-Narcotics Police based in Miraflores, Guaviare failed to apprehend or even question the paramilitaries who killed at least four people. According to residents who spoke later to government authorities, police left their barracks only to collect the bodies of the dead. The Anti-Narcotics Police commander later confirmed to a journalist that police neither patrolled the town nor investigated the killings, a shocking passivity in the face of such atrocities.[211]

Police frequently and publicly describe whole populations as guerrillas or sympathetic to them and withdraw police protection, in part as punishment for their perceived allegiance. This is especially apparent after guerrilla attacks on towns, known as *tomas*. The police attitude reflects a profound disregard for international humanitarian law and of their own duty, as defined by Colombia's laws. In effect, police punish civilians for their perceived support for insurgents or, worse, allow and encourage a paramilitary attack to occur.

For instance, after a guerrilla attack on Chalán, Sucre that resulted in the deaths of eleven officers in March, 1996, General Serrano told journalists, "If the civilian population fails to collaborate with us, well, we'll withdraw the police and let the guerrillas enter and finish them off." His assistant, Gen. Luis Montenegro, now head of the DAS, echoed his words, calling residents "[guerrilla]

---

[210]Lt. Daniel Horacio Mazo Cardona and agents Carlos Alberto Rentería Lemos and Luis Alfredo Berrocal Moreno are under arrest, charged by the attorney general's office with creating paramilitary groups. Press Release, "Aseguran a policías paramilitares de La Ceja, Antioquia," Attorney General's Office, March 30, 1998.

[211]We are not aware of any credible investigation into the behavior of the Anti-Narcotics Police unit in this case. Human Rights Watch interview with town authorities, San José del Guaviare, May 5, 1997; Letter to Human Rights Watch from town authorities, October, 1997; and Tod Robberson, "Killings could cost Colombia: Human-rights review may cut off U.S. aid," *Dallas Morning News*, January 10, 1998.

accomplices... The people of Chalán don't deserve the police they have... The people either support [guerrillas] or support us."[212]

In the case of Chalán, instead of reinforcing the police, commanders withdrew their officers from Chalán and six nearby municipalities. In the weeks following, paramilitaries threatened and killed dozens of local teachers, community leaders, and farmers, prompting hundreds of families to flee. More than a year after the attack, police had still not returned to Chalán, and its mayor was forced to move his office to a larger city for safety reasons. The same threats to remove the police were repeated in several towns in 1996 and 1997.

"Recently, General Serrano said that he wanted to withdraw all police officers from southern Bolívar, after a guerrilla takeover of a town," one government investigator told Human Rights Watch. "He said his men were being massacred by the indolence of the civilian population and didn't deserve their protection."[213]

Many police commanders have an openly hostile attitude to human rights and the people who defend them by reporting on violations. "Whoever complains about human rights to you is by definition a guerrilla," commented Antioquia Deputy Commander Col. Antonio D'León Martínez in an interview with Human Rights Watch.[214]

After the Catholic Church sponsored workshops on human rights in El Peñol, Antioquia in March 1998 and invited local police, organizers learned that police planned to attend only to "take notes and photograph those present," which organizers interpreted as an attempt to identify and later persecute human rights defenders and discourage residents from taking part. Subsequently, the workshop organizers began receiving telephone death threats, which they attributed to police.[215]

It is important to note, however, that some police officers have courageously defended civilians from attacks from all sides and have investigated

---

[212]"Chalán no merece la Policía: Montenegro," *El Heraldo*, March 14, 1996; and "Farc asesinan a 11 policías en Chalán, *El Tiempo*, March 14, 1996.

[213]Human Rights Watch interview with government investigator, Barrancabermeja, Santander, June 28, 1996.

[214]Human Rights Watch interview, Medellín, Antioquia, July 2, 1996.

[215]Letter from Father Javier Giraldo, Justice and Peace, to Gen. Rosso José Serrano, National Police commander, April 17, 1998.

paramilitaries. We have reported in the past, for example, that the police commander in Aguachica, Cesar told government prosecutors about army support for paramilitaries responsible for several massacres.[216]

When paramilitaries told the police commander of Peque, Antioquia that they would begin a "cleansing of the town" on December 6, 1997, and told him to detain and deliver certain people to them, he refused to comply. When paramilitaries attempted to enter by force that evening, police resisted. Nevertheless, over the next two days, paramilitaries set up roadblocks outside town, killing at least five. Only on December 8 did the army appear. However, the paramilitaries had enough time to pack up and leave the area via the major highway that connects Peque to Medellín.[217]

Like members of the armed forces, members of the police are often tried for alleged abuses by military tribunals. More police officers than soldiers have been convicted of human rights-related crimes in these tribunals. Increasingly, cases involving police are being sent to civilian courts, as we note below. Cases involving civil damages are also frequent, and the National Police have consistently been found liable for wrongful death and damages.

In 1997, for instance, a court in Arauca found the National Police liable for the 1989 murder of Arauquita personero Jorge Álvaro Flórez Santiz and ordered the institution to pay the family the equivalent of 1,000 grams of gold. In a separate proceeding, the officer involved was sentenced to twenty-two years in prison.[218]

Murder

Jorge Eliécer López, Gustavo Adolfo Díaz, and Edinson Echeverry: López and Echeverry, who were soldiers, and Díaz, a mechanic, were detained by SIJIN agents based in Palmira, Valle on February 8, 1996. According to an investigation

---

[216]In March 1998, Internal Affairs ordered that army Maj. Jorge Alberto Lázaro Vergel be removed from service for his role in forming and deploying paramilitary groups. The following June, the Attorney General's Office issued an arrest warrant for Lázaro for a 1994 murder. "Destitución para oficial," *El Tiempo*, March 6, 1998; "Asegurados ex sargentos de ejército," *El Tiempo*, June 18, 1998; and Human Rights Watch/Americas, *Colombia's Killer Networks*, pp. 48-50.

[217]"'Cumplí con mi deber'," *El Colombiano*, December 10, 1997; and CINEP and Justice and Peace, *Noche y Niebla*, October-December 1997, p. 46.

[218]"Policía pagará por muerte de personero," *El Tiempo*, November 4, 1997.

by the Public Advocate's Office in Cali, eight police officers operating in an area known as Aguaclara detained the three as suspected guerrillas near a fruit stand and forced them into one of their vehicles. The bodies of López and Echeverry were found several days later on the banks of the Cauca River. To our knowledge, Díaz's body has not been found.[219] Subsequently, police investigated the incident and concluded that Second Lt. José Fernando Montoya Castellanos had violated police regulations by planning and ordering the abduction and killings. Montoya was removed from the force along with the four officers who took part. Also removed from the force were Commander Olga Lucía Largo and two officers who helped cover up the killings.[220] In July 1998, all eight were convicted and sentenced to prison for murder.[221]

Fabio Fonseca Guerrero: This former mayor of Uribia, La Guajira was killed by six members of the Anti-Narcotics Police near Puerto Chimare as he accompanied a group of civic leaders to a meeting on July 17, 1996. The group was apparently ambushed by police officers who fired without warning. Six officers were later accused of carrying out the attack.[222] At the time of this writing, the case was before a military tribunal.[223]

José David Negrette, Guillermo Martínez, and Alejandro Teheran: Negrette, Martínez, and Teheran were detained along with John Negrette by a four-man

---

[219]Letter to Public Advocate's Office from Hernando Toro Parra, regional Public Advocate's Office, Cali, Valle, November 25, 1997; and Justice and Peace, *Boletín*, Vol. 9, No. 1, January-March, 1996, p. 46.

[220]Letter from Lt. Col. Gustavo de Jesús Agudelo Carrillo, Subcomandante, Valle Police, to National Police Human Rights Office, November 28, 1997.

[221]"Por asesinato, condenan a ocho ex policías," *El Tiempo*, July 25, 1998; and Letter to Public Advocate's Office from Hernando Toro Parra, regional Public Advocate's Office, Cali, Valle, November 25, 1997.

[222]Letter to Public Advocate's Office from Wilder Rafael Guerra Millán, regional Public Advocate's Office, Riohacha, La Guajira, December 1, 1997; and CINEP and Justice and Peace, *Noche y Niebla*, No. 1, July-September, 1996, p. 22.

[223]Letter to Human Rights Watch from Gen. Leonardo Gallego, Anti-Narcotics Police, November 11, 1997.

police patrol under the command of Francisco Guzmán in a Tierralta, Córdoba bar on February 13, 1997. Forced to board a police vehicle, the four were taken to a site known as Puente de las Torturas (Bridge of Tortures). John Negrette managed to disarm Officer Diego Guzmán [no relation to the commander], then shot and killed him before fleeing. Subsequently, police beat and executed their three remaining captives. Once he had fled to nearby Montería, John Negrette presented himself to police, turned in Guzmán's revolver, and told what had happened. Nevertheless, the initial police report of the incident listed the three men as guerrillas killed in combat.[224] Internal Affairs is investigating the case.[225] A later police report corrected their version of events, acknowledging that the three civilians had been executed by Officer Francisco Guzmán, who also fired on the police vehicle to simulate a guerrilla attack. At the time of this writing, Guzmán had been formally removed from the police force and was awaiting trial by a military tribunal in the Las Mercedes prison in Córdoba. The other three officers were suspended and awaiting trial by civilian courts.[226]

Torture

Jesús Cevardo Giraldo, Álvaro Viera Díaz, Carlos Arias Alberto Giraldo, and John Francisco Cruz Romero: These individuals were detained as suspected guerrillas in Santafé de Bogotá by police on February 21, 1996, and tortured with near-suffocation, beatings, and mock executions. The four were suspected of having taken part in the murder of the son of Gen. (ret.) Ricardo Emilio Cifuentes five days earlier. According to their lawyer, the torture took place within the first ten hours after their arrest. Giraldo and Viera were later released, while Arias and Cruz were formally charged with murder.[227]

Martín Jerez Balquicet and Teobaldo Díaz Márquez: These young men were detained as suspected guerrillas by a police patrol on November 16, 1997 in the Las

---

[224]CINEP and Justice and Peace, *Noche y Niebla*, No. 3, January-March, 1997, p. 41; and José Fernando Hoyos, "En Tierralta la muerte hizo su ronda," *El Tiempo*, February 23, 1997.

[225]Letter to Human Rights Watch from Jesús Orlando Gómez López, Internal Affairs delegate for human rights, November 28, 1997

[226]Letter from Lt. Col. Germán Alonso Bernal, subcomandante, Córdoba Police, to Human Rights Division, National Police, November 28, 1997.

[227]Justice and Peace, *Boletín*, January-March 1996, p. 48.

Granjas neighborhood of Barrancabermeja, Santander. During their arrest, they were kept incommunicado. Human rights groups reported that police beat them with sticks and their fists.[228]

Misuse of the red cross emblem

Florencia, Caquetá: On August 22, 1996, National Police officers used a red cross, the internationally-protected emblem for medical workers, ambulances, and medical facilities, on a vehicle used to transport smoke and tear gas grenades in their effort to break up a peasant protest march. In an interview with Human Rights Watch, National Police Human Rights Officer Col. Julio Moreno claimed that the laws of war do not apply to this incident, since police were acting to maintain public order, not fight guerrillas. However, we believe this interpretation seriously mischaracterizes the evidence. At the time, the department of Caquetá was under emergency legislation because of the marches, which the government repeatedly described as organized by guerrillas.[229] The police violated the ban contained in Article 12 of Protocol II against misuse of the emblem. To their credit, Colombian government investigators have aggressively investigated the incident. The Internal Affairs delegate for the judicial police filed formal charges against the former commander of the Caquetá police, Col. José Edilberto Rojas, for illegal use of the emblem, prohibited by Article 169 of the military penal code.[230] Also charged were his assistant, Lt. Col. Fabio Sánchez Múnera; Maj. Humberto Guarín Rojas; Sgt. Luis Alfonso Barajas; agent Giovany Yepes, who drove the vehicle; and agent Rigoberto Jara Andrade.[231]

Other acts that violate international humanitarian law

Caicedo, Antioquia: In only two years, this Cauca Valley town was attacked five times – three times by the FARC and twice by the ACCU. After a 1996 FARC attack, National Police left the town, claiming that its residents were sympathetic to guerrillas (see case in ACCU section). As proof, police cited the fact that store owners obeyed a FARC edict threatening them with death if they sold police food,

---

[228]CINEP and Justice and Peace, *Noche y Niebla*, No. 6, October-December 1997, p. 41.

[229]Human Rights Watch interview with Col. Julio Moreno, National Police, Santafé de Bogotá, May 8, 1997.

[230]Alejandro Valencia Villa, *Derecho Humanitario para Colombia*, pp. 213-214.

[231]"Cargos contra policía por uso indebido de emblemas," *El Tiempo*, April 11, 1997.

clothing, or medicine, forcing police to truck in supplies.[232] In 1997, police returned and built a new barracks that shared a wall with Caicedo's Catholic Church. Predictably, the FARC attacked again on October 15, 1997, destroying the church along with the barracks.[233] Although we hold the FARC responsible for a violation, since they apparently set explosives under the wall the structures shared and did nothing to minimize damage to the church, a protected structure, the police also committed a violation by constructing the barracks to share a common wall with the church, in effect using it as a shield from attack. Given Caicedo's history of FARC attacks, a future attempt to attack police there was predictable and should have dissuaded the National Police from locating a barracks next to a church. According to Article 58 (b) and (c) of Protocol I, parties to the conflict shall, to the maximum extent feasible, avoid locating military objectives within or near densely populated areas and take the other necessary precautions to protect the civilian population, individual civilians and civilian objects under their control against the dangers resulting from military operations.

Special Vigilance and Private Security Services (CONVIVIR)

> *We are paramilitaries, macetos, or CONVIVIR, whatever the hell you want to call us.*
> *– Commander Cañón, CONVIVIR leader, Santander*
> *1997*

In 1994, the Colombian government announced a plan to establish "Special Vigilance and Private Security Services" (Servicios de Vigilancia y Seguridad Privada), later renamed CONVIVIR. CONVIVIRs were meant to be formed in combat areas, where the government said it could not fully guarantee public safety. Authorized by Decree 356, these groups were to be made up of individuals who petition the government for a license to "provide their own security... in areas of high risk or in the public interest, which requires a high level

---

[232]Human Rights Watch interview with Col. Julio Moreno, National Police, Santafé de Bogotá, May 8, 1997.

[233]Eight officers were killed in combat. "Ocho policías muertos en toma guerrillera a Caicedo," *El Espectador*, October 17, 1997; and "Vuelan iglesia para atacar a la Policía," *El Colombiano*, October 17, 1997.

of security."[234] Unlike paramilitary groups, outlawed in 1989, CONVIVIRs enjoy explicit government support.

Human Rights Watch visited one CONVIVIR in Rionegro, Antioquia, in 1996. At the time, then-Antioquia Gov. Álvaro Uribe Vélez and his vice-governor, Pedro Juan Moreno, were outspoken supporters of CONVIVIRs. Considered a model association, the Rionegro CONVIVIR counted among its members Moreno and seventy others, anonymous except to the government and local army and police chiefs. We were accompanied by Vice-Governor Moreno, the local police chief, and army Col. Guillermo Cock, in charge of setting up new CONVIVIRs in Antioquia.

The Rionegro CONVIVIR covered the municipalities of Rionegro, home to the international airport that serves Medellín, La Ceja, and Retiro. Upon obtaining a government license, CONVIVIR members contributed a monthly fee, which covered the salaries of CONVIVIR employees, equipment, vehicles, and expenditures for office space. Each member bought a radio for his or her ranch, which allowed communication with the central office staffed twenty-four hours a day by young men hired by the CONVIVIR to monitor radio frequencies and patrol the area.

If a CONVIVIR member noticed suspicious activity, the member would radio the central office, where he or she would be identified by a number code corresponding to the ranch. CONVIVIR employees also conduct intelligence operations and provide information to the police and army.[235]

When we visited, the Rionegro CONVIVIR was based in an apartment in a residential complex. Opposite a playground and amid closely-spaced apartments, nothing distinguished the CONVIVIR door from a residence. According to the CONVIVIR administrator, an employee who asked to be identified as "Mario," he

---

[234]Defense Ministry, Decree 356, República de Colombia, February 11, 1994, pp. 19-20; and Resolution 368, April 27, 1995.

[235] After our visit, Governor Uribe told the newsweekly *Semana* that Human Rights Watch had found "nothing irregular" in the Rionegro CONVIVIR. As this section demonstrates, quite the opposite is true. Human Rights Watch visit to Rionegro, Antioquia, July 4, 1996; and "Mano dura," *Semana*, October 15, 1996.

and his employees were retired soldiers recommended for the job by Medellín's Fourth Brigade. None wore uniforms or any visible CONVIVIR identification.[236]

Mario told us that the Rionegro CONVIVIR worked closely with the security forces to patrol and respond quickly in emergencies. Information collected by the CONVIVIR on its regular patrols, he noted, had been provided to the security forces and used to mount operations. A CONVIVIR representative also joined local authorities for periodic meetings to discuss security matters. By the end of 1996, some Antioquia CONVIVIRs had also met with ICRC representatives and had received information on international humanitarian law.[237]

Like companies that sell security services to banks, commercial establishments, and private offices, CONVIVIRs are supervised by the Superintendency for Vigilance and Private Security (Superintendencia de Vigiliancia y Seguridad Privada), a government agency within the Defense Ministry that issues licenses and is charged with monitoring their activities.[238]

From the start, CONVIVIRs were controversial even within the government. They gained immediate support among influential groups, among them ranchers, businesspeople, some municipal officials, and the security forces, in particular the army.[239] Others, including then-Interior Minister Horacio Serpa, said they feared a return to 1980s-style paramilitary activity, a concern echoed by some human rights groups. Defense Minister Fernando Botero assured the public that CONVIVIRs would operate under intense scrutiny and that only individuals without criminal records would be allowed to join.[240]

---

[236] In contrast, private security companies who arm their employees are required by law to clothe their employees in uniform with visible identification. CONVIVIRs and private security companies are supervised by the same government agency. Human Rights Watch interview with Mario, Rionegro, Antioquia, July 4, 1996; and Resolution 1846, December 29, 1995.

[237] Human Rights Watch interview with Mario, Rionegro, Antioquia, July 4, 1996; and "Cruz Roja se reunió con las Convivir," El Tiempo, January 16, 1997.

[238]Human Rights Watch interview with Hermán Arias Gaviria, Superintendente de Vigiliancia y Seguridad Privada, Santafé de Bogotá, May 15, 1997.

[239]Jesús Ortiz Nieves, "Rumors of Friction between Botero, Serpa," El Tiempo, FBIS, Latin America, December 13, 1994.

[240]"Defense Minister issues communiqué," El Espectador, FBIS, Latin America, December 7, 1994; and Human Rights Watch visit to Rionegro, Antioquia, July 4, 1996.

CONVIVIR and International Humanitarian Law

Human Rights Watch believes that CONVIVIRs dangerously blur the distinction between civilians and combatants, putting civilians at increased risk of attack. In cases detailed in this report, we show that some CONVIVIRs have taken a direct role in hostilities in close coordination with the army and police and have committed serious violations of the laws of war, in some cases with government-supplied weapons.

Since these groups are licensed by the state, we consider them state agents acting under official authority. When they commit abuses, the Colombian government is ultimately responsible.

In general, the government has failed to properly supervise and control CONVIVIRs. Like other perpetrators of political violence in Colombia, CONVIVIR members implicated in abuses have largely gone uninvestigated and unpunished.

A key to the blurring of the distinction between civilians and combatants is the enlistment of anonymous civilians who operate without uniform or visible insignia and in unmarked vehicles. Indeed, the government takes advantage of this anonymity by permitting CONVIVIRs to set up operations in civilian areas, as was the case with the Rionegro CONVIVIR. We have also received credible reports that some CONVIVIR members in northeastern Antioquia work while hooded.

Although CONVIVIR proponents claim the groups are closely supervised by local authorities, our investigation found that CONVIVIRs work almost exclusively with local army and police commanders, who are not required to share this information with civilian authorities.[241] Indeed, elected officials, like mayors, are often unaware of who belongs to a CONVIVIR, how and where they operate, if they have obtained the proper license, or even if one exists within their jurisdiction.

For instance, in 1997, Mayor Gloria Cuartas wrote Antioquia Governor Uribe to express concern about plans to form CONVIVIRs in Apartadó without notifying her. "I don't believe it is prudent to continue to arm, legally or illegally, the civilian population, especially since in this town we have representatives from every state security agency," she wrote. "Daily, private individuals gain increasing

---

[241]Human Rights Watch interview with Mario, Rionegro, Antioquia, July 4, 1996; Human Rights Watch interview with Hermán Arias Gaviria, Superintendency, Santafé de Bogotá, May 15, 1997.

control over weapons, which directly affects the ability of elected officials to do their job."[242]

Mayor Cuartas received a response from Vice-Governor Moreno. Using insulting language, he referred her to the army for any questions about CONVIVIRs.[243] As Cuartas pointed out when she wrote a second time to Governor Uribe, it was disturbing that civilian authorities who strongly support CONVIVIRs could not or would not answer questions from the mayor of the city where CONVIVIRs were supposed to provide security.[244]

Indeed, some army officers have ignored the license requirement and set up and supported CONVIVIRs without consulting the Superintendency. For example, the Las Colonias CONVIVIR in Lebrija, Santander, was set up by Gen. Fernando Millán at the Fifth Brigade base he commanded. The Las Colonias CONVIVIR operated throughout 1997 without a license but with army support according to the testimony of former members. The group regularly extorted money from residents and allegedly committed a series of killings, robberies, and death threats and included among its members known paramilitaries from the Middle Magdalena region.[245]

When the Attorney General's Office investigated the case, the army high command prevented prosecutors from questioning Millán, then interposed a jurisdictional dispute, claiming that since Millán was on active service and carrying out his official duties, the case should be tried before a military tribunal. As prosecutors later argued, the setting up of paramilitary groups cannot be considered an act of service, a conclusion upheld in 1997 by Colombia's Constitutional Court. Nevertheless, the judicial body that resolves these disputes continues to rule in favor of military tribunals, where officers are swiftly acquitted.[246]

---

[242]Letter to Gov. Álvaro Uribe from Apartadó Mayor Gloria Cuartas, April 10, 1997.

[243]A similar letter was also sent to Human Rights Watch. Letter to Mayor Gloria Cuartas from Pedro Juan Moreno, April 17, 1997; and letter to Human Rights Watch from Vice Gov. Pedro Juan Moreno, March 20, 1997.

[244]Letter from Mayor Cuartas to Governor Uribe, April 29, 1997.

[245]Testimony of Carlos Julio Espitia Hernández to the Attorney General's Office, October 20, 1997; and testimony of Luis Antonio Jaimes to the Attorney General's Office, January 30, 1998.

[246]"Quién debe investigar al general Fernando Millán?", El Tiempo, August 21, 1998.

We are also concerned at the absence of proper government supervision and control of CONVIVIRs. Although CONVIVIRs can play an integral role in counterinsurgency operations, the government office in charge of supervising them, the Superintendency, does not have the staff or resources to properly train CONVIVIR employees in human rights and international humanitarian law, supervise their operation, or review the records of CONVIVIRs that have been accused of abuses.

"The 'Convivir' associations have been operating without effective control or adequate supervision," in the words of the Office of the U.N. High Commissioner for Human Rights.[247]

For example, although by law CONVIVIR licenses should be reviewed every two years, by mid-1997, the Superintendency had suspended all visits to the field for lack of personnel. At that time, the superintendent automatically renewed all licenses for an additional two years, without having even visited most associations.[248]

As Human Rights Watch discovered, even serious government authorities have difficulty agreeing on the exact number of groups licensed as CONVIVIRs. Although the president's office claimed to have registered only 414 CONVIVIRs by 1997, press and other accounts cited other authorities saying there were as many as 600 or more CONVIVIRs.[249] In the department of Chocó, for instance, departmental authorities reported in January 1998 that of the five CONVIVIRs operating in Chocó, only one was licensed.[250]

Just as authorities appear unable to agree on the exact number of CONVIVIRs, they have failed to account for what type of weapons, if any, the government issues to CONVIVIRs. Although the government repeatedly assured

---

[247]Commission on Human Rights, "Report by the United Nations High Commissioner for Human Rights," 54th Session, E/CN.4/1998/16, March 1, 1998.

[248]Equipo de Alternativa, "CONVIVIR, embuchado de largo alcance," *Alternativa*, March 15-April 15, 1997, pp. 9-16; and Juanita Darling, "Armed Civilian Groups Add Fuel to Ongoing Colombian Firefights," *Los Angeles Times*, September 28, 1997.

[249]Human Rights Watch interview with Hermán Arias Gaviria, Superintendency, Santafé de Bogotá, May 15, 1997; and Alfredo Molano, "'Las Convivir, un medio para acercarnos a una guerra de carácter civil y irregular,'" *Utopías*, Año V, No. 48, September 1997, pp. 10-11.

[250]"Las convivir de Chocó, se ajustan a la ley o desaparecen," *El Tiempo*, January 10, 1998.

Human Rights Watch that CONVIVIRs would not be armed with special weaponry, during our investigation we found that the government repeatedly issued these groups weapons restricted for the sole use of the armed forces.[251]

By 1996, these weapons included 422 submachine guns, 373 nine mm. pistols, 217 repeating rifles, seventeen mini-Uzi machine guns, seventy rifles, and 109 thirty-eight-caliber revolvers, according to the office of the Superintendency of Vigilance and Private Security.[252] Although Superintendent Arias assured Human Rights Watch in 1997 that no restricted weapons had been issued to CONVIVIRs, three of the forty-seven CONVIVIRs registered with his signature received weapons that year that were restricted for the sole use of the armed forces, including Galil rifles, mortars, grenades, and M-60 machine guns.[253]

Lack of accountability has led to other serious problems. The Superintendency has proved unable and even uninterested in preventing known paramilitaries from joining CONVIVIRs. Indeed, some army officers opposed the creation of CONVIVIRs in the Urabá region because they believed that there was a high risk of paramilitary infiltration.[254] Repeatedly, Human Rights Watch was told that only "decent people" – *gente de bien* – would be allowed to join

---

[251]In Colombia, firearms are classified under three categories according to Decree 2535, promulgated in 1993: high calibre and automatic firearms restricted for the sole use of the armed forces; firearms restricted for the sole use of individuals carrying valuables or employed by security companies; and firearms available to the public that are licensed by the army. Since CONVIVIRs were created, Colombian government officials repeatedly misled groups asking about weapons and CONVIVIRs by asserting that members would only have access to the third category of weapon, available to any Colombian citizens who has made the proper request. Human Rights Watch interview with Amb. Juan Carlos Esguerra, Washington, D.C., November 16, 1995.

[252]We base this on a list of weapons disbursements provided to Human Rights Watch by the office of the Superintendency of Vigilance and Private Security.

[253]Human Rights Watch interview, Santafé de Bogotá, May 15, 1997; and Equipo de Alternativa, "Convivir, embuchado de largo alcance," *Alternativa*, March 15-April 15, 1997, pp. 9-16.

[254]Human Rights Watch interview with Col. (ret.) Carlos Velásquez, Santafé de Bogotá, May 12, 1997.

CONVIVIRs.[255] As is clear, however, the definition of "decent people" is entirely subjective and is often used in Colombia as a euphemism for civilians who support paramilitaries as a way of "cleansing" the country of guerrillas.

When Human Rights Watch asked Superintendent Arias what measures he had taken to insure that paramilitaries did not join, he answered that they review all criminal convictions in a court of law. But since so few paramilitaries have been prosecuted or even captured, we asked, what other measures had he taken. "Anyone who would volunteer for a CONVIVIR has to be a decent person," he answered, a tautology that fails entirely to address the very real problem of paramilitary infiltration.

Indeed, the Superintendency has supplied known paramilitaries with military-style weapons. For example, nine months after police named brothers Martiniano and Roberto Prada Gamarra as suspects in the 1995 Puerto Patiño massacre of eight men in the department of Cesar, the Superintendency approved the Pradas as members of the Renacer CONVIVIR, which operated in the Puerto Patiño area.[256] Martiniano successfully petitioned the government for a 9-mm submachine gun for his personal use along with nine other submachines guns for the "Los Arrayanes" CONVIVIR.[257] In May 1998, the Attorney General's Office formally accused eight men, including Roberto Prada Gamarra, with having carried out the Puerto Patiño massacre.[258]

In practice, some CONVIVIRs make no distinction between illegal paramilitary groups, which they embrace, and their own organizations. For example, when butchers from Lebrija, Santander were told to attend a Las Colonias CONVIVIR meeting, they found armed men who demanded that merchants pay them a monthly quota or face the consequences, interpreted as a death threat. When

---

[255]"Defense Minister issues communiqué," *El Espectador*, FBIS, Latin America, December 7, 1994; and Human Rights Watch visit to Rionegro, Antioquia, July 4, 1996

[256]Roberto Prada Delgado, son of Prada Gamarra, was approved as the security chief of the Renacer CONVIVIR. Defense Ministry, Superintendency Resolution 1496, November 14, 1995; and Human Rights Watch/Americas, *Colombia's Killer Networks,* pp. 42-60.

[257]Roberto Prada Gamarra was arrested in 1996 and is currently incarcerated in Bogotá's El Modelo prison. Defense Ministry, Superintendency, Comité de Revisión y Coordinación de Trámites, Acta No. 012, May 2, 1996; and Human Rights Watch interview with Human Rights Unit, Attorney General's Office, Santafé de Bogotá, May 15, 1997.

[258]Centro de Información de Colombia, Press Bulletin No. 338, "Fiscalía entrega resultados de investigaciones sobre masacres," May 19, 1998;

one of the merchants asked if the group was paramilitary, also known in the region as macetos, the commander, a retired army officer, replied, "We are paramilitaries, macetos, or CONVIVIR, or whatever the hell you want to call us."[259]

When Human Rights Watch presented evidence that known paramilitaries belonged to the Renacer CONVIVIR to the Superintendent in a meeting, he claimed that since no Prada had been convicted in a court of law at the time the CONVIVIR license was issued, he saw no impediment to approving his membership in a CONVIVIR. This response clearly demonstrates that the Superintendency lacked any will to keep known human rights criminals out of the CONVIVIRs.[260]

Salvatore Mancuso is another CONVIVIR member currently being prosecuted for forming paramilitary groups. Known as "El Mono," Mancuso is a well-known Córdoba rancher currently wanted by the authorities for his role in massacres carried out in the departments of Bolívar, Cesar, Córdoba, and Sucre. Mancuso has used paramilitaries to force farmers from productive land, which he then buys for cut-rate prices. Despite his criminal record, Mancuso is registered as the official representative of two CONVIVIRs, one in Sucre and one in Córdoba, called Asociación Horizonte, Ltd. Government investigators believe he is an adviser to Carlos Castaño and the ACCU.[261]

In similar cases, after the UC-ELN's "Héroes de Anorí" Front ambushed the Al Sol CONVIVIR on July 27, 1997 near Anorí, Antioquia, among the six killed was a paramilitary known locally as "The Fox" (El Zorro), believed to have ordered the April 23, 1997 murder of Campamento personero Emilio de Jesús Penagos. "The Fox" was later identified as Leopoldo Guerrero Torres, an army non-commissioned officer.[262] In another case, police discovered that one of the

---

[259]Testimony of Germán Peña Hernández to Attorney General's Office, January 22, 1998.

[260]Human Rights Watch interview with Hermán Arias Gaviria, Superintendency, Santafé de Bogotá, May 15, 1997

[261]Human Rights Watch interview with Human Rights Unit, Attorney General's Office, Santafé de Bogotá, December 4, 1997; and Human Rights Watch interview with humanitarian aid worker, Santafé de Bogotá, June 25, 1996.

[262]Human Rights Watch interview with Rafael Rincón, Medellín personero and president of the National Association of Personeros, Medellín, Antioquia, December 10, 1997; "Cinco muertos en ataque del ELN en Anorí," El Tiempo, July 28, 1997; and CINEP-Justice and Peace, Noche y Niebla, No. 5, July-September, 1997, p. 145.

paramilitaries killed during the massacre of fourteen people in La Horqueta, Cundinamarca, on November 21, 1997, was the legal representative of the La Palma CONVIVIR, based in San Juan de Urabá, Antioquia.[263] In some areas, CONVIVIR jobs are considered stepping stones to important paramilitary commands or ways for known paramilitaries to form groups that appear to enjoy government approval.[264]

Indeed, the danger of once again giving government support to paramilitary groups prompted Attorney General Alfonso Gómez to oppose the creation of CONVIVIRs as a violation of Decree 1194, promulgated in 1989, which prohibits the formation of paramilitary groups. "With the appearance of 'Convivir,' the Colombian state has once again fallen in the mistake of promoting 'armed actors' that worsen problems of illegal repression and war without quarter."[265]

Also dangerous is the army's use of CONVIVIRs to monitor legal political activity, contributing to the atmosphere of danger and threat that permeates public service in Colombia. For example, in September 1997, the chief of staff of the army's Fourth Brigade wrote Antioquia CONVIVIRs urging them not only to collect "information to be used to neutralize and/or impede the plans of subversive cartels," but also investigate "candidates... to determine their political affiliation and degree of acceptance within the population. Determine if they sympathize with democratic institutions, the government, the military forces, and what their level of influence is."[266]

CONVIVIRs have also endangered the civilian population, in violation of the guarantees contained in Protocol II. In one incident, families fleeing political violence in the Nudo del Paramillo region of Antioquia were prevented from traveling by a CONVIVIR in the town of Dabeiba. Dabeiba Mayor Gabriel Eduardo González told authorities that the CONVIVIR president had told local

---

[263]"Para muerto en la Horqueta era de Convivir," *El Tiempo*, January 15, 1998.

[264]Human Rights Watch interview with government investigator, Medellín, Antioquia, December 10, 1997.

[265]Statement by Attorney General Alfonso Gómez Méndez to the Constitutional Court, August 26, 1997.

[266]Letter to Antioquia CONVIVIRs from Fourth Brigade Chief of Staff Col. Juan Octavio Triviño Herrera, September 12, 1997; and "Escándolo por circular del Ejército," *El Tiempo*, October 8, 1997.

transportation companies not to transport emergency food or pick up the displaced, a group he summarily dismissed as "guerrillas."[267]

By the end of 1997, CONVIVIRs had been linked to at least thirty-five criminal investigations involving homicide, torture, and other serious crimes according to the Office of the U.N. High Commissioner for Human Rights.[268] In August, President Samper acknowledged that some CONVIVIRs had "assum[ed] combat roles" and had committed abuses, prompting the government to suspend the creation of new CONVIVIRs.[269]

In November 1997, the Superintendency reorganized CONVIVIRs into two categories: "Special Services," companies authorized to provide security in high risk areas or protect special installations, like multinational corporations; and "Community Services" (Servicios Comunitarios), which work at the local level and would include neighborhood associations or cooperatives.[270]

The same month, the Constitutional Court ruled on a challenge to CONVIVIRs submitted by fifteen human rights groups. In a five to four vote, the court upheld the decree legalizing CONVIVIRs, but stipulated that members and employees of "Community Services" groups could not collect intelligence for the

---

[267]Human Rights Watch interview with María Girlesa Villegas, regional Public Advocate's Office, Medellín, Antioquia, December 9, 1997; and "Investigarán a jefe de Convivir en Dabeiba," El Tiempo, December 3, 1997.

[268]Commission on Human Rights, "Report by the United Nations High Commissioner for Human Rights," 54th Session, E/CN.4/1998/16, March 1, 1998.

[269]CONVIVIRs have also been implicated in other types of abuses that go beyond the scope of this report, including so-called "social cleansing" killings of indigents, street children, suspected drug addicts, and thieves. In Medellín, for instance, where twelve CONVIVIRs were reportedly operating by the end of 1997, residents reported frequent incidents of CONVIVIR employees shooting down street people and pedestrians they suspected of robbery. "Las Convivir se han desbordado: Samper," El Tiempo, August 16, 1997; "Suspenderán la creación de nuevas CONVIVIR," El Tiempo, August 18, 1997; Human Rights Watch interviews with Medellín residents, December 7-11, 1997; Letter to President Ernesto Samper from Rafael Rincón, personero, July 7, 1997; and Frank Bajak, "Legality of armed citizens' watch groups in dispute," Associated Press, November 5, 1997.

[270]Orlando León Restrepo, "Gobierno modifica las Convivir," El Tiempo, November 3, 1997.

security forces and could only possess non-military use weapons.[271] By year's end, former CONVIVIRs had returned a reported 237 "restricted use" weapons to the government.[272]

In addition, a government decree implemented a month later required "Community Services" to be supervised by a locally-elected committee, a welcome end to the total anonymity of organization members.[273] Nonetheless, these groups remain out of uniform and poorly supervised. In the first months of 1998, the Superintendency revoked the licenses of dozens of former CONVIVIRs, for failing to return restricted-use weapons and submit records confirming the judicial status of CONVIVIR members.[274]

Massacres

San Roque, Antioquia: According to an investigation by the Attorney General's Office and information collected by human rights groups, seven men, a woman, and a twelve-year-old child set out by car for Puerto Berrío, Santander on August 14, 1996. Mainly businesspeople and land owners, the men were apparently planning to renew their handgun licenses at the Fourteenth Brigade. Near a turn-off known as Brasil, armed men whom government investigators believe belonged to the San Roque CONVIVIR stopped their car and forced its passengers to board another. The woman was released five days later and reported the incident. Government investigators believe the men and child were executed, mutilated, and thrown into the Magdalena River.[275]

---

[271]Claim filed by fifteen groups, August 26, 1997; and Constitutional Court decision, November 7, 1997.

[272]"Gobierno pone en orden a cooperativas de seguridad," *El Tiempo*, December 18, 1997.

[273]Decree 2974, December 16 , 1997.

[274]"Suspenden a 54 Convivir," *El Tiempo*, January 18, 1998.

[275]Letter from Public Advocate's Office, December 4, 1997; and CINEP and Justice and Peace, *Noche y Niebla*, October-December 1997, p. 143.

Murder and Torture

Norte del Cauca: In March 1996, a CONVIVIR calling itself the "Rural Security Cooperative of Northern Cauca" began circulating a list of 103 local residents accused of maintaining ties with guerrillas and criminals, and threatened them with death. Among them were the leaders of area indigenous communities and local farmers. Within a month, on April 11, gunmen believed to belong to the CONVIVIR began to torture and kill those named, among them three Páez Indians near Tacueyó, Cauca: Jaime Conda, Serafín Escué, and Wilmer López. The following May 29, three farmers — Juan Bautista, Marco Tulio Bautista, and Jorge Enrique Zambrano — were shot by presumed CONVIVIR members near Suárez, Cauca.[276] There is no indication that those killed were combatants; in any case, they were not killed in combat, but were detained before being tortured and shot.

Rioblanco, Tolima: Disputes between farmers living near this highland town were complicated in 1996 by the formation of a CONVIVIR, which began targeting and killing suspected guerrilla supporters as well as individuals embroiled in land and other non-political disputes. In an interview with Human Rights Watch, displaced farmers from the area said that the CONVIVIR maintained close ties with local paramilitaries, who were among those who began to identify themselves as CONVIVIR. In addition, CONVIVIR members worked in coordination with the army base in Chaparral, and, disguised by ski masks, would patrol with soldiers. At frequent roadblocks, the CONVIVIR would charge a "war tax" and engage in robbery. Farmers who refused to patrol with them were threatened and accused of supporting the FARC. In the village of Bilbao, farmers said the CONVIVIR circulated a death list of sixty suspected guerrilla sympathizers, a common paramilitary tactic.[277] On September 22, 1996, CONVIVIR members in ski masks seized José Chepe Yate and Ferney Parra from their homes in villages near Rioblanco and executed them. As a result, an estimated 1,300 people from the villages of Maracaibo, Rionegro, Campo Alegre, Peñas Blancas, La Autora, La Ocasión, Lagunas, La Esmeralda, and La Reina fled the area. Subsequently, the same CONVIVIR was implicated in the killing of farmer Javier Leyton, on

---

[276]Justice and Peace, *Boletín*, April-June 1996, pp. 10, 48.

[277]Human Rights Watch interview with Rioblanco displaced, Santafé de Bogotá, December 5-6, 1997.

December 31, 1996.[278] After farmers reported these incidents to authorities, soldiers captured five alleged CONVIVIR members, but later released them. At the farmers' request, the army sent the Caicedo de Chaparral Battalion to the region, and some displaced families chose to return. However, CONVIVIR attacks resumed once the army left the area and at least 300 people once again fled.[279] Internal Affairs continues to investigate the case.[280]

Yondó CONVIVIR: On February 3, 1997, residents reported that a CONVIVIR operating with Counterguerrilla Battalion No. 43 "Palagua" tortured and killed four people near the village of San Francisco, among them Norberto Galeano Cuadros, Jesús Antonio Cabal, and Reynaldo Jesús Ríos, all elderly men. The bodies were then dismembered and castrated. The combined unit, which included a soldier identified by residents as "El Zarco," had terrorized surrounding villages for four days previous to the killings, threatening the population, killing farm animals, and torturing farmer Antonio Arévalo.[281]

Las Colonias CONVIVIR: Organized by the Fifth Brigade, this group began operating in Lebrija in 1997 without a license, but with the support of the army and local police commander. According to residents and victims' families, the group committed at least fifteen targeted killings before the director, Commander Cañón, a retired army officer, and the employees he hired were arrested and prosecuted under the Decree 1194, which prohibits the formation of paramilitary groups. Among the cases currently under investigation by the Attorney General's Office are the killings of two Protestants, brothers Oscar and Armando Beltrán Correa,

---

[278]Human Rights Watch interview with Rioblanco displaced, Santafé de Bogotá, December 5, 1997; and Letter to Public Advocate's Office from Santiago Ramírez Calderón, regional Public Advocate's Office, Ibagué, Tolima, November 25, 1997.

[279]Human Rights Watch interview with Rioblanco displaced, Santafé de Bogotá, December 5-6, 1997; "Capturan sindicado de paramilitarismo," *El Nuevo Día*, October 9, 1996; and "'Paras' están libres en Rioblanco," *El Nuevo Día*, October 18, 1996.

[280]Letter to Human Rights Watch from Jesús Orlando Gómez López, Internal Affairs Delegate for Human Rights, November 28, 1997.

[281]Human Rights Watch interview with humanitarian aid workers, Santafé de Bogotá, December 5, 1997; Amnesty International Urgent Action further information on 05/97, February 11, 1997; and CINEP and Justice and Peace, *Noche y Niebla*, No. 3, January-March, 1997, p. 33.

taken captive by the Las Colonias CONVIVIR as they headed to work on July 29, 1997 and killed on the road leading from Lebrija to the hamlet of La Puente. Apparently, the CONVIVIR accused them of passing information to the guerrillas.[282] On September 4, 1997, father and son Leonardo and José Manuel Cadena were forced out of their home by CONVIVIR members and killed according to a family member's testimony to the Attorney General's Office, apparently because the CONVIVIR accused the Cadenas of bringing food to guerrillas.[283] According to a former CONVIVIR member who was also an army informant, during its months of operation, the Las Colonias CONVIVIR went on frequent operations with army units, setting up roadblocks and detaining suspected guerrillas and criminals.[284] In December 1997, three civilian members of the Las Colonias CONVIVIR were arrested in connection with these killings. As we detailed above, the Attorney General's Office is investigating Fifth Brigade commander Gen. Fernando Millán and his staff for their role in setting up paramilitary groups. Human Rights Watch holds the government responsible for these killings, a serious violation of the ban in Common Article 3 and Protocol II against killing civilians. In this case, CONVIVIR members also extorted money from civilians by threatening them with death.

---

[282]Report from Miguel Antonio Rico Machado, chief, SIJIN (Santander) Homicide Division, to the Attorney General's Office, December 5, 1997.

[283]Testimony of Ana Mercedes Cadena to Attorney General's Office, October 6, 1997.

[284]Testimony of Nilson Eduardo Ramírez to the Attorney General's Office, December 23, 1997.

IV. PARAMILITARY VIOLATIONS OF INTERNATIONAL HUMANITARIAN LAW

Each night they kill groups of five to six defenseless people, who are cruelly and monstrously massacred after being tortured. The screams of humble people are audible, begging for mercy and asking for help.

– Judge Leonardo Iván Cortés, Mapiripán, Meta
July 1997

At the time of this writing, there are at least seven groups allied under the name United Self-Defense Groups of Colombia (Autodefensas Unidas de Colombia, AUC): the Peasant Self-Defense Group of Córdoba and Urabá (Autodefensas Campesinas de Córdoba and Urabá, ACCU), the largest and most public group; the Eastern Plains Self-Defense Group (Autodefensas de los Llanos Orientales, also known as Los Carranceros, after their leader, Víctor Carranza); the Cesar Self-Defense Group (Autodefensas del Cesar); the Middle Magdalena Self-Defense Group (Autodefensas del Magdalena Medio), the group with the longest history; the Santander and Southern Cesar Self-Defense Group (Autodefensas de Santander y el sur del Cesar); the Casanare Self-Defense Group (Autodefensas del Casanare); and the Cundinamarca Self-Defense Group (Autodefensas de Cundinamarca).

Applying the laws of war to the AUC gives them no special status or recognition. As we showed in the section devoted to the Colombian state forces, AUC units operate frequently in direct coordination with the Colombian security forces. In this report, we refer to them as paramilitaries because of this historical and continuing relationship with the Colombian military. Within Colombia, these groups can also be referred to as "self-defense" groups, a description the AUC uses.

However, the AUC does act independently, and has a separate command structure, source of weapons and supplies, and operation planning. The AUC leader, Carlos Castaño, has repeatedly stated a willingness to pledge his forces to respect the laws of war. Nevertheless, he has qualified that pledge by stating he would not respect the rights of guerrilla fighters *hors de combat* or civilians he suspects of guerrilla collaboration, an exception that renders his purported commitment almost meaningless.

AUC

The AUC is a descendant of Muerte a Secuestradores (Death to Kidnappers, MAS), an alliance formed in the 1980s between the Colombian military, the police, and Middle Magdalena businessmen and ranchers. At the time, the army and paramilitaries characterized their activity as necessary to fend off guerrilla incursions.[285]

By 1983, however, Internal Affairs had registered over 240 political killings by MAS, whose victims included elected officials, farmers, and community leaders. In his report, Internal Affairs chief Carlos Jiménez Gómez identified fifty-nine active-duty members of the police and military who belonged to MAS, including the commander of the army's Bomboná Battalion. In an interview with Human Rights Watch, Carlos Castaño, AUC founder and Colombia's most powerful paramilitary leader, traced his first involvement in paramilitary activity to the training he received in the early 1980s at the Bomboná Battalion.[286]

Castaño began as a guide, fought with troops, and identified suspected subversives.[287] Meanwhile, his elder brother, Fidel, was amassing a fortune from drug trafficking. Fidel invested his earnings in land, and became one of northern Colombia's most powerful ranchers. With Fidel's profits as well as contributions from landowners and businessmen, the Castaños decided to form their own army in the mid-1980s, known as "Los Tangüeros," after the Castaño ranch called Las Tangas.[288]

---

[285]Human Rights Watch interview with AUC founder Carlos Castaño, July 9, 1996; and Carlos Medina Gallego, *Autodefensas, Paramilitares y Narcotráfico en Colombia* (Santafé de Bogotá: Editorial Documentos Periodísticos, 1990).

[286]In numerous press interviews, Fidel and Carlos Castaño have maintained that they went to the army after the Fourth Front of the FARC kidnapped their father, Jesús, who died in guerrilla custody. For more on the history of the Castaño family, see Germán Castro Caycedo, *En Secreto* (Santafé de Bogotá: Planeta, 1996), pp. 141-232.

[287]Human Rights Watch interview with Carlos Castaño, July 9, 1996.

[288]Fidel Castaño denied involvement in drug trafficking and claims that his considerable fortune was earned through cattle ranching and an art dealership. However, his role as enforcer for the Medellín Cartel is amply documented by many sources consulted by Human Rights Watch, including the National Police and the U.S. Embassy, which dedicated dozens of cables to his exploits between 1990 and 1994. These were released to Human Rights Watch through our Freedom of Information Act (FOIA) request. "Yo fui creador de los Pepes," *Semana*, May 31, 1994, pp. 38-45.

"Guerrillas can act outside the law, so this battle is not equal," Carlos Castaño told Human Rights Watch in an interview. "We realized we could use the same tactics as the guerrillas and adopt their methods of combat."[289]

It was on Las Tangas, for example, that foreign mercenaries and active-duty army officers taught paramilitaries and professional hit men who worked for drug kingpins how to shoot, make bombs, and ambush people in the mid-1980s.[290]

The Castaño strategy produced a particularly violent record, described by one government commission as "one of the most tragic chapters in this country's recent history of violence." For example, on January 14, 1990, the Tangüeros kidnapped and killed forty-two people from the Urabá town of Pueblo Bello, apparently revenge for the earlier killing by the EPL of several Castaño gunmen.[291] Months later, the bodies of six of those taken were found in unmarked graves holding a total of twenty-four bodies at Las Tangas and Jaraguay, another Castaño ranch.[292]

---

[289]Human Rights Watch interview with Carlos Castaño, July 9, 1996.

[290]A tanga is a bird native to the Córdoba plains. In 1998, the Attorney General's Human Rights Unit issued formal arrest warrants for several of the foreign mercenaries who taught at Las Tangas, including the Israeli Yair Klein. Human Rights Watch interview with El Caramelo survivors, Montería, Córdoba, October 16, 1992; "Testimonio clave," *Semana*, September 28, 1993, pp. 44-47; and Americas Watch, *The "Drug War" in Colombia: the Neglected Tragedy of Political Violence* (New York: Americas Watch, 1990), pp. 19-23.

[291]Comisión de Superación de la Violencia, *Pacificar la Paz: Lo que no se ha negociado en los acuerdos de paz* (Santafé de Bogotá: Instituto de Estudios Políticos y Relaciones Internacionales (IEPRI), 1992, pp. 25, 160-161.

[292]"Identificados sólo 7 cadáveres en Córdoba," *La Prensa*, April 19, 1990.

Fidel Castaño was convicted *in absentia* for his role in that massacre.[293] Carlos Castaño has admitted his family's role in the Pueblo Bello massacre, but claimed that it was "an error" due to poor training. "Our military force had grown enormously, and sometimes the men used the weapons for bad purposes," he said.[294]

Massacres by the Tangüeros caused massive forced displacement throughout the late 1980s, as the inhabitants of entire villages left in fear.[295] According to one group that works with the displaced, abandoned land would then be purchased cheaply by the same traffickers-turned-landowners funding the Castaño army, fueling the campaign to rid the region of guerrillas and their perceived supporters.[296]

This trend continues, with drug traffickers buying huge tracts abandoned by fleeing families. "Land-buying by drug traffickers changes the war's course, because these new land owners become part of the paramilitary structure," commented Alejandro Reyes, a sociologist who has studied political violence, in an interview with Human Rights Watch. "It is then that the traffickers begin to defend themselves territorially."[297]

---

[293]A court also found Fidel guilty *in absentia* of conspiracy (*concierto para delinquir*) for having helped carry out the 1988 killings of seventeen banana workers on the La Honduras/La Negra and Punta Coquitos plantations. The court issued a sentence of twenty years, upheld by the Supreme Court. In addition, Fidel was convicted of the kidnappings and murder of Sen. Alfonso Ospina and has been formally accused by the Attorney General's Office of ordering the 1988 Segovia massacre of fifty people. "Corte condena a 'Rambo'," *El Tiempo*, February 17, 1994; "Condena de 30 años para Fidel Castaño," *El Tiempo*, June 28, 1997; and Centro de Información de Colombia, Press Bulletin No. 338, "Fiscalía entrega resultados de investigaciones sobre masacres," May 19, 1998.

[294]Human Rights Watch interview with Carlos Castaño, July 9, 1996.

[295]Human rights groups also recorded the activity of smaller private armies working for powerful local businessmen and landowners. All operated with the tolerance and occasional open support of the army. Human Rights Watch interview with forcibly displaced family, Montería, Córdoba, October 16, 1992.

[296]Human Rights Watch interview, Montería, Córdoba, October 16, 1992.

[297]Human Rights Watch interview with Alejandro Reyes, Santafé de Bogotá, December 6, 1997.

The Tangüeros established a clear pattern of operation, which continues to be used by the AUC. At first, rumors of an imminent attack, graffiti, and written death threats circulate. On the chosen night, heavily armed men drive in and begin pulling people from their homes to be killed. No one we interviewed in the department of Córdoba in 1992, including government authorities, was aware of any clash between the Tangüeros and the security forces; to the contrary, known paramilitary leaders would often sleep in military installations apparently as protection from guerrilla attack.[298]

In the village of El Tomate, for example, considered by paramilitaries to be sympathetic to the EPL, armed men commandeered a public bus and killed five passengers on August 30, 1988. Gunmen executed ten more El Tomate residents after dragging them from their homes. They burned twenty-two houses and the public bus, with the driver shackled to the steering wheel.[299]

People who were perceived to be sympathetic to guerrillas or their ideology — including teachers, community leaders, trade unionists, human rights defenders, and religious workers — were also considered legitimate targets even though they took no active part in conflict. Often, it was the work itself that put them at risk. Among the victims of the Tangüeros was Sergio Restrepo, a Jesuit priest who administered the Tierralta parish in Córdoba. Apparently, Restrepo became a target because of his work with the poor, identified as being pro-guerrilla and communist. A Castaño gunman shot and killed him in 1988 outside the Jesuit parish house.[300]

As the Castaños themselves have acknowledged, some of the victims were also bystanders, killed by mistake.

After other massacres carried out by Middle Magdalena paramilitaries and their army patrons in 1989, including the killing of two judges and ten government investigators at La Rochela, Santander, the government of Virgilio Barco issued Decree 1194, which established criminal penalties for civilians and members of the armed forces who recruit, train, promote, finance, organize, lead, or belong to "the armed groups, misnamed paramilitary groups, that have been formed into death

---

[298]Human Rights Watch interviews in Montería, Córdoba, October 16-18, 1992.

[299]Human Rights Watch interview with El Tomate survivors, Montería, Córdoba, October 16, 1992.

[300]Human Rights Watch interview, Tierralta, July 8, 1996.

squads, bands of hired assassins, self-defense groups, or groups that carry out their own justice."[301]

Despite this decree, neither Fidel nor Carlos Castaño have ever been arrested for their roles in directing a private army or ordering massacres, though both have multiple outstanding convictions and warrants for their arrests.[302]

By 1990, EPL guerrillas were decimated by the combined action of the army and the Tangüeros. In August, Fidel Castaño and some paramilitaries from the Middle Magdalena offered to hand over their weapons if the EPL disbanded, an agreement that led to the demobilization of over 2,000 EPL militants on March 1, 1992. Castaño also delivered some weapons to authorities. Through a family foundation, called the Foundation for the Peace of Córdoba (Fundación por la Paz de Córdoba, FUNPAZCOR), the Castaños donated land, money, and cattle for hundreds of former guerrillas to set up small businesses, farms, market networks, schools, and training programs.[303]

Nevertheless, peace was short-lived. By the time former EPL members had formed Esperanza, Paz y Libertad, a legal political party, the FARC had expanded its activities in northern Colombia, occupying much of the EPL's former territory. Some EPL members rejected the terms of the negotiations and returned to combat. For that reason, Carlos Castaño told us, his family decided to reactivate its private army as the ACCU and convert it into a national force to defeat guerrillas.

---

[301]Translation by Human Rights Watch from Decree 1194. That year, paramilitaries working for drug traffickers also killed three presidential candidates: Bernardo Jaramillo, Carlos Pizarro, and Luis Carlos Galán.

[302]Despite their seemingly disastrous legal status, the Castaños have maintained regular and close contact with the security forces throughout the 1990s. In 1992, Fidel Castaño had a falling-out with Medellín Cartel leader Pablo Escobar, formed a group known as "People Persecuted by Pablo Escobar," also called "Los Pepes," and helped authorities locate and kill the fugitive trafficker on December 2, 1993. As Fidel Castaño stated in an interview with the newsweekly *Semana*, the Pepes supplied information to the authorities and attacked Escobar associates and lands, forcing Escobar to go on the run. The Pepes were considered fundamental to the government's success in tracking down Escobar. "Yo fui creador de los Pepes," *Semana*, May 31, 1994, pp. 38-45.

[303]These details come from a summary of FUNPAZCOR activities given to Human Rights Watch by its director, Sister Teresa Gómez Alvarez, in Montería, Córdoba, on July 8, 1996.

In press interviews, Carlos Castaño has claimed that his elder brother Fidel vanished on an overland trip from Colombia to Panama in 1994, not long after writing to then-Interior Minister Horacio Serpa of his desire to take part in peace negotiations with the government and guerrillas. The offer bore no fruit. Since Fidel's disappearance, Carlos has become the leader of the ACCU and later the AUC.[304]

"By 1993, we had 600 guns. We began to establish 'fronts' in other regions to fight the guerrillas. A front would be established at the request of people living in the region who were willing to pay for it."[305]

The ACCU quickly became Colombia's most organized and largest paramilitary group. Although each front has a local leader, Castaño says that all coordinate through a central command. Castaño is the commander-in-chief. Like the guerrillas they consciously emulate, the ACCU has a general staff (*estado mayor conjunto*) made up of the leaders of each regional paramilitary group. Regional groups also have a general staff (*estados mayores regionales*). The fighting force is divided into two types of unit: stationary groups, known as local self-defense associations (*juntas de autodefensas locales*) and support groups (*grupos de apoyo*); and mobile groups (*frentes de choque*), better trained and equipped and able to move quickly throughout Colombia.[306] Among the men pledged to the ACCU are former EPL guerrillas, some of whom surrendered directly to the ACCU.[307]

Both local and special fighters receive a base salary plus food, a uniform, weapons, and munitions. The funds to cover these expenses come from local

---

[304]"Revelan carta de 'Rambo' a Serpa," *El Tiempo*, September 20, 1994; and "'Fidel Castaño está muerto,'" *Semana*, July 9, 1996, pp. 32-38.

[305]Human Rights Watch interview with Carlos Castaño, July 9, 1996.

[306]Human Rights Watch interview with Carlos Castaño, July 9, 1996; and ACCU Statutes.

[307]For example, in July 1996, an EPL group that had refused the government amnesty in 1992 gave itself up to the ACCU and some former guerrillas were incorporated into its ranks. Continued rivalry between Esperanza, some of whose sympathizers have joined the ACCU, the FARC, and EPL guerrillas who refused to demobilize is believed to be at the root of much of the political violence registered in Urabá since 1991. For more, see the sections in this report on the EPL and the FARC. "60 guerrilleros buscan su reinserción social," *El Tiempo*, July 31, 1996.

ranchers and businesspeople.[308] There is also an emerging body of evidence linking Castaño to drug trafficking in Antioquia and Córdoba, a business that has earned his family millions.[309]

One businessman explained to Human Rights Watch how he had been told to attend a meeting that Castaño had called in northern Antioquia to collect funds for a new ACCU unit. "Each person was expected to pay a quota of between U.S. $3,000 to $5,000, and everyone knew what it was for," he told us.[310]

In contrast to the 1980s, when the Castaños' army was essentially a regional force, the ACCU sponsored a national summit to form an alliance of like-minded groups in December 1994, which led to the founding of the AUC. [311] Within the AUC, according to Castaño, "Each front is autonomous and responsible for its region in terms of funds and should take responsibility for or reject responsibility for actions that are attributed to them."[312] However, regions share munitions, weapons, and even men.[313] Observers agree that Castaño exerts ultimate control over the AUC and has the clearest plans for its future.[314]

Castaño denies that he works with the army, though he says there is "sympathy" between the ACCU and the security forces. On occasion, he told Human Rights Watch, if the paramilitaries find themselves fighting guerrillas and the army appears, "it's natural that we would combine forces with the army to

---

[308]Human Rights Watch interview with Carlos Castaño, July 9, 1996; and ACCU Statutes.

[309]Human Rights Watch interview with Antioquia businessman, Guarné, Antioquia, December 11, 1997; "Apreciación situación actual narcotráfico en Medellín," Departamento Administrativo de Seguridad, April 1, 1998.

[310]Human Rights Watch interview with Antioquia businessman, Guarné, Antioquia, December 11, 1997.

[311]Primera Cumbre de las Autodefensas de Colombia, December, 1994; "Paramilitares se habrían unido," *El Tiempo*, April 20, 1997.

[312]Translation by Human Rights Watch. Bibiana Mercado and Orlando León Restrepo, "Urabá: el fin de la pesadilla," *El Tiempo*, September 28, 1997.

[313]Ibid.

[314]Francisco Santos, "Proyecto contrainsurgente," *El Tiempo*, April 29, 1997.

defeat a common enemy."[315] During their Third Summit, the group acknowledged a continuing relationship with the armed forces, which "want to use us, because it is well known that we are the ones who, in the last instance, put ourselves into combat and in a good number of antiguerrilla operations."[316]

Indeed, evidence is abundant and consistent that Castaño frequently coordinates with the army, including on high-profile political killings. For instance, the Attorney General's Office formally accused Castaño of involvement in the 1994 murder of Colombian Sen. Manuel Cepeda, carried out with the alleged assistance of the army's Ninth Brigade.[317]

The ACCU began its campaign to eliminate guerrillas in northern Urabá, then expanded south into the departments of Antioquia, Chocó, Bolívar, and Sucre. By the time we spoke with Castaño in 1996, he claimed to have over 2,000 trained, armed, and equipped fighters distributed among five fronts in addition to his headquarters in San Pedro de Urabá. Colombian government analysts estimate the same armed strength, augmented by hundreds more depending on the location where Castaño plans an operation.[318]

By the end of 1996, the AUC included paramilitaries from the Middle Magdalena, led by Ramón Isaza, and the eastern plains, led by Víctor Carranza.[319] At that time, the AUC planned new fronts in the departments of Guaviare and Putumayo, leapfrogging to Colombia's southernmost border.[320] For its part, the ACCU has also crossed Colombia's northern border with Panama in pursuit of guerrillas, who have for years used the thinly populated area as a refuge.[321]

---

[315]Human Rights Watch interview with Carlos Castaño, July 9, 1996.

[316]"Tercera Cumbre Nacional," Movimiento Autodefensas de Colombia, 1996.

[317]Castaño is also being investigated for his alleged participation in the killing of presidential candidate Bernardo Jaramillo, a member of the Patriotic Union Party, in 1990. "A juicio Castaño," El Colombiano, October 22, 1997; and Human Rights Watch interview with Human Rights Unit, Attorney General's Office, Santafé de Bogotá, December 4, 1997.

[318]Human Rights Watch interview with Colombian government intelligence analyst, Santafé de Bogotá, December 2, 1997.

[319]III Cumbre Nacional, Movimiento Autodefensas de Colombia, 1996.

[320]"Guerra en el fin del mundo," Semana, February 16-23, 1998.

[321]Human Rights Watch interview with Carlos Castaño, July 9, 1996.

After the ACCU was linked to ninety killings over a space of twenty-two days in late 1996, the Colombian government announced a "full offensive" against them and a U.S. $1 million reward for information leading to Castaño's capture.[322]

Over the following months, however, the security forces made no effort to find and arrest him. Indeed, Castaño continued to meet normally with reporters, municipal and national government officials, and representatives of the church in areas he controlled. When the reward was repeated a year later, this time paired with Castaño's photo, the government promised to send a special, police-led team against him.[323]

As of this writing, the Attorney General's Office and police had captured some paramilitary leaders, including Víctor Carranza. However, Castaño himself remains unhindered and has launched a new offensive in the department of Putumayo.[324]

The AUC and International Humanitarian Law

The AUC has recognized some principles of international humanitarian law and accepts training in the laws of war from the ICRC. However, the group has yet to conform their behavior in the field to these standards. Instead, the AUC has called for "negotiations" with guerrillas to "reach an agreement that would permit the civilian population to be excluded from the conflict and in this way comply with International Humanitarian Law," ignoring the fact that no negotiations are needed to apply these standards immediately.[325] Talks with government representatives have been sporadic, but ongoing.[326]

---

[322]"Precio a la cabeza de Carlos Castaño Gil," *El Tiempo*, December 11, 1996.

[323]On December 3, 1997, the government issued Decree 2895, which created a "Search Block" (Bloque de Búsqueda) to capture and investigate paramilitary groups. The Search Block is headed by the defense minister.

[324]"Critican ofrecimiento de recompensa por Castaño," *El Tiempo*, January 10, 1997; "Ganaderos se alían con paras," *El Espectador*, January 14, 1997; and Bibiana Mercado and Orlando León Restrepo, "Urabá: el fin de la pesadilla," *El Tiempo*, September 28, 1997.

[325]Translation by Human Rights Watch. Letter from Estado Mayor-AUC, to José Noé Rios, presidential peace counselor, November 27, 1997.

[326]See, for instance, Serpa's announcement that he would talk to the ACCU. "Polémica por diálogos con las autodefensas," *El Tiempo*, January 4, 1996.

Within the AUC, the ACCU has the most receptive position. ACCU statutes prohibit fighters from forcibly recruiting members and attacking individuals who take no part in the conflict. Fighters who disobey the statutes, it states, will be punished and potentially expelled.[327]

In other material, the AUC has prohibited the recruitment of combatants under eighteen years of age; forced displacement; and the kidnapping or forced disappearance of civilians.[328]

"In the past, the self-defense groups committed errors," Castaño told two reporters from the daily *El Tiempo* in 1997. "It was the result of a lack of professionalization and ignorance, but we have begun a process of recuperation. We carried out a kind of coup d'etat on certain groups. We took away their guns and expelled their men. We carried out a clean-up, and in that way unified the movement."[329]

At the same time, however, Castaño has argued that the nature of Colombia's war — with many combatants out of uniform uniforms or any identification — makes strict standards difficult if not impossible to apply.[330] Instead, he has advocated a "creole" version of international humanitarian law, adaptable to Colombia's irregular warfare.[331]

"We have not shot people indiscriminately," he told the magazine *Cambio 16* in December 1997. "Massacres don't exist... The only thing I accept is that I kill guerrillas *hors de combat*."[332]

After a detailed review of cases, Human Rights Watch has concluded that far from respecting the laws of war, the AUC depends on the explicit, deliberate,

---

[327]Although the ACCU refers to an internal rules document, which we requested, we were never provided with a copy. AUC, "Naturaleza Político-Militar del Movimiento," June 26, 1997; and ACCU statutes.

[328]AUC, "Colombia Libre," August 1997, No. 2.

[329]Translation by Human Rights Watch. Bibiana Mercado and Orlando León Restrepo, "Urabá: el fin de la pesadilla," *El Tiempo*, September 28, 1997.

[330]Human Rights Watch interview with Carlos Castaño, July 9, 1996.

[331]Bibiana Mercado and Orlando León Restrepo, "'Las Farc infiltraron listas de los partidos tradicionales'" *El Tiempo*, September 29, 1997.

[332]"'Esta guerra no da más," *Cambio 16*, December 15, 1997.

and systematic violation of these standards in order to wage war. Government investigators, church officials, humanitarian aid groups, and victims of AUC attacks agree that Castaño and the AUC have paid only lip service to the protections contained in Common Article 3 and Protocol II. To the contrary, the AUC has repeatedly and energetically flouted international standards by committing massacres, executing civilians and combatants *hors de combat*, torturing, mutilating corpses, circulating death threats, torture, forcing displacement, taking hostages, and looting, among other violations.

"People die because they live in areas dominated by guerrillas and because they are seen by the paramilitaries as supporting them," one government intelligence analyst told Human Rights Watch.[333]

In 1997, the Data Bank recorded at least 155 massacres apparently committed by units allied under the AUC, making it responsible for the vast majority of killings in violation of the laws of war in Colombia.[334] In that same time period, the Attorney General's Office formulated accusations in 271 cases implicating AUC members, many involving massacres.[335]

For its part, the ACCU, the AUC's most powerful member, denies hundreds of reports that its members routinely torture captives and mutilate and decapitate the bodies of people it has executed.[336] However, such reports are consistent, widespread, and based on credible sources. Such practices are not only routine, but are a deliberate strategy. Of the 150 cases of torture registered by the Data Bank in 1997, 141 were attributed to paramilitary groups. Of those, most involved individuals tortured and then killed. In many cases, bodies were also dismembered, decapitated, and mutilated with machetes, chain saws, and acid.[337]

In interviews, Carlos Castaño can be forthright and unapologetic about tactics that flout the laws of war. In an interview with journalist Germán Castro Caycedo, Castaño said that the Tangüero strategy of purposefully massacring the

---

[333]Human Rights Watch interview with intelligence analyst, Santafé de Bogotá, December 2, 1997.

[334]CINEP and Justice and Peace, *Balance 1997*, p 6.

[335]Human Rights Watch interview with Human Rights Unit, Attorney General's Office, Santafé de Bogotá, December 4, 1997.

[336]Letter to Human Rights Watch from the ACCU, July 27, 1997.

[337]CINEP and Justice and Peace, *Balance 1997*, p. 4-5.

civilians they believed brought guerrillas food, medicine, and other supplies was a useful one that the AUC has energetically employed.

"We realized that we could isolate [guerrillas] and saw that this was a strategy that had very good results," Castaño said. "Today, we continue to apply the same mechanism [in Urabá]... with the same excellent results we experienced then."[338]

In its conclusions to its third summit in 1996, the AUC provided a virtual hit list of those it considers military targets, completely ignoring the careful distinctions combatants are required to make to protect civilians. "All of the inhabitants of a region dominated by any of the [groups in conflict] are potential combatants, be they active sympathizers who take no direct part in the conflict but do assume the key responsibility of transmitting orders and information, establishing lines of communication, providing supplies of every type, infiltrating the enemy, 'collecting' funds, and acting as political commissars,... or passive sympathizers, who take on the duty of seeing, hearing, and especially knowing nothing."[339]

An ACCU pronouncement circulated in the department of Bolívar in December 1996 encapsulates Castaño's strategy. ACCU fighters planned to carry out a population census, the pronouncement said, to distinguish between "people who are dedicated to working honorably from those... who will be detained and executed." The latter category included "those who assist [guerrillas] ideologically or with material support, because in this way we are striking at the guerrillas' foundation and contributing to the work of their destruction."[340]

As is clear, these statements and the behavior of AUC units in the field reflect a profound rejection of the laws of war even as Castaño has learned to praise them in public documents and interviews.

Throughout 1996 and 1997, AUC units established a clear pattern of violations of the laws of war. A unit would enter a village, execute civilians believed to support guerrillas, and leave. In hundreds of cases, as sociologist Alejandro Reyes pointed out in the daily *El Espectador*, massacres of civilians achieved a definite, albeit brutal purpose.

---

[338]Translation by Human Rights Watch. Germán Castro Caycedo, *En Secreto* (Santafé de Bogotá: Planeta, 1996), pp. 153-154.

[339]"Naturaleza Político-Militar del Movimiento," AUC, June 26, 1997.

[340]Translation by Human Rights Watch. "Al pueblo del Departamento de Bolívar, Que pretenden las Autodefensas Campesinas de Córdoba y Urabá," December 1996.

"The massacre of those suspect of guerrilla ties [by paramilitaries] serves as an efficient notification to the population to sever any ties of support they may have with guerrillas," he noted. "Many of those who may have sympathized with guerrillas get scared and flee the region. Then the self-defense groups organize their own local support network, preferably of families who have lost members to the guerrillas. As a result, the self-defense groups consider the region recovered from their enemies."[341]

For example, on April 2, 1997, an estimated 200 ACCU members crossed the border into Panama and entered the villages of La Bonga and Titiná, Panama, settled by Colombian refugees. Paramilitaries reportedly executed three residents after dragging them from their homes. A fourth, Remberto Arrieta, was killed as he attempted to escape. Although the ACCU, which claimed responsibility for the attack, said the dead were guerrillas, human rights groups, who interviewed witnesses later, described them as a lumberjack, a peasant woman, and two farmers, who paramilitaries accused of assisting guerrillas, not taking a direct role in hostilities. Subsequently, many fled the region.[342]

When Human Rights Watch asked Carlos Castaño why the ACCU had killed several butchers in and around Tierralta, Córdoba, in 1996, his answer both recognized the group's responsibility for the killings and demonstrated its policy of violating the laws of war. Guerrillas, Castaño said, steal cattle from ranchers, then trade the stolen herd for cattle belonging to small farmers. When the small farmers take the stolen cows to the local slaughterhouse, butchers buy them. Therefore, Castaño reasoned, butchers assist guerrillas and relinquish their status as non-combatants. "The killing of butchers was to send a message that people could no longer provide this economic support to the guerrillas," he told Human Rights Watch.[343]

Castaño has also admitted targeting for attack leftist politicians simply because of their views, violating the protection guaranteed civilians by the laws of war. The conclusions to the AUC's First Summit in 1994 state that as long as guerrillas continue to execute security force members and the families of

---

[341]Translation by Human Rights Watch. Alejandro Reyes Posada, "El negocio de las masacres: ganancias privadas y costos públicos," *El Espectador*, January 19, 1997.

[342]Letter to Human Rights Watch from the ACCU, July 27, 1997; CINEP and Justice and Peace, *Noche y Niebla*, April-June, 1997, No. 4, p. 25; and Luis Alberto Milo Rueda, "Temen otra invasión 'para' en Panamá," *El Tiempo*, May 28, 1997.

[343]Human Rights Watch interview with Carlos Castaño, July 9, 1996.

paramilitaries, they will consider "political and trade union operatives of the extreme left" as prime targets, in essence a policy of violating the laws of war by deliberately targeting civilians.

Castaño reaffirmed this position in 1997, when he told reporters that his forces would kill candidates perceived as supporting guerrillas.[344]

This violates the laws of war, which protect even a civilian who speaks out in support of a party to the conflict so long as that civilian takes no direct role in hostilities. Also, the laws of war make no exception for abuses committed because an enemy commits them; all sides are bound to uphold the laws of war regardless of whether their enemies do so.

Also targeted are human rights defenders who report on paramilitary abuses. After the Santander and Southern Cesar Self-Defense Group killed eleven residents and arbitrarily detained at least thirty-four others in Barrancabermeja on May 16, 1998, human rights leaders protested and called on authorities to investigate.[345] Subsequently, the paramilitary group, which belongs to the AUC, circulated a threat naming Osiris Bayther, president of the Regional Committee for the Defense of Human Rights (Comité Regional para la defensa de los Derechos Humanos, CREDHOS) a Colombian human rights group that covers the Middle Magdalena region, and declaring her a "military target" for allegedly working in coordination with guerrillas. On June 4, government investigators announced that

---

[344]Translation by Human Rights Watch. Bibiana Mercado and Orlando León Restrepo, "'Las Farc infiltraron listas de los partidos tradicionales'" *El Tiempo*, September 29, 1997.

[345]Julio César Niño Orozco, "Paras de Santander, autores de masacre," *El Espectador*, May 28, 1998.

Joint burials of massacre victims, like this one in Barrancabermeja in 1998, have become common in Colombia. © Agencia Toma

paramilitaries had told them that at least twenty-three of those detained had been shot and their bodies burned, a serious violation of the laws of war.[346]

To counter accusations of abuses committed by the AUC, Castaño says that his group first consults at least three unconnected intelligence sources to prove that a prospective target is a combatant before carrying out a killing. To reporters, Castaño has said that suspects are only killed after being sentenced by a panel of three paramilitary judges, who must gather evidence from two independent sources before issuing a verdict.[347]

Nevertheless, Human Rights Watch collected evidence showing that rarely does the AUC even follow these grossly inadequate procedures before killing those it accuses of supporting guerrillas. Instead, talk of gathering evidence and panels of judges appears to be part of a cynical public relations effort to justify the unjustifiable: the massacre and executions of non-combatants and combatants *hors de combat*.

---

[346]"Asesinados 25 jóvenes secuestrados hace 19 días," *El Tiempo*, June 4, 1998.

[347]Joshua Hammer, "'Head Cutters' at War," *Newsweek*, June 2, 1997.

Human Rights Watch was able to test the AUC's "trial proceedings" on the case of one individual well known to us who, Castaño had said, had been proven to be a guerrilla by his so-called independent intelligence sources. According to Castaño, the individual had supplied tents, food, and medicines to guerrillas and had traveled in guerrilla-held areas. As a result, Castaño noted, his name was on a death list.

We pointed out that the individual, a humanitarian aid worker, was at the time in question assisting hundreds of families forcibly displaced by the armed conflict. The individual may have handed supplies to a guerrilla; however, the individual's job was to distribute tents, food, and medicines to displaced families, not distinguish between guerrillas dressed as civilians and non-combatants, and deny aid on that basis. At no time did the individual take a direct role in hostilities.

Castaño conceded that his sources were sometimes unreliable and may not have taken the individual's duties into account. However, it was clear that this type of reasoning has, for the AUC, turned almost anyone living and working in areas where guerrillas are present into a target.[348]

Massacres

Caicedo, Antioquia: After an April 12, 1996 assault by the FARC in which one police officer was killed, the National Police withdrew from this town. Despite the desperate pleas of local authorities urging them to stay, police officials charged that residents supported guerrillas and therefore did not merit protection.[349] Eight days later, the ACCU seized the town and forced its residents to the central square. Working from lists of names, the armed men selected four people — Dario Restrepo, Caladino González, Jorge Eliécer Castro, and Isaías González — and killed them. All were merchants the ACCU accused of selling supplies to

---

[348]Human Rights Watch interview with Carlos Castaño, July 9, 1996.

[349]Letter from Aracelly Tamayo Restrepo, personera, to Col. Hugo Pulido, National Police adviser, May 17, 1996; Human Rights Watch interview with Antioquia deputy commander Col. Antonio D' León Martínez, Medellín, Antioquia, July 2, 1996; and "Las Farc atacaron a Caicedo en Antioquia," *El Tiempo*, April 14, 1996

guerrillas.[350] In an interview, the ACCU claimed responsibility for the killings.[351] The fact that a merchant living in a war zone sells goods to one side or the other does not convert them into a target.

Media Luna, Cesar: Traveling in three pick-up trucks, an estimated sixty ACCU members seized this village around noon on October 27, 1996, after cutting telephone lines. The armed men executed seven residents and abducted seven others, one of whom was found dead the next day. The remaining six were reported as forcibly disappeared.[352] Before leaving, the men painted machine guns and the letters "ACCU" on walls.[353] Afterwards, the media reported that the ACCU was circulating a death list of 200 names of suspected guerrilla supporters.[354] The Attorney General's Office is currently investigating the ACCU's involvement in the massacre.[355]

Colosó, Morroa, and Toluviejo, Sucre: On December 3 and 4, 1996, an estimated thirty members of the ACCU entered the town of Colosó and seized Elsa Rosa Silgado, a police inspector, and two others, who were later executed. The next day, this same group set up a roadblock outside Colosó and detained seven travelers, four of whom were killed on the spot. Later the same day, the group surrounded a party in Colosó and detained thirty people whose names appeared on their lists. After announcing that they would "clean" the area of guerrillas, the men released their captives and continued on to Pichilín, where they killed two men, leaving their bodies in the road. Finally, in the village of Varsovia, the ACCU killed seven

---

[350]When the FARC attacked Caicedo, the army reacted by sending helicopters to strafe the surrounding area. However, the army did nothing when paramilitaries seized the town. Human Rights Watch interview with a government investigator, Medellín, Antioquia, July 2, 1996; and Justice and Peace, *Boletín*, April-June 1996, p. 12.

[351]Human Rights Watch interview with Carlos Castaño, July 9, 1996.

[352]Amnesty International Urgent Action 251/96, November 1, 1996.

[353]CINEP and Justice and Peace, *Noche y Niebla*, October-December 1996, p. 27.

[354]"Six die, nine disappear in Colombian massacre," Reuters, October 27, 1996; and "Autodefensas amenazan a La Guajira y Cesar," *El Tiempo*, November 9, 1996.

[355]Human Rights Watch interview with Human Rights Unit, Attorney General's Office, Santafé de Bogotá, December 4, 1997.

villagers. All told, sixteen people were slain. According to police, the location and identification of bodies was especially difficult since they were spread over a radius of thirty-five kilometers. Many of the victims were found with their hands bound behind their backs and multiple shots to the head.[356] In the days after the massacre, an estimated 350 farmers fled the area in fear. The ACCU continued to circulate pronouncements saying that guerrilla collaborators would be killed.[357] After an investigation by the attorney general's office, arrest warrants were issued for fourteen men identified as ACCU members.[358]

Mapiripán, Meta: From July 15 through July 20, 1997, the ACCU seized the town of Mapiripán, Meta, killed at least thirteen people, and threatened others with death. An investigation by human rights groups concluded that paramilitaries had arrived in the region via chartered airplane, which landed at the San José del Guaviare airport days before the massacre. This case also illustrates the deadly results of the army and police policy of acquiescence in paramilitary killings. Local army and police units ignored repeated phone calls from a civilian judge in the area asking for help to stop the slayings. At dawn on July 15, an estimated 200 heavily-armed ACCU members arrived and began rounding up local authorities and forcing them to accompany them. Among those they searched for were peasants who had taken part in a 1996 department-wide protest against coca eradication and the government's failure to provide viable economic alternatives for the region. ACCU men detained residents and people arriving by boat, took them to the local slaughterhouse, then bound, tortured, and executed them by slitting their throats. The first person killed, Antonio María Herrera, known as "Catumare," was hung from a hook, and ACCU members quartered his body, throwing the pieces into the Guaviare River. At least two bodies — those of Sinaí Blanco, a boatman, and Ronald Valencia, the airstrip manager — were

---

[356]This was one of the massacres that prompted the Colombian government to issue its first reward for information leading to the capture of Carlos Castaño. Letter to Human Rights Watch from Gen. Harold Bedoya, Commander, Colombian Armed Forces, July 2, 1997; and "Autodefensas masacran a 16 campesinos en Sucre," *El Tiempo*, December 6, 1996.

[357]Laureano Romero Colley, "Autodefensas anuncian nueva masacre en Sucre," *El Tiempo*, December 17, 1996.

[358]Letter to Ernesto Carrasco, Attorney General's Office, from Human Rights Unit of Attorney General's Office, May 14, 1997.

decapitated.[359] Judge Leonardo Iván Cortés reported hearing the screams of the people they brought to the slaughterhouse to interrogate, torture, and kill throughout the five days the ACCU remained in the area. In one of the missives he sent to various regional authorities during the massacre, he wrote: "Each night they kill groups of five to six defenseless people, who are cruelly and monstrously massacred after being tortured. The screams of humble people are audible, begging for mercy and asking for help."[360] ACCU leader Carlos Castaño took responsibility for the massacre, and told reporters that an ACCU "shock front" of seventy men executed thirteen people, and threw some bodies in the Guaviare River. Arriving only days after the ACCU left, authorities located five bodies, though the ICRC estimated to reporters that as many as twenty more may have been killed and thrown into the Guaviare River.[361] Castaño denied reports of torture, yet promised "many more Mapiripans" for Colombia in subsequent press interviews.[362] Hundreds of people fled the region, including Judge Cortés, who was forced to leave Colombia with his family because of threats on his life. The Attorney General's Office is currently investigating the ACCU's involvement in the massacre and has

---

[359]The report by the representative of the attorney general who recovered Valencia's body noted that the head was found ten meters away from the body, which was found on the river bank. Formato Nacional de Acta de Levantamiento de Cadaver, July 20, 1997.

[360]Translation by Human Rights Watch. "Nadie quiso evitar masacre," *Cambio 16*, November 3, 1997.

[361]The lack of a precise body count is due to several factors. Because it is in a coca-growing area, Mapiripán has a large, transient work force made up mostly of young men, who work the coca fields, and young women, who work as prostitutes; permanent residents often do not know their names or recognize people only by their nicknames. Also, many of the bodies were thrown into the Guaviare River, and little attempt was made to search its banks for remains. Before dumping the bodies, witnesses say, paramilitaries eviscerated them to make sure they would not float. Finally, people abandoned the area so quickly after the massacre that it was difficult for authorities to confirm if those missing were dead or forcibly displaced. Bibiana Mercado and Orlando León Restrepo, "Urabá: el fin de la pesadilla," *El Tiempo*, September 28, 1997; and "'Soy el ala moderada de las autodefensas'," *Cambio 16*, December 22, 1997.

[362]Castaño had announced his intention to move a unit to the Guaviare in a July 1997 release. "Frente Guaviare: Autodefensas Unidas de Colombia-AUC, July 1997.

issued arrest warrants for Castaño and two of his men for planning and carrying out the killings.[363] The Internal Affairs continues to investigate official involvement.[364]

Despite Judge Cortés's eight telephone pleas for help along with the calls of at least two others, neither the police nor the army's "Joaquín París" Battalion in nearby San José reacted until the ACCU had left town. As a result of their internal investigation, the army put Seventh Brigade Commander Gen. Jaime Humberto Uscátegui on administrative duty for failing to act promptly to stop the massacre and detain those responsible. The armed forces also claimed to be investigating Maj. Hernán Orozco Castro, acting commander of the "Joaquín París" Battalion, Maj. Horacio Galeano, and Capt. Luis Carlos López. In an interview, General Bonett told Human Rights Watch that General Uscátegui would not be promoted and that his career was over. However, Human Rights Watch subsequently learned that General Uscátegui was returned to active duty without any apparent punishment. It is also noteworthy that the army, which controls the San José airport, claimed that it had not registered the arrival of the ACCU's chartered airplane despite a policy of registering every arriving plane and passenger, including Human Rights Watch representatives during a May 1997 visit.[365]

Murder and Torture

Edilma Ocampo and Stella Gil: Ocampo and Gil, her daughter, were seized at their home by paramilitaries belonging to the ACCU on February 21, 1996, in the village of Las Cañas, near Turbo, Antioquia. According to human rights groups, the paramilitaries, some of whom were hooded, bound them and accused them of being guerrillas. "For them, we have a special treatment," they reportedly said. The paramilitaries beat them, then decapitated them. Afterwards paramilitaries cut open

---

[363]Human Rights Watch interview with Human Rights Unit, Attorney General's Office, Santafé de Bogotá, December 4, 1997; and "Primera decisión judicial por masacre de Mapiripán: Carlos Castaño, nueva medida de aseguramiento," *El Tiempo*, July 5, 1998.

[364]Letter to Human Rights Watch from Jesús Orlando Gómez López, Internal Affairs Delegate for Human Rights, November 28, 1997; and Human Rights Watch telephone interview with María Cristina Caballero, *Cambio 16*, November 5, 1997.

[365]Human Rights Watch interview with General Bonett, Santafé de Bogotá, December 12, 1997; "'Nadie quiso evitar masacre'," *Cambio 16*, November 3, 1997; and "Investigación contra 4 militares y 5 civiles por masacre de Mapiripán," *El Tiempo*, October 15, 1997.

their torsos and placed Gil's body over Ocampo's. Paramilitaries told villagers they had six months to completely abandon the village. If not, they promised, they would return and burn everything in their path.[366]

Héctor Hernán Correa, Jairo de Jesús Sepúlveda, and William de Jesús Villa García: Correa, a mentally retarded man, was in his home in La Granja, Antioquia, when an ACCU unit of an estimated twenty men arrived on June 11, 1996. Residents rushed to close doors and windows, but paramilitaries began to beat down the door of Correa's house. As Correa's elderly father hid in the bathroom, he and his mother crouched in the kitchen. A paramilitary burst into the kitchen, grabbed Correa, pulled him into the living room, and shot him dead. The mother was dragged to the living room, where she saw her dead son. "Where are the weapons?" the paramilitary demanded. When the man asked if the person he had killed was her husband, Correa's mother said yes, hoping to protect her husband, still hidden in the kitchen. Before leaving, paramilitaries sacked the Correa home, taking clothing, a radio, and even Correa's school photo framed on the wall. That day in La Granja, the ACCU also killed Jairo de Jesús Sepúlveda, a teacher they dragged from a sports center, and Correa's cousin, William de Jesús Villa García, who had been shot from the ladder where he had been painting a house. Before leaving, the paramilitaries reportedly told residents, "This is just the beginning" and they were going to continue to act until they "got rid of everyone who had something to do with the guerrillas." Three days later, the Correa family abandoned La Granja.[367]

Guillermo León Barrera Henao, Francisco Javier Taborda Taborda, and Álvaro Vásquez: Barrera and Taborda, both professional drivers, were taken from their homes by ACCU members on June 13, 1996 in the Chocó hamlet known as El Siete. Paramilitaries forced them to sit beneath an image of the Virgin Mary before torturing and executing them.[368] The same paramilitaries then attempted to commandeer a vehicle being driven by Vásquez, who refused to hand over his keys. He was dragged out of his vehicle and shot, and his vehicle was burned. The

---

[366]Justice and Peace, *Boletín*, January-March 1996, p. 37.

[367]Human Rights Watch interviews with La Granja survivors, Medellín, Antioquia, December 11, 1997; and Justice and Peace, *Boletín*, April-June 1996, p. 70.

[368]Letter to Human Rights Watch from Raymundo Moreno Lobon, regional advocate-Chocó, November 28, 1997.

ACCU painted graffiti in the area saying, "Death to snitches, get out guerrillas of the southwest, ACCU." The ACCU also distributed a flyer taking responsibility for the killings.[369]

Corregimiento Coyongal: Paramilitaries belonging to the ACCU seized this Magangué, Bolívar, village on December 9, 1996 and detained three residents, Pedro Nolasco Arroyo Martínez, Tomás López, and Jacobo Rivera. ACCU members accused them of helping guerrillas. Arroyo and López worked on the boats that provide public transportation and Rivera sold street food. Two days later, residents found their corpses, which showed signs of torture.[370] A year later, the area was still plagued by paramilitary violence, and ACCU checkpoints along the river continued to operate without interference from the government.[371]

Eli Gómez Osorio: This El Carmen de Viboral, Antioquia personero investigated reports that members of the Barbacoas Battalion worked with paramilitaries and had raped local women in 1996. After soldiers visited the farmers who had filed the complaints to force them to withdraw them, Gómez held a meeting with Fourth Brigade Commander Gen. Alfonso Manosalva (now deceased) to complain. Afterwards, he began receiving threats. On November 26, 1996, men believed to belong to the ACCU intercepted him in town and shot him dead.[372]

José Miguel Domicó: A member of the Emberá-Katío indigenous community, Domicó was seized by the ACCU near his village in the Dabeiba region of Antioquia on December 21, 1996. Hours later, Domicó's body was found with several gunshot wounds. The ACCU accepts responsibility for killing Domicó, but

---

[369]Justice and Peace, *Boletín*, April-June 1996, p. 70; and "Muerte a Guerrilleros y Militantes," Movimiento de Autodefensas Campesinas de Urabá and Córdoba.

[370]CINEP and Justice and Peace, *Noche y Niebla*, October-December 1996, p. 53.

[371]Letter from Carlos Rodríguez, CCJ, to John Donaldson, president, Inter-American Commission on Human Rights, Organization of American States, February 24, 1998.

[372]Human Rights Watch interview with Rafael Rincón, Medellín personero and president of the National Association of Personeros, Medellín, Antioquia, December 10, 1997; and Human Rights Watch interview with Carlos Castaño, July 9, 1996; and ACCU Statutes.

claims he was engaged in planting mines.[373] While Domicó may have been a combatant, in this case, he was clearly *hors de combat* when he was killed.

Marino López: On February 27, 1997, about sixty armed and uniformed ACCU members arrived in Vijao, Chocó, and set up three machine guns on tripods. After indiscriminately strafing the town, where some guerrillas were living, they captured twenty residents who they accused of supporting guerrillas. Residents were given three days to leave the area. While paramilitaries were searching the town house by house, they discovered a military uniform and munitions in the home of Marino López. Although López and residents insisted the material belonged to someone else, paramilitaries took López to the nearby river, decapitated him, then cut off an arm and a leg before throwing his body into the river. Residents told humanitarian aid workers that paramilitaries kicked López's head like a soccer ball before discarding it.[374] Government investigators refused to travel to the area for security reasons.[375]

Claudio Manuel Pérez, Javier Galarcio, and Álvaro Taborda: These three teachers were captured and killed by the ACCU for allegedly carrying out the FARC bombing of FUNPAZCOR and the Córdoba Ranchers Federation in Montería, Córdoba, in 1996. In a letter to Human Rights Watch, the ACCU claimed that it had convicted the three after an investigation.[376] Subsequently, Castaño played for the *New York Times* a tape of Taborda's purported confession, in which he said that he sold information that allowed the FARC to plant the October 1996 bomb that killed four passers-by.[377] Taborda's body remains unaccounted for. Currently, the

---

[373]CINEP and Justice and Peace, *Noche y Niebla*, October-December 1996, p. 53; and letter to Human Rights Watch from the ACCU, July 27, 1997.

[374]Letter to Human Rights Watch from humanitarian aid worker, June 1997; Letter from Father Javier Giraldo, Justice and Peace, to President Ernesto Samper, March 12, 1997; and CINEP and Justice and Peace, *Noche y Niebla*, January-March 1997, p. 36.

[375]Colombian government's response to cases submitted to the office of the U.N. High Commissioner for Human Rights, January-June, 1997.

[376]Letter to Human Rights Watch from the ACCU, July 27, 1997; and "Gobierno anuncia medidas contra las autodefensas," *El Tiempo*, January 15, 1997.

[377]Diana Jean Schemo, "Anti-Rebel Groups Become the Terror of Colombia," *New York Times*, March 26, 1997.

Attorney General's Office is investigating the ACCU for the killings.[378] Based on this information, we cannot determine if these three individuals were combatants. However, even if they were FARC members, they were protected by Article 7 of Protocol II, which prohibits the killing of combatants *hors de combat*. Moreover, the ACCU's procedure makes it clear that its leaders have no intention of implementing anything remotely resembling a fair trial for detainees, as required by Protocol II, Article 6.

Diego Márquez Zapata: Paramilitaries identified as ACCU members forced this local leader and human rights committee member from his home on March 18, 1997 and shot him dead fifty meters away. Márquez had reported in July 1996 that he had come into the possession of a "black list" circulated by the Salgar, Antioquia police commander and apparently obtained by the ACCU. The list was addressed to the army's Cacique Nutibara Battalion, and identified five people, including Márquez, as guerrillas and guerrilla collaborators.[379]

La Victoria de San Isidro, Cesar: On March 24, 1997, the ACCU seized this village and forced the 600 residents to gather in the central square at 4 a.m. William Pérez Durán, a town council member, and Calixto Oñate, a resident, attempted to flee and were shot dead. As paramilitaries searched the houses, they took money and jewelry. According to a report by village residents, "they said that they would kill everyone on their lists and that they would burn all of the large stores that sold to the guerrillas and kill their owners." As the ACCU fighters left, they took with them seven residents. Approximately 300 meters beyond the village, they executed Edelfonso Rangel Contreras and José Daniel Quintero, whose body showed signs of torture. One of the villagers, Manolo Durá, reported that a paramilitary cut off

---

[378]Human Rights Watch interview with Human Rights Unit, Attorney General's Office, Santafé de Bogotá, December 4, 1997; and letter to Human Rights Watch from Sandra Peñaloza Cuevas, Oficina de Asuntos Internacionales, Attorney General's Office, June 6, 1997.

[379]Human Rights Watch interview with María Girlesa Villegas, Public Advocate's Office, Medellín, Antioquia, December 9, 1997; Amnesty International Urgent Action 85/97, March 26, 1997; and CINEP and Justice and Peace, *Noche y Niebla*, January-March 1997, p. 50.

a piece of his beard and the skin attached to it as a "memento" of the visit. The remaining captives were released.[380]

Juan Camacho Herrera: After six months of rumors that the ACCU planned to seize the town of Rio Viejo, Bolívar, an estimated sixty heavily armed men arrived on April 25, 1997 and forced residents to gather in the central square. There, they executed Juan Camacho Herrera, a street vendor, and decapitated him. They did it, residents told journalists, saying, "This is to give you an example of how guerrillas should be killed." Paramilitaries had also searched for the Rio Viejo mayor, who managed to flee out the back door of his house as armed men kicked in the front door. Unable to locate him, they destroyed part of his house and looted personal belongings.[381] To return, Mayor Luis Santiago de la Rosa told authorities, would be to "dig my own grave." Mayor de la Rosa later resigned.[382]

Luis Fernando Rodríguez, Darío de Jesús Londoño Vargas, and José Jairo Blandón: The public bus these three men were traveling on near Betulia, Antioquia, was stopped at an ACCU roadblock on May 17, 1997. Rodríguez and Londoño were passengers; Blandón was the driver's assistant. Paramilitaries with lists of names forced them off the bus and killed them. Authorities found ACCU literature around the bodies when they were recovered later. Authorities also told the press that the men's bodies had been doused with a corrosive liquid which caused their skin to peel off.[383]

---

[380]Letter to Human Rights Watch from La Victoria residents, March 1997; CINEP and Justice and Peace, *Noche y Niebla*, January-March, 1997, p. 50; and "Autodefensas matan a 9 personas," *El Tiempo*, March 25, 1997.

[381]Urgent Action, CREDHOS, April 1997; Letter from the Comité Permanente por la Defensa de los Derechos Humanos de Bolívar, May 14, 1997; and "'Paras' dan látigo en el sur de Bolívar," *El Tiempo*, April 30, 1997.

[382]Translation by Human Rights Watch. "Más Ejército para el sur de Bolívar," *El Tiempo*, May 2, 1997; and "Renuncian dos alcaldes en Bolívar," *El Tiempo*, June 26, 1997.

[383]CINEP and Justice and Peace, *Noche y Niebla*, April-June, 1997, p. 37; and "Accu matan a 3 campesinos en Betulia," *El Tiempo*, May 19, 1997.

Taking of hostages

Guerrilla family members: From July through November, 1996, the ACCU took hostage at least twenty family members of FARC and ELN combatants, holding them under threat of death as retribution for guerrilla hostage-taking. None of the hostages were themselves involved in guerrilla activity.[384] The ACCU took responsibility for the following kidnappings, and some hostages were allowed to see ICRC representatives and correspond with family during their captivity. In its Third Summit report, the AUC concluded that the tactic "has proved its efficiency in demoralizing the enemy" and should be continued. All of the hostages were later released.[385] Among the hostages were:

■   José Ricardo Sáenz Vargas, the brother of Guillermo León Sáenz Vargas or "Alfonso Cano," a member of the FARC's General Secretariat. Sáenz was taken by ACCU members on July 24, 1996. Along with other hostages, he was released under the auspices of the ICRC and Catholic Church on March 28, 1997.[386]

■   Carmen Emilia de Arango, the mother of Luciano Arango Marín, who uses the name Iván Márquez as a member of the FARC's General Secretariat. Arango was taken on October 16, 1996 with her daughter and Luciano's sister, Edna Maritza Arango. Along with Isabel Ruiz de Chamorro, mother of an UC-ELN commander known as "Ernestino,"

---

[384]In a letter to Human Rights Watch, the ACCU admitted responsibility for these hostage-takings. Letter to Human Rights Watch from the ACCU, July 27, 1997.

[385]Human Rights Watch interview with Pax Christi, Washington, D.C., May 12, 1998.

[386]In a confused incident, a former guerrilla-turned-army informant told the magazine *Alternativa* that Sáenz had in fact been kidnapped by ACCU members working with the army's Twentieth Brigade, which drafted him to take part. The informant later recanted. However, Human Rights Watch has received corroborating information indicating that the Twentieth Brigade took part in the kidnappings and executions of guerrilla family members (see case of Jorge Velandia in the army section). "Colombia: armed groups release civilians," *ICRC News*, April 3, 1997; Equipo de Alternativa, "'Ejército secuestró al hermano de Cano,'" *Alternativa*, January 15-February 15, 1997, pp. 18-19; and "Pille el detalle," *Alternativa*, February 15-March 15, 1997, pp. 14-15.

Carmen was released on December 2, 1996, while Edna was released on March 28, 1997.[387]

■ Janeth Torres Victoria, sister of Hernando Torres Victoria, who uses the name Pablo Catatumbo as a FARC commander. Torres was taken in Cali on July 29. She was released on December 16, 1996.[388]

■ Leonor Palmera de Castro, sister of Ricardo Palmera, known as "Simón Trinidad" as a FARC commander. Palmera was taken in Valledupar on August 25, 1996. She was released on March 28, 1997.[389]

■ Guillermo López Nieto and his two children, Germán López Bustos and Diana María López, were taken by ACCU members who identified themselves as members of the Attorney General's Office on September 13, 1996 in Medellín, Antioquia. López's other son, Bernardo, is a member of the EPL. The ACCU returned to their home the same day to get other relatives, who had already fled. The three López family members were released later that month.[390]

■ Nuria Carvajal Reales, sister of William Manjarres, who uses the name Adan Izquierdo as a FARC commander, and her husband, Luis Alberto Montoya, were taken near Santa Marta, Magdalena on November 10, 1996. They were released on March 28, 1997.[391]

---

[387]"Colombia: armed groups release civilians," *ICRC News*, April 3, 1997; and "Paramilitares liberaron madres de jefes guerrilleros," *El Colombiano*, December 20, 1996.

[388]CCJ, *Colombia, Derechos Humanos y Derecho Humanitario: 1996*, p. 67.

[389]"Colombia: armed groups release civilians," *ICRC News*, April 3, 1997; and "'Cada noche sueño con la liberación de Leonor'," *El Tiempo*, March 26, 1997.

[390]"Los 'paras' van a la universidad," *El Tiempo*, February 18, 1997.

[391]"Colombia: armed groups release civilians," *ICRC News*, April 3, 1997; and Carlos Alberto Giraldo, "Informó Pax Christi en Ginebra," *El Colombiano*, April 9, 1997.

Attacks on medical workers, installations, and ambulances
Luz Marina Arteaga: According to human rights groups, this doctor and two store owners were taken captive by the ACCU on March 3, 1996, near Mutatá, Antioquia. Paramilitaries later killed the store owners. During the two days she was held, Arteaga was told by paramilitaries that "they would exterminate all of the people in the town who had even the smallest relationship with guerrillas." Arteaga was released, apparently to carry this message to other residents.[392]

Bolívar medical workers: After a series of attacks on southern Bolívar towns that included threats to medical workers, departmental medical authorities reported that seven villages – including Tiquisio and Rio Viejo, mentioned above – were completely without medical care, since doctors, nurses, and medical workers had fled out of fear for their lives. In repeated incursions, ACCU members had demanded that medical workers provide them with a list of the guerrillas they had treated.[393]

Norberto and Silvio Baquiaza Tascon: According to a human rights group, these brothers were at a Christmas party when paramilitaries who identified themselves as ACCU members seized the village of San Juan del Ité on December 25, 1997. Firing indiscriminately, paramilitaries seriously wounded two men, including Norberto. Silvio took Norberto to a clinic in the town of Puerto Berrío, Antioquia, where he was given first aid and put onto an ambulance that would take him to Medellín. However, the ambulance was stopped by hooded paramilitaries near El Porce. They forced the brothers to leave the ambulance, then executed them with shots to the head.[394]

Threats against civilian population
October municipal elections: The ACCU prohibited campaigning in towns throughout the departments of Bolívar, Magdalena, and Cesar, threatening those belonging to leftist political parties with death for their supposed links to guerrillas. Politicians who were suspected of negotiating agreements with guerrillas in their

---

[392]Justice and Peace, *Boletín*, January-March 1996, p. 60.

[393]"Por violencia, siete municipios sin médicos," *El Tiempo*, April 30, 1997; and "Amenazan a médicos y maestros," *El Tiempo*, May 3, 1997.

[394]CREDHOS, "S.O.S por Yondó (Antioquia)", Barrancabermeja, February 12, 1998; and CINEP and Justice and Peace, *Noche y Niebla*, October-December 1997, p. 49.

regions were also threatened. In an interview with *El Tiempo*, Carlos Castaño took responsibility for the threats.[395]

Non-combatants: The ACCU denies that it threatens the civilian population. Rather, the ACCU "warns... [The ACCU] wants to prevent harm and teach the population about the harm done to it by guerrillas."[396] However, reports of threats and the actions carried out when threats are not heeded are numerous and credible. A threat issued by the ACCU to the communities of Carmen de Atrato, Bolívar, Betania, Salgar, "or anyplace in southeastern Antioquia" takes responsibility for the killings of Guillermo Barrera, Álvaro Vásquez, and Francisco Javier Taborda, all accused of "collaborating with the Juan Camilo and Ernesto Che Guevara Fronts of the ELN." The document goes on to "sentence to death" twenty-six people, including someone identified only as "the village doctor."[397] Telephoned and written death threats from the ACCU in 1997 led two government investigators working on massacres where the ACCU was implicated to leave the country for their safety. In a letter, the AUC warned that if they "insisted in their persecution and partial attitude toward civil antisubversive organizations, we will be obligated to take up our weapons against the subversives hidden in these institutions."[398] The AUC has also repeatedly threatened the civilian population that if they travel to certain areas, they will be declared "military objectives" and killed. In October 1997, the AUC notified pilots and charter air companies that if their flew to Puerto Alvira or Barranco de Mina, Guainía, their aircraft would be "destroyed or brought down by any of our units." Companies immediately suspended the thirty-three

---

[395]"Autodefensas boicotearán las elecciones," *El Tiempo*, May 28, 1997; and Bibiana Mercado and Orlando León Restrepo, "'Las Farc inflitraron listas de los partidos tradicionales'" *El Tiempo*, September 29, 1997.

[396]Letter to Human Rights Watch from the ACCU, July 27, 1997.

[397]Human Rights Watch obtained a copy of this threat, which was circulated in 1996. "Muerte a Guerrilleros y Militantes," Movimiento de Autodefensas Campesinas de Urabá and Córdoba.

[398]Human Rights Watch interview, December 11, 1997.

daily flights to the region, causing shortages in food and medicine and prompting residents to flee.[399]

---

[399]Human Rights Watch telephone interview with Rocío López, regional Public Advocate's Office, Villavicencio, Meta, October 28, 1997; and "Las Auc crean zona de restricción aérea," *El Colombiano*, October 22, 1997.

V. GUERRILLA VIOLATIONS OF INTERNATIONAL HUMANITARIAN LAW

FARC

*The FARC calls it popular justice, but what they do is kill people
without consulting with anyone.*

> – *Guaviare resident,*
> *May 5, 1997*

The Revolutionary Armed Forces of Colombia (Fuerzas Armadas Revolucionarias de Colombia, FARC) had its beginnings in the civil conflict known as La Violencia, which began with the assassination of presidential candidate Jorge Eliécer Gaitán on April 9, 1948. At first a loose association of peasant self-defense groups, this mostly rural movement came increasingly under the influence of the Communist Party and declared itself a revolutionary army in 1964.[400]

An early member, former highway inspector Manuel Marulanda Vélez, or "Tirofijo" (Sure Shot), remains in command. By 1997, reports estimated that Marulanda had at least 8,000 troops distributed among an estimated sixty-two rural fronts, three urban fronts, and nine elite units, modeled on the army's specialized counterinsurgency brigades.[401] The FARC, which also calls itself the FARC-People's Army (Ejército del Pueblo, FARC-EP) is present throughout Colombia, and is considered strongest militarily in the southern Colombian departments of Caquetá, Putumayo, and Guaviare.[402]

---

[400]Comisión Internacional, *25 años de lucha por la paz, democracia y soberanía* (Comisión Internacional FARC-EP, May 1989), pp. 23-27. For a history of the FARC, see Eduardo Pizarro Leongómez, *Las FARC: de la autodefensa a la combinación de todas las formas de lucha* (Santafé de Bogotá: IEPRI/Tercer Mundo, 1991).

[401]Human Rights Watch interview, Colombian intelligence service, Santafé de Bogotá, December 2, 1997; and Bibiana Mercado and Orlando León Restrepo, "Farc alimentan la línea dura," *El Tiempo*, June 29, 1997.

[402]Human Rights Watch interview with Gen. Carlos Ospina, Mobile Brigade Two, San José del Guaviare, May 6, 1997.

By most accounts, the FARC has a highly centralized command that depends directly on Marulanda and his associates, known as the General Secretariat. As of this writing, the General Secretariat consists of seven individuals, each responsible for specific regions or duties, like international outreach. In addition, the FARC has a General Staff (*Estado Mayor*) responsible for military operations and the blocks (*bloques*), which join several fronts as regional forces.[403]

Although the organization operates over a vast and rugged territory and field commanders can be out of touch with central command, the many sources consulted by Human Rights Watch agreed that Marulanda and his staff maintain tight control over their units and strategy. The FARC itself claims that its policies and actions are determined by its high command, not individual commanders.[404]

Throughout the 1990s, Colombia's security forces have attempted to wrest legitimacy from the FARC by terming it a "narcoguerrilla" group dedicated not to political goals, but to the drug trade.[405] Although it is clear that the FARC does collect revenue from the illegal narcotics trade, there is no evidence that the FARC actively exports narcotics from Colombia.[406] The available evidence makes clear that the FARC uses a variety of illegal activities, including kidnapping for ransom, to fund its war. The FARC's relationship with drug traffickers is similar to its relationship with ranchers, businesspeople, and multinational corporations

---

[403]As of this writing, the members of the General Secretariat are believed to include Marulanda, commander in chief; Jorge Briceño, known as "Mono Jojoy" and in command of FARC units in much of southern Colombia; Alfonso Cano, responsible for ideology; Noel Matta, known as Efraín Guzmán or "El Viejo Efraín"; Timoleón Jiménez, known as "Timochenko"; Iván Márquez; and Raúl Reyes, responsible for international outreach. Conclusiones, Octava Conferencia Nacional de las FARC, May 3, 1993; and "El nuevo No. 1," *Semana*, September 10, 1996, pp. 50-51.

[404]Human Rights Watch interview with Marco León Calarcá, Frente Internacional-FARC, Mexico City, July 13, 1996.

[405]One example is a book widely distributed by the army that equates the FARC with the Medellín and Cali cartels, criminal syndicates dedicated to the export of cocaine and heroin. Major Luis Alberto Villamarín Pulido, *El Cartel de las FARC* (Santafé de Bogotá: Ediciones El Faraón, 1996).

[406]Interview with U.S. Ambassador Myles Frechette, Santafé de Bogotá, May 7, 1997.

throughout Colombia. The FARC levies a fee, or "war tax," on all commercial enterprises under threat of violence.[407]

The FARC and International Humanitarian Law

The FARC claims that it respects international humanitarian law. Writing to Human Rights Watch, the International Commission told us that there are "regulations that punish FARC members who commit acts that harm the civilian population."[408] However, when pressed in an interview, a FARC spokesperson told Human Rights Watch that guerrillas consider Protocol II and Common Article 3 "open to interpretation."[409]

Indeed, Human Rights Watch has found little evidence that the FARC makes an attempt to conform its methods to international standards, which its members flagrantly violate in the field. Despite repeated requests, the FARC has not provided Human Rights Watch with a copy of its regulations, current combat manuals, trial procedures, or rules of engagement, nor has it responded to our submission of a list of detailed cases, some included in this report, of alleged violations committed by the FARC.

When the FARC perceives a political advantage, it emphasizes its respect for international humanitarian law, as in the case of sixty soldiers captured after an armed forces-FARC clash at the Las Delicias base in the department of Putumayo in 1996 and released ten months later. The laws of war applicable in Colombia give captured combatants no special status, but provide for their humane treatment and safe release, which the FARC respected.[410]

---

[407]In November 1997, the army announced that it had prohibited officers from using the word "cartel" when referring to guerrillas. Nevertheless, officers continue to use the term, especially when lobbying for increased U.S. security assistance to fight what they term a "narco-guerrilla" threat. "Ejército prohíbe llamar 'cartel' a grupos guerrilleros," *El Tiempo*, November 21, 1997.

[408]Letter to Human Rights Watch from the International Commission of the FARC-EP, June 15, 1996.

[409]Human Rights Watch interview with Marco León Calarcá, Frente Internacional-FARC, Mexico City, July 15, 1996.

[410]On June 15, 1997, the FARC also released ten navy sailors captured the previous January. For a summary of the Las Delicias case, see "Guerrilla," *Semana*, June 9-16, 1997.

However, in dozens of other, less publicized cases, when no political advantage is apparent, the FARC makes little if any attempt to abide by international humanitarian law.

Investigators who have interviewed field commanders reported to us that the group remains "inflexible" on key questions, including an end to the executions of captured paramilitaries and hostage-taking.[411] "The FARC says that the civilian population has to be the objective in this type of war," a humanitarian aid worker in regular contact with the group told Human Rights Watch. "The day the FARC fully accepts international humanitarian law, they believe, will be the day their war ends."[412]

In a FARC combat manual obtained independently by Human Rights Watch, there is no mention of international humanitarian law or any standing order to ensure that civilians are unharmed by FARC operations. In its single reference to captured prisoners, the manual states that "it is not necessary to execute the enemy when he is defenseless, when he is wounded." However, in the same manual, commanders are told to "execute criminals of the local security forces who have distinguished themselves for their bestial actions."[413]

A document supplied to us by the FARC's International Front cautions guerrillas to "study and apply international humanitarian law according to the conditions of our revolutionary war." In the same document, however, combatants are authorized to carry out executions, restricted only by the need to obtain "express authorization for each case from the leadership of the organization."[414]

---

[411]Human Rights Watch interview with independent investigators, Santafé de Bogotá, June 26, 1996.

[412]Human Rights Watch interview, Santafé de Bogotá, June 25, 1996.

[413]Translation by Human Rights Watch. *Manual de Operaciones de las FARC* (no date), pp. 110, 142.

[414]Translation by Human Rights Watch. The FARC told us that this document had been approved at the group's first summit of commanders, but did not provide a date. *Normas de Comportamiento con las Masas*, FARC-EP.

Perhaps the most terrifying evidence of the FARC's disdain for international humanitarian law is its willingness to massacre.[415] The FARC carried out at least twelve massacres in 1997.[416]

Investigators pinpoint 1991 as the year the FARC began to massacre perceived political rivals in the Esperanza political party formed by amnestied EPL guerrillas and their supporters. The FARC and its urban militias were believed responsible for 204 murders of Esperanza members and amnestied EPL guerrillas from 1991 to 1995.[417]

"The FARC began to kill Esperanza members, because they believed that their political control of the area was in jeopardy," says Col. (ret.) Carlos Velásquez, at the time chief of staff of the army's Seventeenth Brigade, based in Carepa.[418]

The FARC also targeted people living in areas identified as under Esperanza influence.[419] Among them was the neighborhood of La Chinita in Apartadó, Antioquia. On January 22, 1994, FARC guerrillas surrounded a school fund-raising party, killing thirty-five and wounding twelve. Among the dead were three children.[420] Some victims were bound and shot execution-style, including a

---

[415]The tactic of massacres has been in the FARC's arsenal since the 1960s. For more details, see Maria Victoria Uribe and Teófilo Vásquez, *Enterrar y Callar: las masacres en Colombia, 1980-1993*, Volume 2, (Santafé de Bogotá: Comité Permanente por la Defensa de los Derechos Humanos, 1995). Human Rights Watch interview with humanitarian aid workers, Santafé de Bogotá, June 26, 1996.

[416]These figures are based on 1996 and 1997 statistics compiled by the Data Bank.

[417]Not all of the victims were confirmed to be non-combatants, however. Although many amnestied EPL members turned in their weapons after the 1991 demobilization, others continued as combatants and formed so-called "popular commands" to attack those suspected of supporting the FARC. "Listado de personas asesinadas pertenecientes a Esperanza Paz y Libertad," Fundación Progresar, February 1996.

[418]Human Rights Watch interview, Santafé de Bogotá, May 12, 1997.

[419]Human Rights Watch interview with Mario Agudelo, Esperanza, Santafé de Bogotá, May 13, 1997.

[420]"Masacre de La Chinita," a report by the Sección para la Vida, la Justicia y la Paz del Secretariado Nacional de Pastoral Social, the Fundación Comité de Solidaridad con los Presos Políticos (CSPP), the Corporación Colectivo de Abogados "José Alvear Restrepo,"

FARC militant who apparently refused to fire on civilians.[421] Since, twenty-seven people have been convicted for their participation in the massacre.[422]

The FARC has denied its role in the La Chinita massacre.[423] However, a mountain of evidence compiled by government investigators and corroborated by research done by other reliable groups points directly at the FARC.

In 1995, the FARC enemies list expanded to include people suspected of supporting or merely sympathizing with paramilitaries, who began a bloody advance to push guerrillas out of former strongholds like Urabá. In August and September 1995, the FARC and its urban militias carried out at least five massacres, often involving individuals known to be former EPL guerrillas, Esperanza party members, or suspected paramilitary supporters. However, many victims probably had nothing to do with politics or the conflict. Among them were the massacres of six people at La Heladería "La Campesina," on August 12; Churidó, with four victims, and Mapaná, with five victims, both on August 19; Finca Los Cunas, with fifteen victims, on August 29; and Bajo el Oso, with twenty-four victims, on September 20. Often, victims were bound and beaten before being executed.[424]

Another common violation by the FARC is the killing of combatants *hors de combat,* expressly prohibited in Common Article 3 to the Geneva Conventions and Articles 4 of Protocol II. In practice, the FARC routinely executes captured security force officers, people it suspects of support for paramilitaries, and those suspected of treason or so-called revolutionary crimes within its own ranks. In

---

the Comisión Andina de Juristas-Seccional Colombiana (now Colombian Commission of Jurists), the Comité Permanente para la Defensa de los Derechos Humanos, the Fundación Progresar, CINEP, and the magazine *Colombia Hoy,* August 1994.

[421]Human Rights Watch interview with government investigator, Santafé de Bogotá, June 6, 1995.

[422]Letter to Human Rights Watch from Luis Manuel Lasso Lozano, office of the presidential human rights counselor, December 12, 1997.

[423]Human Rights Watch interview with Marco León Calarcá, Frente Internacional-FARC, Mexico City, July 13, 1996.

[424]These massacres took place in the Urabá region of Antioquia. Human Rights Watch interview with Col. (ret.) Carlos Velásquez, Santafé de Bogotá, May 12, 1997; and Human Rights Watch interview with CINEP, Santafé de Bogotá, June 26, 1996.

regions like Urabá, for instance, where such executions are common, it is vox populi that the FARC kills paramilitaries who have been captured and disarmed.[425]

To Human Rights Watch, a FARC spokesperson confirmed that these executions are carried out once they are approved by Marulanda and the General Secretariat.[426] According to the armed forces, nine soldiers were killed *hors de combat* by the FARC in 1997.[427]

The FARC also holds so-called popular trials for civilians accused of misdeeds, like rape, spouse abuse, theft, or failing to pay a "war tax." For minor crimes, the accused are warned twice. If they do not rectify their behavior, they can be summarily executed. "The FARC calls a community meeting, and the guerrillas hear everyone's testimony," one Guaviare farmer told us. "There can be drastic punishment when they decide on guilt, like an execution."[428]

Another Guaviare resident commented: "The FARC calls it popular justice, but what they do is kill people without consulting with anyone." He estimated that in the first five months of 1997, at least thirty people had been killed in "popular trials" because of alleged ties to paramilitary groups in and around his town. "It's the law of the trigger," another resident commented.[429]

Human Rights Watch found no evidence to support the assertion made by the FARC that it only kills the accused after giving them a fair trial, required by Article 6 of Protocol II. Indeed, the FARC rarely if ever informs the accused of the charges against him or her or the trial procedure the FARC intends to follow. During the trial, the accused are not allowed a proper defense. Our evidence demonstrates that the accused are presumed guilty during the trial and are often tried *in absentia.* Finally, there is no appeals process. Therefore, all killings carried

---

[425]Human Rights Watch interview with a humanitarian aid worker, Apartadó, Antioquia, July 5, 1996.

[426]Human Rights Watch interview with Marco León Calarcá, Frente Internacional-FARC, Mexico City, July 13, 1996.

[427]"Relación de personal fallecido fuera de combate pero por acción del enemigo en el año 1997," Colombian Army, May 8, 1998.

[428]Human Rights Watch interviews with farmers, San José del Guaviare, Guaviare, May 5, 1997.

[429]Human Rights Watch interview with El Retorno residents, San José del Guaviare, Guaviare, May 5, 1997.

out as a result of so-called popular trials by the FARC are serious violations of the laws of war.

Another frequent violation of the laws of war by the FARC is hostage-taking, commonly referred to in Colombia as kidnapping. In the past, the FARC promised to stop kidnapping. During the 1984 negotiations that led to the formation of the Patriotic Union Party, for instance, the FARC agreed that "once again we will condemn and withdraw authorization from kidnapping, extortion, and terrorism in all of its forms and work to end these practices."[430]

Nevertheless, kidnapping by the FARC continued and increased notably in 1997. According to País Libre, an independent research group, the FARC carried out at least 408 kidnappings that year alone.[431]

Alfonso Cano, a member of the General Secretariat, told a Colombian journalist in May 1997 that while the leadership had "prohibited" kidnapping, some FARC units continued to kidnap for "political and economic reasons," a freedom of action incongruent with the organization's otherwise strict command structure.[432] Indeed, Human Rights Watch interprets the General Secretariat's failure to enforce the ban on hostage-taking as tacit support for an egregious violation of the laws of war.

Both killings and kidnappings are used against civilians to spread terror, a violation of Article 13 (2), which prohibits "acts or threats of violence the primary purpose of which is to spread terror among the civilian population." In the months leading up to October 1997 municipal elections, FARC guerrillas killed, threatened, and kidnapped dozens of mayors, town council members, and candidates, who were told to resign or face death. Among the departments most pressured were Antioquia, Bolívar, Caquetá, Cundinamarca, Guaviare, Huila, Meta, Nariño, Putumayo, and Tolima.[433]

---

[430]Translation by Human Rights Watch. Acuerdo entre la Comisión de Paz y las FARC-EP, Mesetas, Meta, March 28, 1984.

[431]Letter to Human Rights Watch from Francisco Santos, País Libre, July 3, 1998.

[432]"El mundo de Alfonso Cano," *Semana*, May 26-June 2, 1997.

[433]"Las Farc amenazan elecciones en Cundinamarca," *El Tiempo*, August 31, 1997; "Siguen amenazas de las Farc contra elecciones," *El Tiempo*, October 17, 1997; and letter to Human Rights Watch from Volmar Pérez Ortiz, national director, Office of Complaints, Public Advocate's Office, December 12, 1997.

The FARC threat was so determined, in fact, that the group felt obliged to issue a confirmation via the Internet. "The position of the FARC-EP in relation to the upcoming elections continues irrevocably to be the same: complete sabotage," which in practice consisted primarily of killing and threatening civilians who were candidates or outgoing officials.[434]

In a March 1998 letter to the daily *El Tiempo*, General Secretariat member Alfonso Cano gave a rationale for such violations: "We order the mayors to modify their antisocial conduct... And we show the tricky ones how illegitimate they are... We are warning them that we will not permit more trickery... But this does not change the fact that some mayors who support paramilitary activity take an active role in the war. They are protagonists."[435]

But even when there are no elections, the FARC has frequently and openly advocated tactics that violate international humanitarian law. In an interview published in the FARC magazine *Resistencia Internacional*, for instance, FARC commander Marulanda recommends attacks on "any civilian factories and trucks," claiming that such attacks "destroy the source [of the government's] wealth, so that they will be unable to maintain this war over a long period."[436]

As we have noted, the laws of war demand that FARC make specific and careful decisions about potential military targets. If the destruction or neutralization of a factory makes no specific contribution to military action in the circumstances ruling at the time, the FARC is bound to refrain from attacking regardless of whether or not an attack would, over the long term, hamper the state's ability to fight.

Repeatedly, the FARC announces its intent to violate the laws of war in advance. In one circular distributed in the Urabá region and via the Internet in September 1996, the FARC warned the residents of Urabá to travel between the towns of Santa Fe de Antioquia and Turbo only on Thursdays and Fridays between

---

[434]"El Bloque Sur de las FARC-EP informa a la Opinión Pública," Montañas del Caquetá, October 17, 1997.

[435]"'Encuentros en el exterior son etapas superadas'," *El Tiempo*, March 29, 1998.

[436]"O mandan las Fuerzas Armadas o el Presidente de la República," *Resistencia Internacional*, May 1991, pp. 7.

the hours of 6 a.m. and 6 p.m. Travelers at all other hours, the circular warns, "will be considered legitimate military targets."[437]

However, the laws of war do not give the FARC or any party to the conflict the power to declare who is and who is not a military target. In a similar vein, the FARC warned journalists who wrote what guerrillas deemed to be "apology for militarism" and radio and television stations that broadcast political advertisements that they would also be considered targets. One example of "apology for militarism," a General Secretariat circular noted, was printing the statements of Armed Forces Commander Harold Bedoya.[438]

Those who violate these dictates have been captured and even killed, as the following cases demonstrate. But it is not only when its edicts are violated that the FARC attacks civilians; often, it is simply an opportunity presenting itself. For instance, in 1997, two days after four European tourists entered the Colombian nature reserve Los Katíos on foot from Panama, the FARC's Fifty-Seventh Front kidnapped them, demanding U.S. $15 million for their release.[439]

During an army operation to rescue the tourists, guerrillas apparently executed two of their captives; two others survived. Indeed, the execution of kidnap victims during rescue operations is not unusual. In the case of U.S. missionaries detailed below, evidence strongly suggests that the two were executed by the FARC before soldiers could reach them. In an interview with the daily *El Tiempo*, businessman Alejandro Vásquez Moreno said that his FARC captors had repeatedly warned him that in any clash, "the first one to fall will be you." After thirty-one days in captivity, Vásquez managed to escape without paying the U.S. $5 million ransom demanded.[440]

In the Guaviare, the young men who harvest coca leaves can also be targeted for seemingly arbitrary reasons. Bishop Belarmino Correa told Human Rights Watch that he knew of the FARC executions of two young men from an area of the department of Boyacá where paramilitaries are active. "The only crime

---

[437]Communiqué from the Bloque "José María Córdoba" of the FARC-EP, September 1996.

[438]"Farc amenazan a periodistas," *El Tiempo*, June 23, 1997; and "Amenazas contra los medios en Popayán," *El Tiempo*, October 17, 1997.

[439]"Dramático rescate de extranjeros en Chocó," *El Tiempo*, March 5, 1997; and "El mundo de Alfonso Cano," *Semana*, May 26-June 2, 1997.

[440]"Una mula lo llevó por el camino de la libertad," *El Tiempo*, November 24, 1997.

these boys committed was having identification cards from Muzo [an emerald-mining area controlled by paramilitary leader Víctor Carranza], which made guerrillas suspect that they belonged to a paramilitary group," Bishop Correa said. "People may report on army abuses, but they will rarely mention guerrilla crimes, out of fear."[441]

There are other ways that the FARC forces civilians into the conflict. For instance, one well-known guerrilla tactic is the so-called "laundering of cattle" (*lavado de ganado*). Guerrillas will herd stolen cattle to an area of small farmers, then trade them for legal animals. Farmers cannot refuse to trade, for fear of reprisals, even though they know that ranchers and the paramilitaries they fund will inevitably come to search for their property. Guerrillas then sell the "laundered" cattle to slaughterhouses.

"This involves the farmer in the conflict, often unwillingly," one humanitarian aid worker told us, referring to how paramilitaries then treat farmers who have accepted stolen cattle. "That's why we've seen the killings of so many butchers and truck drivers recently. Because they have slaughtered or transported the 'laundered' cattle, they are seen as a party to the conflict, even though they may have had no choice in the matter."[442]

Massacres

Finca Osaka: On February 14, 1996, a FARC militia stopped a bus carrying over forty workers to the banana farm known as Finca Osaka, near Carepa, Antioquia. The militia forced the bus to detour to a secluded spot and began checking identity cards. The seven FARC members singled out ten men and one woman and executed them with shots to the head at the side of the road. Some passengers managed to flee and hide in a nearby irrigation ditch, and one man survived by shielding himself with the bodies of the dead. Another managed to escape despite being wounded. Witnesses told government investigators that a FARC militia member called "Papujo" was in charge.[443] "Papujo" and four others were later

---

[441]Human Rights Watch interview, San José del Guaviare, Guaviare, May 6, 1997.

[442]Human Rights Watch interview, July 8, 1996.

[443]Human Rights Watch interview with Human Rights Unit, Attorney General's Office, Santafé de Bogotá, July 11, 1996; and CCJ, *Colombia, Derechos Humanos y Derecho Humanitario: 1996*, p. 28.

arrested and charged with taking part in the massacre.[444] In an interview, the FARC took responsibility for the killings, but claimed that the individuals were combatants and belonged to the "popular commands" run by former EPL members to kill FARC supporters.[445] Even if some among the victims were "popular command" members, the killing is a violation of the ban against killing combatants *hors de combat*. Indeed, the FARC's definition of combatants often includes civilians, and we have received numerous, credible reports that the FARC killed former EPL members who had accepted a government amnesty and ceased taking part in hostilities, thereby regaining their protected status as civilians.

Alto Mulatos/Pueblo Bello: Located in Urabá, these towns were the site of a double massacre by the Fifth and Fifty-Ninth Fronts of the FARC on May 4 and 5, 1996. According to police, the FARC began the attack in Alto Mulatos, where they executed seven people after tying them up in front of family members and neighbors. Next, guerrillas set fire to seven civilian houses.[446] Guerrillas left four of the bodies inside the burning houses, making identification almost impossible. The same group continued the same day to nearby Pueblo Bello, killing seven. Two of the bodies were also severely burned and only identified months later.[447] Among the dead were Aura Castro, sixty-five, and Humberto Ramos, seventy, a married couple. Guerrillas forced Castro and Ramos to sit on an outdoor platform used to display a statue of the Virgin Mary, where they were summarily executed. Residents told government investigators that guerrillas seeking Gustavo Díaz captured his wife, two young daughters, and daughter-in-law, locked them inside their home, and burned them alive. Investigators believe the attack may have been in retaliation for an earlier paramilitary massacre since guerrillas considered Alto

---

[444]Human Rights Watch interview with Human Rights Unit, Attorney General's Office, Santafé de Bogotá, July 11, 1996; and "Reabierto paso en la vía a Urabá," *El Tiempo*, September 24, 1996.

[445]Human Rights Watch interview with Marco León Calarcá, Frente Internacional-FARC, Mexico City, July 13, 1996.

[446]"16 campesinos masacrados: más víctimas de una guerra sucia," *El Colombiano*, May 6, 1996.

[447]Letter to Human Rights Watch from Enalba Rosa Fernández Gamboa, office of the presidential human rights counselor, May 30, 1996.

Mulatos and Pueblo Bello to be paramilitary strongholds.[448] Months later, Alto Mulatos was deserted, its residents among the ranks of the forcibly displaced.[449] In these instances, the FARC committed multiple violations of the laws of war, among them the murder of civilians, torture, the mutilation of bodies, collective punishment, acts of perfidy, and indiscriminate attack against civilian homes. The act of burning people who were still alive and the bodies of the dead appears to have been a deliberate attempt to add an act of terror, also prohibited, and meant to provoke forced displacement.

Riosucio, Chocó: During intense combat between the FARC, the ACCU, and the army in this region, the FARC attacked the Riosucio police post on January 9, 1997, then retreated through the villages of Nueva Luz and Bajirá. On the Villa Ligia ranch outside Bajirá, guerrillas singled out four individuals they accused of collaborating with paramilitaries. Guerrillas bound, executed, and decapitated them. Continuing on to Nueva Luz, guerrillas killed resident Neir Manga Hernández, also accused of supporting paramilitaries.[450] It is unclear what information guerrillas used to accuse these individuals. However, based on available evidence, Human Rights Watch believes that the individuals were civilians and therefore protected by the laws of war.

San José de Apartadó: To protest political violence, the 850 residents of this Urabá town declared themselves a "peace community" and neutral to the conflict on March 23, 1997. The declaration was in part a reaction to a wave of killings by the FARC and paramilitaries working with the army. For instance, on September 8, 1996, FARC members entered the village and with list in hand seized and executed Gustavo de Jesús Loaiza, president of a local Neighborhood Action Committee (Junta de Acción Comunal, JAC); Samuel Arias, president of a local cooperative; and local leaders Juan González and María Eugenia Usaga, who was pregnant. All four had been forced to flee their homes two months earlier, and had signed an agreement with the government accepting terms for their return. Days before

---

[448]Human Rights Watch interview with government investigator, Apartadó, Antioquia, July 5, 1996.

[449]Carlos Alberto Giraldo, "Alto Mulatos: la violencia, la estampida," *El Colombiano*, December 2, 1996.

[450]CINEP and Justice and Peace, *Noche y Niebla*, No. 3, January-March, 1997, pp. 86-87; and "Nuevo éxodo de campesinos en Riosucio," *El Tiempo*, March 4, 1997.

guerrillas arrived, the four had accompanied government representatives who toured the region to report on political violence.[451] On October 6, 1997, guerrillas from the Fifty-Eighth Front approached a group of twenty San José de Apartadó residents as they were repairing roads near the hamlet of La Cristalina. Guerrillas questioned them about the community's decision not to sell the FARC food and pressed them on why the FARC had not been consulted about the "peace community." Guerrillas complained that this decision favored paramilitaries. Ramiro Correa, a leader who had supported the "peace community" proposal, responded that the Fifth Front had been consulted and had approved. The guerrillas departed. When they returned later that afternoon, guerrillas chose Ramiro Correa, Luis Fernando Espinosa, and Fernando Aguirre, claiming that they would be "reprimanded" (*llamada de atención*). Three minutes later, members of the work party heard shots from an automatic weapon. The next day, a local priest, an ICRC representative, and two community members found the three, who had been executed.[452]

El Hobo, Huila: On June 21, 1997, an estimated fifteen FARC militants attacked ten police officers who were carrying out a routine search in the El Pato bar.[453] According to witnesses interviewed by police, guerrillas began the attack by detonating a five-kilo bomb packed with screws, pieces of chain, staples, and nails at the bar's entrance.[454] Next, they opened fire on the bar from a nearby park. Killed by the bomb blast and bullets were Liliana Suárez, Mercedes Gutiérrez Arias, Martha Cecilia Arévalo, and María Lozada, all prostitutes who had been sitting outside the bar and in plain view. Photographs taken after the attack show the four women still seated in their chairs on either side of the entryway, the walls

---

[451]Instituto de Capacitación Popular, *?Hacía dónde va Colombia? Una mirada desde Antioquia: 1996*, p. 107; CINEP and Justice and Peace, *Noche y Niebla*, No. 1, July-September 1996, p. 52; and "Asesinados 4 dirigentes comunales en Apartadó," *El Mundo*, September 8, 1996.

[452]Urgent Action from Justice and Peace, October 9, 1997; and "En Urabá asesinan a miembros de Comisión de Neutralidad," *El Tiempo*, October 8, 1997.

[453]Letter to Public Advocate's Office from Jesús Antonio Silva Urriago, regional Public Advocate's Office, Neiva, Huila, November 25, 1997.

[454]Report from police explosives expert Javier Briñez Vera to SIJIN, June 22, 1997.

behind them pockmarked from the explosion and gunfire.[455] Bartender Rigoberto Montealegre Andrade, inside at the time, died later of gunshot wounds. In their escape, guerrillas attempted to commandeer a local bus, firing on it when the driver refused to stop. Three passengers were seriously wounded. In their second attempt to secure a vehicle, guerrillas killed farmer Jack Róbinson, who happened to be driving by at the time, and seized his vehicle.[456] Guerrillas failed to take into account the possible civilian casualties that would result from an attack on police under the circumstances ruling at the time. Their behavior after the attack was also a violation, since they fired on a civilian vehicle that did not qualify as a military target, injured civilian passengers, killed a civilian, and stole a vehicle.

Koreguaje Indians: On July 20, 1997, FARC guerrillas reportedly killed five Koreguaje Indians who lived near Milan, Caquetá. All five – Jorge Camacho, Aliner Gutiérrez, Elias and Tirso Valencia, and Aristides Gasca – had been previously threatened by the FARC. Five days later, guerrillas entered the nearby village of San Luis at 6:00 a.m., gathered up its residents, separated men from women and children, and compared the identity documents of the adults against written lists that they carried with them. After separating out seven men, guerrillas bound them, forced them down the path that leads to the cemetery, and executed them. Villagers found the bodies lying face down in a circle with the feet of the dead at its center.[457]

Murder and Torture
Missionaries: FARC militants seized New Tribes missionaries Steve Welsh and Timothy Van Dyke from a mission boarding school near Villavicencio, Meta, on January 16, 1994. Guerrillas prevented them from communicating with family members for over a year. In mid-1995, relatives managed to begin negotiations for their release. As members of the FARC's Fifty-Third Front were taking the missionaries to a release point near Medina, Cundinamarca, on June 16, they encountered a Seventh Brigade army unit. Fighting broke out. When soldiers

---

[455]The photographs were taken by Technical Investigation Unit (Cuerpo Técnico de Investigación, CTI) investigators attached to the Attorney General's Office.

[456]Report from Hugo Garzón Rueda, Chief, Hobo Station, to Huila Police Department, June 22, 1997; and "Farc mataron a 6 personas en un bar," *El Tiempo*, June 23, 1997.

[457]CINEP and Justice and Peace, *Noche y Niebla*, No. 5, July-September 1997, pp. 86, 88.

reached the spot where guerrillas had been, they found the bodies of the two missionaries. According to autopsies carried out in the United States, both men were shot several times at point-blank range.[458] Evidence, including eyewitness testimonies collected by the Attorney General's Office, point to the FARC as their executioners. Thirteen FARC members, among them Henry Castellanos Garzón, alias "Romaña," leader of the Fifty-Third Front, have outstanding arrest warrants for the killings.[459] Guerrillas committed multiple violations in this case by taking hostages, then executing them.

Luis Hernán Zambrano Enríquez, Pedro Mauricio Valencia Alzate, and Salvador Becerra: These soldiers — Second Sergeant Zambrano, Second Private Valencia, and enlisted man Becerra – were captured by the FARC near Labranzagrande, Boyacá, on March 11, 1996, according to the army. Another soldier who guerrillas later released and who did not report torture told reporters that guerrillas had cut off the three men's fingers, beat them, burned them, then shot them in the back. Guerrillas released him, the soldier said, "so that you could tell how [the FARC] bring[s] intelligence dogs to justice." Army photographs taken of the bodies of Zambrano and Valencia show several fingers missing and burns on their faces, arms, and legs. One of the bodies was missing large pieces of skin on the upper arms.[460]

Chalán, Sucre: The FARC opened an attack on the Chalán, Sucre police station by detonating a bomb strapped to a donkey's back on March 12, 1996. According to press reports, four officers — Jhonny Buelvas, Deider José Díaz Paternina, José Ramírez Montes, and Dario Giraldo García – were executed after surrendering. Guerrillas apparently doused the remains of some of the officers with gasoline and

---

[458]Human Rights Watch telephone interview with U.S. Embassy, January 28, 1997; and "Farc asesinó a dos misioneros de E.U.," *El Espectador*, June 21, 1995.

[459]As of this writing, none were in custody. Human Rights Watch interview with Human Rights Unit, Attorney General's Office, Santafé de Bogotá, December 4, 1997.

[460]"Atroz muerte de tres soldados," *El Espectador*, April 27, 1996; and Fuerzas Militares de Colombia, Inspección General, Oficina de Derechos Humanos, "Infracciones al derecho internacional humanitario cometidas por los grupos subversivos," 1997, p. 23.

set them afire inside the station, leaving cadavers unrecognizable.[461] The use of a "donkey bomb" also qualifies as perfidy, since it is disguised in such a way as to imitate a form of transportation commonly used by area peasants and invites the confidence of the security forces by pretending to be a civilian object protected by the laws of war.

Caquetá officials: In 1996 and 1997, at least six elected officials and government workers in the department of Caquetá were assassinated by the FARC. On June 20, 1996, governor Jesús Angel González Arias and his driver, Orlando García, were on their way to a meeting with members of the FARC's Fifteenth Front to negotiate the release of congressman Rodrigo Turbay Cote when guerrillas killed them near Paujil. Previously, González had criticized government measures that curtailed basic rights as well as guerrilla threats against Caquetá residents.[462] Three days before his death, González had conditioned any possible political talks with the FARC on Turbay's release.[463] The same day that González was killed, guerrillas shot Solano mayor Demetrio Quintero Rentería in front of the local Caja Agraria. His replacement, Edilberto Hidalgo Anturi, was himself killed by the FARC on October 6 in San Antonio de Getuchá. A third mayor, Edilberto Murillo Ortega, and three associates — Bernardo Uribe, director of a government agrarian service, Miguel Uribe Tobón and Nelson Trujillo Herrera, were also killed by the FARC in San Antonio de Getuchá on February 17, 1997, apparently because of Murillo's support for CONVIVIR.[464] Although Human Rights Watch has documented cases where some CONVIVIRs have crossed the line dividing civilians from combatants, the fact that a civilian may have spoken out in support of CONVIVIRs or supported

---

[461]"Farc asesinan a 11 policías en Chalán," *El Tiempo*, March 14, 1996; and "Asalto Guerrillero a la población de Chalán, Sucre," División Derechos Humanos, Inspección General, Policía Nacional, 1996. The FARC accepted responsibility for the attack in an April 1996 press release. The guerrillas claim that they killed eleven police officers, but give no further details. Press release, Febrero-Abril 1996.

[462]Human Rights Watch interview with CINEP, Santafé de Bogotá, May 4, 1997; and "Delito de opinión," *Semana*, June 25, 1996.

[463]"Gobernador reclama libertad de Turbay," *El Tiempo*, June 18, 1995.

[464]Human Rights Watch interview with Caquetá residents, Santafé de Bogotá, May 8, 1997; Letter to Defensoría from Edgar Ernesto Urueña, Defensoría Seccional, Florencia, Caquetá, December 3, 1997; and "'Convivir, objectivo militar,'" *El Tiempo*, February 28, 1997.

their formation does not rob that civilian of their protected status. We have no evidence suggesting that these mayors took an active role in hostilities. Therefore, their assassinations are serious violations of the laws of war.

Abelardo Tejada Durán: This peasant leader represented coca farmers in the department of Caquetá and helped negotiate an end to widespread protests against the government's forced eradication efforts in 1996. Reportedly, on January 4, 1997, he was in his home near San Vicente del Caguán when FARC guerrillas arrived and asked for water. Once they finished, they seized and executed Tejada. Apparently, they accused Tejada of supporting the government in talks to resolve peasant protests. FARC attacks against local leaders were increasingly common in 1997 as rumors spread of a paramilitary advance in the department.[465] Support for a political point of view that guerrillas opposed would not, if true, turn Tejada from a civilian into a combatant so long as he took no active role in hostilities.

Frank Pescatore: An American geologist working in the department of La Guajira, Pescatore was kidnapped and held for ransom by the FARC's Fifty-Ninth Front on December 10, 1996. After the FARC notified authorities, Pescatore's body was found shot to death on February 23, 1997. He had been killed with a shot through his left arm that reached into his chest. Left for five to six days in a remote area, his body had been eviscerated, packed with lime and clothing, and crudely sewn up and bound with rope, apparently to prevent animal depredation.[466] The case is currently being investigated by the regional prosecutor in Barranquilla.[467] Although guerrillas may have meant to preserve his body by eviscerating him, in other cases we are aware of, guerrillas have been able to deliver bodies without going to such extremes. We consider the mutilation a failure to decently dispose of the dead and refrain from despoiling them, as required by Article 8 of Protocol II.

---

[465]Human Rights Watch interview with Caquetá residents, Santafé de Bogotá, May 8, 1997; and "Matan a vocero de campesinos cocaleros," *El Tiempo*, January 10, 1997.

[466]Human Rights Watch telephone interview with a U.S. Embassy source, January 28, 1997; and "Recuperan cadáver de ingeniero estadounidense secuestrado," *El Tiempo*, February 27, 1997.

[467]Letter to Public Advocate's Office from Wilder Rafael Guerra Millan, regional Public Advocate's Office, Riohacha, La Guajira, December 1, 1997.

Pedro León Agudelo: On April 14, 1997, Pedro Agudelo, seventeen, was killed when he opened an envelope containing a book bomb addressed to his father, Mario, a leader of the Esperanza political party. The package had been delivered to the father's Medellín office, then forwarded to his home. There, Agudelo gave the book, titled *Ethics for Medicine*, to his son, an aspiring medical student. Pedro was killed instantly. Mario Agudelo believes the bomb was sent by the FARC and forms part of a pattern of attacks on Esperanza members.[468] A year earlier, he told Human Rights Watch, the FARC attempted to kill him with a grenade. His leg remains deeply scarred by the attempt.[469] Days after Pedro's death another book bomb was sent to Esperanza member Teodoro Díaz, currently the mayor of Apartadó, Antioquia, but was discovered before it was detonated.[470]

Liliana Londoño Díaz: This young woman was seized at a FARC roadblock on May 4, 1997, apparently because she was the girlfriend of an army lieutenant based in the area. Several days later, her body was found near Caracolí, in Urabá.[471] As a non-combatant, Londoño was protected by the laws of war regardless of any relationship she might have had with a combatant.

Félix Antonio Vélez White: This agronomist and cattle rancher was traveling near Cañas Gordas, Antioquia, when FARC guerrillas reportedly stopped his vehicle on August 6, 1997, and killed him. The FARC had repeatedly threatened the Vélez family in the past. Vélez's mother, Graciela White de Vélez, had been kidnapped and killed by the FARC in 1991, and Vélez himself had been kidnapped on two

---

[468]The case is being investigated by the Medellín regional prosecutor. Letter to Human Rights Watch from Luis Manuel Lasso Lozano, office of the presidential human rights counselor, December 12, 1997.

[469]In the bar where Agudelo was sitting when the grenade exploded, María Bernarda Lora was killed and six others injured. Human Rights Watch interview with Mario Agudelo, Santafé de Bogotá, May 13, 1997.

[470]Before his inauguration as mayor in January 1998, Díaz received new death threats from the FARC. "Frustran atentado con otro libro bomba," *El Tiempo*, April 16, 1997; and "Farc impediría posesión de alcalde de Apartadó," *El Colombiano*, December 31, 1997.

[471]Letter to Human Rights Watch from San José de Apartadó leaders, June 1, 1997; Human Rights Watch interview with María Girlesa Villegas, regional Public Advocate's Office, Medellín, Antioquia, December 9, 1997; and CINEP and Justice and Peace, *Noche y Niebla*, No. 4, April-June 1997, p. 105.

previous occasions. The guerrillas had also threatened to kidnap his sons.[472] An investigation by forensic specialists showed that Vélez had been severely beaten and burned, with some fingernails torn out, before being assassinated with three shots to the head.[473]

John Jairo Cardona Patiño: This police officer was assassinated by members of the FARC's Thirty-Sixth Front after being taken from a public bus on August 10, 1997 near Sabanalarga, Antioquia. According to police, Cardona, on his way to a training workshop, was carrying his uniform and a police-issue revolver in his luggage. After the FARC stopped the bus and forced the passengers off, they found the uniform and gun and identified Cardona as a police officer.[474] According to press reports, Cardona was bound before being led away.[475] Guerrillas allowed the remaining passengers to continue their journey. Police say that Cardona was forced to kneel at the roadside and was executed with shots through the mouth.[476]

Emberá Katío leaders: With their lands in one of the most dangerous areas of Colombia—in the Urabá foothills joining Antioquia's banana region with the western spur of the Andes—this indigenous group has lost members to both paramilitaries and guerrillas. Since 1986, when the FARC first executed six Emberá Katío leaders, the Antioquia Indigenous Organization (Organización Indígena de Antioquia, OIA) has attempted to negotiate a neutrality agreement with guerrillas, which was finally formalized in 1989. However, on January 20, 1997, the FARC violated the agreement by assassinating Joaquín Domicó in Cañero. The following September 17, Ivan Dario and Jairo Domicó were killed near Surambaicito. Less than a month later, on October 13, the OIA reported that FARC guerrillas abducted Mario Domicó and his son, David, from a meeting they were attending in the village of El Porroso. Mario was a founder of OIA and a medical

---

[472]Letter to Human Rights Watch from Pedro Juan Moreno, a personal friend of Vélez, vice-governor of Antioquia, September 17, 1997; and "Guerrilla mata a un hacendado," *El Tiempo*, August 8, 1997.

[473]Letter to Human Rights Watch from Antioquia Gov. Álvaro Uribe, August 8, 1997.

[474]Case summary, Human Rights Office, National Police, 1998.

[475]"Condenan asesinato de Policía," *El Colombiano*, August 12, 1997.

[476]Case summary, Human Rights Office, National Police, 1998.

worker. David was a bilingual teacher at El Porroso until being forced to resign after receiving threats. Witnesses told the OIA that the men were led away in different directions, then shots were fired. The bodies were discovered the next day.[477] Subsequently, an estimated 400 Katíos fled to nearby Mutatá as internally displaced.[478] Human Rights Watch believes these individuals were civilians and therefore protected by the laws of war.

Anzá, Antioquia: On November 14, 1997, guerrillas from the FARC's Thirty-Fourth Front killed Anzá mayor César Velásquez Montoya as he ate breakfast in his home. Hours later in nearby Guintar, guerrillas assassinated town councilman Juan Francisco Montoya Torres and a local resident, Antonio Abad Caro Ospina.[479] Subsequently, residents told Human Rights Watch that guerrillas held a meeting in Guintar to claim responsibility for the killings and accuse their victims of supporting the ACCU. When Human Rights Watch visited Anzá and Guintar in December 1997, residents still lived in fear of an attack by either the FARC or the ACCU.[480] Support for a party to the conflict would not by itself, if true, make these individuals into military targets.

Taking of hostages

Missionaries: New Tribes missionaries David Mankins, Richard Tenenoff, and Mark Rich were seized by FARC militants on January 31, 1993, from the Kuna Indian village in Panama where they worked. After maintaining intermittent radio contact throughout 1993, during which guerrillas demanded a ransom of U.S. $5 million, the FARC suspended contact.[481] According to New Tribes, in February

---

[477]Letter to Human Rights Watch from the OIA, October 16, 1997; and "Asesinados dos líderes indígenas," El Colombiano, October 15, 1997.

[478]U.S. Committee for Refugees, Colombia's Silent Crisis: One million displaced by violence (Washington, D.C.: U.S. Committee for Refugees, 1998), p. 32.

[479]"Farc asesinaron al alcalde de Anzá," El Tiempo, November 16, 1997; and CINEP and Justice and Peace, Noche y Niebla, No. 6, October-December 1997, p. 110.

[480]Human Rights Watch visit to Anzá and Guintar, Antioquia, December 10, 1997; and "Guerrilla se atribuyó asesinato de alcalde," El Colombiano, November 19, 1997.

[481]Letter to Human Rights Watch from wives Lorraine Van Dyke, Sandy Welsh, Patti Tenenoff, Nancy Mankins, and Tania M. Rich, May 10, 1995; and Case summary, New Tribes Mission, June 1997.

1997, the FARC contacted a Costa Rican diplomat who later informed them that Mankins, Tenenoff, and Rich were alive, in good condition, and in FARC custody.[482] The FARC has publicly denied taking the men.[483]

Rodrigo Turbay Cote: This congressman was kidnapped by the FARC's Bloque Sur on June 16, 1995, as he campaigned in the department of Caquetá. Son of a local family that had long been politically powerful in the region, Turbay had been elected to Congress for the Liberal Party in 1994.[484] After he was elected president of the House of Representatives, the FARC accused Turbay of having profited personally from a road built in Caquetá and claimed to have kidnapped him in order to investigate and collect a ransom.[485] On May 4, 1997, the FARC released a statement saying that Turbay had drowned while being transported on the Caguán River in Caquetá. Residents found the body floating in the river. An autopsy carried out by government forensic experts confirmed that Turbay had drowned, possibly after falling and hitting his head.[486] Subsequently, the Bloque Sur released a statement acknowledging the kidnapping, which they termed a "prolonged retention," and accused the family of being responsible for its length, "since they refused to pay the fine... we imposed."[487]

---

[482]Testimony before the House International Relations Committee by Dan Germann, Executive Committee, New Tribes Mission, and Tania Rich, Washington, D.C., March 31, 1998.

[483]Guerrillas claim the men were taken by common criminals and members of the security forces intending to damage the FARC's reputation. Comisión Internacional de las FARC-EP México, D.F. December 1997; and Farc-EP Press Release, May 12, 1998 .

[484]"Perfil de Rodrigo Turbay Cote," Cámara de Representantes, 1996.

[485]Human Rights Watch interview with Marco León Calarcá, Frente Internacional-FARC, Mexico City, July 13, 1996.

[486]"Turbay Cote murió ahogado," El Tiempo, June 19, 1997.

[487] "A la opinión pública," Bloque Sur-FARC release, July 18, 1997. The Turbay family accused local politicians of paying the FARC to prolong the congressman's captivity, and three men and one woman were later arrested by the authorities in connection to this claim. "Turbay," Semana, July 7-14, 1997; and "Detenida diputada en el caso Rodrigo Turbay," El Tiempo, September 11, 1997.

Alina Gautier de Ochoa: This retired professor of chemistry was kidnapped by the Thirty-Sixth Front of the FARC on August 3, 1996, from a family farm near San Pedro de Milagros, Antioquia.[488] Apparently, guerrillas worked with known criminals from the area, who carried out the kidnapping and delivered their hostage to the FARC six days later in exchange for a fee. The guerrilla in charge, called "Gustavo" or "El Viejo," demanded a ransom of U.S. $1 million from the family. During her three-month captivity, Gautier broke her hand, but did not receive medical care for it.[489] After her release, Gautier reported that she had spent one night with other kidnap victims, awaiting news of their families and the payment of ransoms.[490] In addition to violating the ban on hostage-taking, the FARC also violated the provision in Article 5 (2) (e), which requires that forces responsible for restricting the liberty of persons provide for their physical and medical well-being.

José Ignacio González: This seventy-three-year-old doctor was kidnapped by members of the FARC's Thirty-Fourth Front on August 14, 1997 from the clinic where he was providing free medical service to patients near Concordia, Antioquia.[491] Moments later, he suffered a fatal heart attack and guerrillas abandoned his body outside town, where it was recovered later that day. At the time, González was also president of the Concordia town council.[492]

October 26 elections: In the months preceding Colombia's 1997 elections, the FARC kidnapped dozens of mayors, town council members, municipal workers, and candidates from the departments of Antioquia, Bolívar, Caquetá, Cundinamarca, Guaviare, Huila, Meta, Nariño, Putumayo, and Tolima, openly

[488]Letter to Human Rights Watch from Ochoa family, September 5, 1996.

[489]Letter to Human Rights Watch from Raúl Reyes, Comisión Internacional-FARC, September 22, 1996.

[490]Human Rights Watch telephone interview with Alina Gautier de Ochoa, January 5, 1997.

[491]"Concejal murió de infarto en manos de las Farc," El Tiempo, August 16, 1997.

[492]Letter to Human Rights Watch from Antioquia Gov. Álvaro Uribe, September 5, 1997.

violating the ban on hostage-taking.[493] In the Guaviare, for example, candidates were told that they would be considered "military objectives" and killed if they continued to campaign after being released.[494] In Caquetá, guerrillas reportedly told one candidate, "We will disappear anyone who puts on a t-shirt that refers to a political candidacy."[495] Upon his release after three days in captivity, Buriticá Mayor José Luis Vélez Hincapié passed to the press a FARC communique declaring all candidates legitimate military targets.[496] Vélez's driver was killed when the mayor was seized.[497] The FARC assassinated other candidates at roadblocks, including Ricardo Jiménez Zuluaga, running for mayor of San Carlos, Antioquia, killed on August 15, 1997.[498] Candidates who defied threats and were elected received new threats from the FARC into 1998. The mayor of Puerto Rico, Caquetá, who had been taken hostage by the FARC, received a new threat in 1998, when the Bloque Sur sent a message to mayors in the departments of Huila, Caquetá, and Putumayo saying that whoever failed to follow their directives would be considered a military target and would suffer serious consequences.[499] It is important to underscore that no force engaged in a conflict can arbitrarily declare a civilian or civilian object a military target. As we have noted, a military target makes, by its nature, location, purpose, or use, an effective contribution to military action. Its total or partial destruction, capture, or neutralization in the circumstances ruling at the time must offer a definite military advantage. Support for a political

---

[493]"Secuestran a candidato a alcaldía en Bolívar," *El Tiempo*, June 4, 1997; "Secuestrado alcalde de Yalí, Antioquia," *El Tiempo*, June 16, 1997;

[494]Human Rights Watch interviews with mayors, San José del Guaviare, Guaviare, May 5-7, 1997; Letter to Human Rights Watch from Volmar Pérez Ortiz, national director, Office of Complaints, Public Advocate's Office, December 12, 1997; "Las Farc amenazan elecciones en Cundinamarca," *El Tiempo*, August 31, 1997; and "Siguen amenazas de las Farc contra elecciones," *El Tiempo*, October 17, 1997.

[495]"Denuncian amenazas de las FARC a candidatos en Caquetá," *El Tiempo*, March 6, 1997.

[496]"Farc reiteran que impedirán las elecciones," *El Tiempo*, June 9, 1997.

[497]"Secuestran a Alcalde de Buriticá y a seis personas más," *El Tiempo*, June 3, 1997.

[498]"Asesinan candidato a Alcaldía de San Carlos," *El Colombiano*, August 16, 1997.

[499]"FARC persigue a desplazados," *El Espectador*, January 6, 1998.

point of view that guerrillas oppose would not make any of these individuals into combatants and therefore military targets so long as they took no active role in hostilities.

Attacks on medical workers, installations, and ambulances

ICRC vehicle: During a routine stop at a roadblock set up by the FARC's Tenth Front between Fortul and Saravena, Arauca, on June 2, 1996, guerrillas shot at a vehicle marked with the red cross belonging to the ICRC. According to reports, guerrillas aimed at the tires and fuel tank while the vehicle was stopped and with an ICRC delegate present. Subsequently, the guerrilla in charge forced the ICRC delegate to sign a document addressed to the Tenth Front commander promising not to report on the incident.[500] This is a serious violation of the protection guaranteed vehicles marked with the red cross, the internationally recognized symbol of protection granted to medical and religious personnel, medical units, and medical transports, as laid out in Article 12 of Protocol II.

Ambulances: Protocol II prohibits not only attacks on vehicles properly identified with the red cross, but also their "inappropriate use." Nevertheless, the FARC has repeatedly violated these protections by attacking marked vehicles or using them to transport troops and weapons. On April 4, 1997, for instance, during an attack on the town of Chámeza, Casanare, guerrillas from the FARC's Thirty-Eighth and Fifty-Sixth Fronts reportedly used an ambulance to transport armed fighters.[501] On August 13, after combat between the FARC and units from the Seventeenth Brigade, the army reported that guerrillas stopped a vehicle carrying a wounded soldier, forced him out, and killed him.[502] The following October 25, the FARC attacked an ambulance marked with a red cross near Puerto Rico, Caquetá, injuring physician Edinson Morales, who was attending a patient giving birth prematurely.[503]

---

[500]"Farc dispararon contra carro de la Cruz Roja," *El Tiempo*, June 3, 1996; and CCJ, *Colombia, Derechos Humanos y Derecho Humanitario: 1996* pp. 79-80.

[501]CINEP and Justice and Peace, *Noche y Niebla*, No. 4, April-June 1997, p. 136.

[502]Letter to Almudena Masarraza, Office of the High Commissioner for Human Rights, from Gen. Rito Alejo del Río Rojas, commander, Seventeenth Brigade, August 21, 1997.

[503]CINEP and Justice and Peace, *Noche y Niebla*, No. 6, October-December 1997, p. 100.

Other acts that violate the laws of war

Arcua, Antioquia: Human Rights Watch has received numerous reports from reliable sources indicating that the Fifth Front of the FARC used unmarked land mines in civilian areas near this Urabá town throughout 1996. During that time, the area was highly contested by paramilitaries and guerrillas and many families fled. One explosives expert commented that the use of land mines in the area was notable since, as a rule, the FARC makes less use of them than other insurgent groups.[504] The FARC confirmed to Human Rights Watch that it uses land mines.[505]

Fourth Brigade: On May 27, 1996, members of FARC militias operating in Medellín attacked the headquarters of the army's Fourth Brigade, located in a residential district. Launched from the summit of a hill known as El Volador, the attack caused little damage to the military installation, but did kill Francisco Sergio Castrillón Zapata, a watchman working nearby, and wounded three civilians, including a child.[506] The attack also damaged two homes.[507]   While the Fourth Brigade is a military target, this attack clearly violated the rule of proportionality by doing more damage to civilians than any direct or strategically important damage to the army. Potential damage to protected structures was foreseeable, and the guerrilla commander in charge should have taken specific measures to prevent or minimize damage to them, ignored in this case.

Montería, Córdoba: At least five times, the FARC has placed bombs near or in front of an office associated with the ACCU in downtown Montería. Guerrillas detonated the first bomb, hidden in a street vendor's cart, on October 21, 1996, near the offices of FUNPAZCOR. Four passersby were reported killed. The bombing followed repeated threats. FUNPAZCOR was founded in 1991 by the family of Carlos Castaño, the leader of the ACCU. Its funds were meant to assist in the demobilization of EPL guerrillas and have gone toward credits for land,

---

[504]Human Rights Watch interviews in Apartadó, Antioquia, July 5 and 6, 1996.

[505]Human Rights Watch interview with Marco León Calarcá, Frente Internacional-FARC, Mexico City, July 13, 1996.

[506]Certificate from Carlos Alberto Vélez Betancur, prosecutor 148, May 28, 1996.

[507]Human Rights Watch interview with Gen. Alfonso Manosalva Flórez, commander, Fourth Brigade, Medellín, Antioquia, July 2, 1996; and "Fuera de peligro, heridos por atentado con morteros," *El Colombiano*, May 28, 1996.

housing, school-building, and community businesses.[508] The FARC reportedly detonated more bombs in central Montería on December 17, 1996, and March 10, July 12, and July 23, 1997. The March bomb wounded seventeen, including a six-year-old girl.[509] The fact that FUNPAZCOR was begun by the Castaño family does not turn it automatically into a military target. These attacks are serious violations of the ban on attacking civilians and civilian objects. In addition, since FUNPAZCOR is located in a busy urban area, any attack risks civilian casualties and therefore should be canceled. This attack also demonstrates the FARC's disregard for the rule of proportionality, which requires that those who plan or decide upon attack must take into account the effects of the attack on the civilian population in their pre-attack estimate." Just as the rules regarding objects that can have dual civilian-military functions demand that there be a direct military advantage evident in such deliberations, so too does the rule of proportionality require that the advantage be specific, not general, and perceptible to the senses. A remote advantage to be gained at some unknown time in the future is not be a proper consideration to weigh against civilian losses.

Atrato River blockade: Beginning in mid-December 1996 and lasting through the following January, the FARC blocked commercial traffic on the Atrato River, which divides the departments of Chocó and Antioquia. According to reports, guerrillas told boat captains who transport goods and passengers that the FARC would destroy their boats if they left port. Much of the area's food and medicine are transported by river.[510] These threats of violence were meant to spread terror throughout the region in violation of Article 13 (2) of Protocol II. Human Rights Watch received credible reports that the FARC fired on boats that defied the threats.[511] Similar acts by the FARC were not unusual at the time. A FARC

---

[508]Human Rights Watch interview with Sister Teresa Gómez, FUNPAZCOR, Montería, July 8, 1996; and "Bomb injures 10 at Police HQ in Northern Colombia," Reuters, October 21, 1996.

[509]"Atentado terrorista en Montería deja 17 heridos," El Tiempo, March 11, 1997; and AUC, "Colombia Libre," August 1997, No. 2.

[510]"Continúa bloqueo del Atrato," El Tiempo, January 14, 1997.

[511]"Farc siguen con la intimidación en el Río Atrato," El Tiempo, January 21, 1997.

communiqué distributed widely in the region warned truck drivers and passengers not to travel or risk attack, another violation of Article 13 (2) of Protocol II.[512]

Caloto, Cauca: On January 12, 1997, the FARC's Sixth Front launched an attack on Caloto, Cauca. Although their main target was the police station, the FARC struck indiscriminately, seriously damaging the fire department, the office of the Colombian Red Cross, a restaurant, court offices, twenty houses, a school, and the hospital. According to government investigators, guerrillas were fully aware that they were damaging a Red Cross office and threatened to do it again. In addition, watchman Héctor Fajardo, guarding the court offices, was reportedly summarily executed by a guerrilla.[513]

Apartadó, Antioquia: The FARC has also bombed hotels where security force personnel and paramilitaries are said to lodge. On February 27, 1997, a FARC bomb in a commandeered garbage truck exploded in front of the Hotel El Pescador, killing ten people.[514] Among them was an eleven-year-old boy.[515]   Fifty-three people were reported injured, among them four police officers. In addition, eight buildings on the same block were reported damaged.[516] Weeks later, authorities captured UC-ELN member Enrique de Jesús Vergara Pacheco, and accused him of having assisted the FARC in the bombing.[517] Any attack against a hotel used to lodge combatants must be carefully planned to avoid civilian casualties, which the

---

[512]Elizabeth Yarce Ospina, "Urabá se queda sin alimentos," *El Espectador*, September 19, 1996; "Tres días cumple retén de las Farc en la vía a Urabá," *El Tiempo*, September 18, 1996.

[513]There was no indication that police used any of the civilian structures, including the Red Cross office or the hospital, during the attack. CINEP and Justice and Peace, *Noche y Niebla*, No. 3, January-March 1997, p. 128; and "Cuatro horas de terror en Caloto," *El Tiempo*, January 14, 1997.

[514]Marisol Gómez Giraldo, "La muerte llegó en carro bomba a Urabá," *El Tiempo*, February 28, 1997.

[515]Marisol Gómez Giraldo, "'Hermanita, no me deje morir'," *El Tiempo*, March 1, 1997.

[516]Marisol Gómez Giraldo, "La muerte llegó en carro bomba a Urabá," *El Tiempo*, February 28, 1997.

[517]"Cae autor de bomba en Apartadó," *El Tiempo*, March 25, 1997.

FARC clearly failed to do in this case. The attack was not carried out in a way that minimized civilian casualties as the rule of proportionality requires. The military advantage the FARC may have gained was clearly outweighed by the death toll.

Calamar mines: Repeatedly in 1997, the FARC placed Claymore mines within the city limits of Calamar, Guaviare, including on the grounds of a school, on the central plaza, and in front of the church. Guerrillas would attempt to detonate the mines when soldiers from the army's "Joaquín París" Battalion would pass by them.[518] This tactic violates the laws of war, specifically the ban on attacks that endanger the civilian population and exclusively civilian objects, like schools. In Calamar, the 500 students who regularly occupy the school were repeatedly endangered by this tactic. Indeed, fear drove twenty teachers to abandon their posts in late 1997. Although residents complained to the FARC, guerrillas continued to use the school as an ambush point when Human Rights Watch visited Guaviare Department in May 1997.[519]

Cadavers: Human Rights Watch has received credible and consistent information about the FARC's use of bodies as booby traps, which qualifies as perfidy under the laws of war. When a booby trap is hidden inside the body of a slain combatant, the party responsible also violates Article 8 of Protocol II, which requires combatants to ensure that the bodies of the dead are treated decorously. After combat between the Colombian army and the FARC near Fomeque, Cundinamarca, on February 16, 1998, soldiers collected the bodies of three soldiers killed the next day. The bodies were flown by helicopter to an army base in Santafé de Bogotá. When the bodies were unloaded, the body of Capt. Luis Hernando Camacho exploded, apparently used by the FARC as a booby trap. Two soldiers were killed and five were wounded.[520] Subsequently, the ICRC issued a

---

[518]The FARC uses the M18A1 (Claymore) mines. It is not a "smart" mine, meaning it never self-destructs. Claymore mines can be used with trip wires or can be detonated manually.

[519]Human Rights Watch interviews with Calamar residents, San José del Guaviare, Guaviare, May 6, 1997,

[520]Report from Col. Germán Galvis Corona, Chief of Staff, Mobile Brigade One, to Regional Prosecutor, February 19, 1998; and "Guerrilla utiliza cadaveres en atentado," El Espectador, February 19, 1998.

communiqué reminding the parties to the conflict that the dead are protected by Protocol II.[521] The FARC denied it had used the body as a booby trap.[522]

---

[521]ICRC press release, February 18, 1998.

[522]FARC press release, February 19, 1998; and "'Encuentros en el exterior son etapas superadas'," *El Tiempo*, March 29, 1998.

UC-ELN

> *Three families were told by the local ELN commander that they were under "investigation" for suspected paramilitary ties. They left rather than risk a guilty verdict, which would have meant an execution.*
>
> — *Middle Magdalena humanitarian aid worker*
> *June 28, 1996*

The National Liberation Army (Ejército de Liberación Nacional, ELN) began in the Middle Magdalena region in 1964, drawing from a pool of guerrillas active during La Violencia. The ELN was almost destroyed in an army offensive at Anorí, Antioquia, in 1973; in 1987, the group merged with a smaller leftist insurgency and added Camilista Union (Unión Camilista, UC) to its name. Twenty years later, analysts considered the UC-ELN to be stronger than ever, with an estimated 3,000 armed militants divided into thirty-five rural fronts, five urban fronts, and several urban militias.[523]

One of the ELN's early leaders, Nicolás Rodríguez Bautista, known as "Gabino," remains a member of the leadership, called the National Directorate (Dirección Nacional), along with Antonio García. Before his death in 1998, Spanish priest Manuel Pérez, known as "Poliarco," was long credited with articulating the group's political philosophy while Rodríguez is believed to direct the group's military actions. Below the National Directorate is the Central Command (Comando Central, COCE), which assembles the commanders of the group's military units, often identified by the names of fallen combatants, battles, or Communist leaders. The UC-ELN is concentrated in the Middle Magdalena region, southern Bolívar, Nariño, Cauca, Valle, and the Colombian departments bordering Venezuela.[524]

---

[523]In an interview with Radio Caracol on June 28, 1998, COCE member Pablo Beltrán claimed that the UC-ELN had over 5,000 armed militants. For a history of the UC-ELN from the perspective of two commanders, see Carlos Medina Gallego, *ELN: una historia contada a dos voces* (Santafé de Bogotá: Rodríguez Quito Editores, 1996). For estimates of troop strength, see "La versión alemana," *Semana*, January 21-28, 1997.

[524]Human Rights Watch interview with Colombian intelligence service, Santafé de Bogotá, December 2, 1997.

Although political and military decisions are made by the UC-ELN leadership, commanders have a great deal more latitude than their counterparts in the FARC. For instance, the Domingo Laín front is known for being among the most radical groups as well as the wealthiest. Control is highly regional, and individual commanders often differ sharply in their tactics on issues like kidnapping, public executions, and extortion.[525] Although the UC-ELN claims to carry out investigations prior to executing captives, to our knowledge these are usually closed procedures where those accused of supposed crimes can be unaware of them and unable to present any defense or appeal.[526]

Currently, the UC-ELN is represented publicly in Colombia by Gerardo Bermúdez Sánchez, known as Francisco Galán, and Carlos Arturo Velandia Jagua, known as Felipe Torres, both serving sentences in Antioquia's Itagüí prison.

The UC-ELN and International Humanitarian Law

The UC-ELN was among the first insurgent groups in Colombia to begin an internal discussion of international humanitarian law. Soon after its organization, the ELN adopted a "Guerrilla Code" (Código Guerrillero) that regulated the behavior of militants in the field. Even as Colombia refused to adopt Protocol II, the UC-ELN called for negotiations aimed at "humanizing" political conflict in Colombia.[527]

A 1995 version of the Guerrilla Code prohibits UC-ELN militants from using civilians as shields during an attack; harming civilians used as shields by an enemy force; launching indiscriminate attacks; failing to advise civilians of the location of land mines; launching attacks aimed at terrorizing civilians; forcing the displacement of civilians; arming children under the age of sixteen; carrying out actions that severely damage the environment; looting; harming vehicles or structures marked with a red cross; and executing prisoners *hors de combat.*[528]

---

[525]Human Rights Watch interviews in the Middle Magdalena region, June 27-July 1, 1996.

[526]Human Rights Watch interviews in the Middle Magdalena region, June 27-July 1, 1996.

[527]Alejandro Valencia Villa, *Humanización de la Guerra,* p. 74.

[528]Letter from Manuel Pérez, released to the press on July 15, 1995.

The COCE released more limited rules in 1996:

1. In times of war, [the ELN] will work to reduce to the maximum unnecessary human sacrifice and suffering by the enemy; this is because combatants will limit their actions to complete only the mission they have been entrusted with; and at all times, they will respect the combatant's ethical code, specifically the rules of behavior of the International Committee of the Red Cross.

2. [The ELN] will give humanitarian treatment to enemies who have surrendered or been wounded in combat and will respect their dignity and provide them with the aid necessary for their condition.

3. Within our ranks, we will not permit or tolerate abuses against the population; they are our reason for being and our relationship with them should be above reproach.

4. Our revolutionary ethic obligates us to be rigorous in avoiding military actions that can harm civilians and our people. This is the essence of our ethics and behavior.

5. It is important to underscore that during armed conflict there are unforseen circumstances and critical situations that can overcome the best intentions. But we, the ELN, are willing to discuss attitudes that, after appropriate analysis, may be punishable if they merit such action, in accordance with our rules of conduct and internal regulations.[529]

Guerrillas accused of violating UC-ELN rules, Galán and Torres told Human Rights Watch, are investigated, sometimes by the community involved. If found guilty, they can be punished with sanctions ranging from reparations to victims, a drop in rank, suspension, or death.[530]

In a response to an 1994 Amnesty International report, the UC-ELN leadership promised to adopt the group's recommendations and added that "anyone who has committed or ordered abuses, deliberate murder, hostage-taking, torture or bad treatment of prisoners will be relieved of their duty or any service that puts

---

[529]Translation by Human Rights Watch. "Nuestra Ética En La Doctrina Militar," Comando Central del ELN, Manuel Pérez Martínez, Nicolás Rodríguez Bautista, Antonio García, 1996.

[530]Human Rights Watch interview with Francisco Galán and Felipe Torres, Itagüí Prison, Antioquia, July 3, 1996.

them in contact with prisoners or others who may be subject to abuses."[531] In a 1997 interview, representatives Francisco Galán and Felipe Torres told Human Rights Watch that the UC-ELN was preparing a legal manual that would allow them to better comply with international humanitarian law.[532]

The UC-ELN has also expressed regret for some violations. After a series of indiscriminate attacks in June and July 1997 in which children were killed, the UC-ELN recognized that "some children have been killed or wounded as a result of our acts of war and we feel that it is an imperative to recognize these as serious errors of lack of foresight or crossfire in the midst of conflict... We will make an effort to avoid repeating this type of regrettable action."[533]

Currently, the UC-ELN claims that 90 percent of its armed militants have regular contact with ICRC representatives. Among Colombian guerrilla groups, the UC-ELN is the most responsive to a discussion of international humanitarian law as well as cases of alleged abuses.[534]

Nevertheless, this openness to discussion is not as yet reflected in changes in behavior in the field. Indeed, under the guise of calling for a "humanization of war," the UC-ELN continues to dispute international humanitarian law instead of conforming their rules of engagement to it. Human Rights Watch has convincing evidence that the UC-ELN flouts the laws of war in the field by targeting and killing civilians and combatants *hors de combat*, taking hostages, and launching indiscriminate attacks. We are aware of no internal investigations of reported abuses or internal investigations of militants who violate the UC-ELN's own rules.

For instance, in a public statement broadcast on July 15, 1995, Manuel Pérez claimed that the UC-ELN accepted Protocol II though it disputed "some terms and categories used in [Protocol II and Article 3 of the Geneva Conventions]." Among the terms he disputed were hostage-taking, attacks, acts of terrorism, sabotage, the definition of dangerous substances, and the distinction

---

[531]Translation by Human Rights Watch. Letter to Amnesty International from Manuel Pérez Martínez, Nicolás Rodríguez Bautista, and Antonio García, January 7, 1995.

[532]Human Rights Watch interview with Francisco Galán and Felipe Torres, Itagüí Prison, Antioquia, March 8, 1997.

[533]Translation by Human Rights Watch. "Principales apartes de la carta del ELN," *El Tiempo*, July 10, 1997.

[534]Human Rights Watch interview with Francisco Galán and Felipe Torres, Itagüí Prison, Antioquia, March 8 and December 8, 1997.

between combatants and non-combatants – in short, every precision contained within the language of both documents. In effect, this acceptance was a non-acceptance and charts the enormous gulf between what the UC-ELN says and its behavior in the field.[535]

"The ELN says the army must respect international humanitarian law, because it gives [guerrillas] a tactical advantage," a humanitarian aid work familiar with the group told Human Rights Watch. "Since they know that the army shouldn't launch rocket attacks against a village, they will send their militants to the homes of farm families to protect themselves."[536]

In an interview with Human Rights Watch, UC-ELN spokespersons Francisco Galán and Felipe Torres welcomed a discussion of international humanitarian law, but disputed attempts to apply the law to their practices. At one point, they suggested that the government intended to use international humanitarian law as a "trap" to weaken insurgencies. It is worth noting that this argument is frequently made by governments to elude responsibility for human rights crimes.

At another point in the interview, they claimed that international humanitarian law was an unattainable ideal and had to be "Colombianized" before it could be applied to them, another argument often heard from governments regarding their failure to abide by human rights treaties.

Ironically, the same argument is used by AUC leader Carlos Castaño, who has called for a "creole" version of the laws of war that would allow, among other things, the killing of combatants *hors de combat* and summary executions of suspected guerrilla collaborators.[537]

Echoing Manuel Pérez's efforts to question the definition of violations, Galán and Torres claimed that before applying international humanitarian law, it

---

[535]Translation by Human Rights Watch. "Declaración pública del comandante Manuel Pérez," July 15, 1995.

[536]Human Rights Watch interview with humanitarian aid worker, Santafé de Bogotá, June 25, 1996.

[537]Bibiana Mercado and Orlando León Restrepo, "'Las Farc inflitraron listas de los partidos tradicionales'" *El Tiempo*, September 29, 1997.

was necessary to "define" what they claimed were vague terms.[538] For instance, the UC-ELN routinely executes paramilitary combatants *hors de combat*. According to a statement by Pérez, they merit "none of the guarantees of prisoners of war."[539] Francisco Galán and Felipe Torres emphasized this exception to Human Rights Watch, adding that the UC-ELN also executes captured spies, including UC-ELN deserters and non-combatants who provide information to the security forces. Non-combatants, Galán and Torres noted, are permitted by the UC-ELN to tell their enemies that guerrillas have passed recently, but not how many, in what direction, or when. Such a blunder, they said, may be punished by forced expulsion or death.[540]

Indeed, the UC-ELN routinely executes soldiers and police officers taken *hors de combat*, often in front of dozens of witnesses. In 1997 alone, the UC-ELN killed at least seventy-one civilians and combatants *hors de combat* according to the Data Bank.[541]

These indefensible killings make a mockery of justice and demonstrate that the UC-ELN has made no attempt to provide a fair trial. Indeed, the UC-ELN rarely if ever informs the accused of the charges against him or her or the trial procedure the UC-ELN intends to follow. During the "trial", the accused is not allowed a proper defense. Our evidence demonstrates that the accused is presumed guilty during the "trial" and is often tried *in absentia*. Finally, there is no appeals

---

[538]ACCU leader Carlos Castaño makes the same argument, asserting that he is willing to accept a "creole" version of international standards — that would allow, for instance, the execution of prisoners taken *hors de combat* — if guerrillas accept the same standards. Human Rights Watch interview with Carlos Castaño, July 9, 1996; Human Rights Watch interview with Francisco Galán and Felipe Torres, Itagüí Prison, Antioquia, July 3, 1996; and Bibiana Mercado and Orlando León Restrepo, "'Las Farc inflitraron listas de los partidos tradicionales'," *El Tiempo*, September 29, 1997.

[539]Translation by Human Rights Watch. "Declaración pública del comandante Manuel Pérez," July 15, 1995.

[540]Galán and Torres noted that the treatment of captured combatants varies from front to front, demonstrating that the group's "Guerrilla Code" may be best termed a suggestion, not standing orders. Human Rights Watch interview with Francisco Galán and Felipe Torres, Itagüí Prison, Antioquia, July 3, 1996.

[541]Human Rights Watch interviews in Magdalena Medio, June 27-30, 1996; and Data Bank, *Balance: 1997*, p. 4.

process. Therefore, all killings carried out as a result of so-called trials by the UC-ELN are serious violations of the laws of war.

In one case, María Elena Molina, the mayor of Tame, Arauca, was seized by the UC-ELN for a so-called political trial on November 23, 1996. During a sixteen-day interrogation by the UC-ELN's Simacota Company during which she was bound and blindfolded, Molina said that she had been questioned about municipal affairs without benefit of any defense counsel, any indication of the charges against her, or any explanations of trial procedures.

"When they began, they made it clear that I would emerge from this political trial either alive or dead," she told reporters after her release. "To be bound and blindfolded in the power of the Simacota Company is the worst test I can imagine.[542]

Others don't get the benefit of even summary proceedings. On April 28, 1997, Julio Acosta Bernal, vice-president of Colombia's House of Representatives, narrowly escaped death when the UC-ELN detonated a car bomb as he passed on his way to the Arauca airport. His bodyguard, DAS agent Carlos León, was killed. The UC-ELN's Simacota Company later took responsibility for the attack in a telephone call to a local radio station.[543]

The UC-ELN also disputes the ban on hostage-taking, claiming that in addition to capturing enemy combatants, its forces engage only in so-called "retention" (*retenciones*) when civilians refuse to pay what the UC-ELN terms "war" or "peace taxes" (*impuestos de guerra o paz*). Unlike kidnapping, which results in personal gain for the criminals that carry them out, UC-ELN spokesperson Torres argues that the ransoms for so-called "retention" benefit society by funding the UC-ELN's war effort. Since the UC-ELN does not use captives as shields, he argues, the UC-ELN rejects the term hostage.[544]

---

[542]Translation by Human Rights Watch. Human Rights Watch interview with government investigator, Arauca, February 2, 1997; and "ELN pone a temblar a la burocracia," *El Corredor*, December 21-January 3, 1997.

[543]Acosta had repeatedly been accused by the UC-ELN of supporting an increased army presence in Arauca. Human Rights Watch interviews with government investigators, Arauca, February 2-3, 1997; and "Herido vicepresidente de la Cámara en Arauca," *El Tiempo*, April 29, 1997.

[544]Human Rights Watch interview with Francisco Galán and Felipe Torres, Itagüí Prison, Medellín, Antioquia, December 8, 1997; and "¿Qué es humanizar el conflicto?" Documento II Derechos Humanos, UC-ELN, May 1995, p. 34.

Human Rights Watch rejects this argument, which ignores the clear language banning hostage-taking in the laws of war and seeks to justify an abhorrent tactic. The laws of war do not exist in order to justify or protect certain tactics, but rather to defend and protect the civilian population. According to País Libre, the UC-ELN carried out at least 412 kidnappings in 1997.[545]

Some hostage-takings end in lurid headlines. In 1996, Colombian authorities captured German national Werner Mauss, who with his wife and the support of the German government had negotiated the release for a reported US $1.5 million of Brigitte Schöene, the German wife of a former BASF Chemicals president based in Colombia.[546] The UC-ELN denied that it had kidnapped Schöene, claiming its involvement was as an "intermediary to secure her release at the request of the German government."[547] However, interviewed after her release, Schöene was unequivocal in her identification of the UC-ELN as her captors.[548]

There are other glaring inconsistencies in UC-ELN rhetoric and practice. While the Guerrilla Code bans attacks on civilians, the UC-ELN consistently tries to deny civilians protection if they fail to support the UC-ELN, ignoring their protected status under the laws of war. For instance, in an interview with Human Rights Watch, Galán and Torres defended the civilians who provide the UC-ELN with information, food, and shelter, and claimed that the laws of war protect them. However, when asked if civilians who provide similar services to the UC-ELN's adversaries were also protected, Galán and Torres did not hesitate to call them "legitimate military targets." Even former soldiers and their family members who take no part in hostilities — clearly protected under the laws of war — remain

---

[545]Letter to Human Rights Watch from Francisco Santos, País Libre, July 3, 1998.

[546]This international scandal led to the arrest of the German couple in Medellín in 1996 and their release a year later. As this report was going to press, the Mausses were helping the German government facilitate peace talks between the UC-ELN and the Colombian government. Katy Barnett, "Playing cat and 'Mauss,'" *Latinamerica Press*, January 16, 1997; Edgar Torres, "Mauss empezó a romper 52 días de silencio," *El Tiempo*, January 8, 1997; and Radio Caracol interview with Pablo Beltrán, COCE member, June 30, 1998.

[547]"Colombia rebels say Bonn asked for kidnap case," Reuters, December 14, 1996.

[548]José Fernando Hoyos, "Cómo se apoderó Werner Mauss de un secuestro," *El Tiempo*, September 7, 1997; and "'Si alguien pagó por el rescate, fue Mauss'," *El Tiempo*, September 8, 1997.

Recuerde también de que el SAPO está en contra de nuestros intereses y nos toca ajusticiarlo donde esté.

This graphic accompanied a UC-ELN death threat against civilians suspected of providing information to the security forces or paramilitaries.

"military targets" to the UC-ELN, according to Galán and Torres.[549]

In a pamphlet distributed in 1996 by the UC-ELN's Ramón Emilio Arcila Front, which operates in eastern Antioquia, civilians are encouraged to provide information to guerrillas. However, they are also warned that anyone who provides information to the security forces or paramilitaries "will be executed on the spot."

This is a policy of violating Protocol II, not upholding it. The words are accompanied by a crude drawing of a mouse-human hanging from a gibbet in a cemetery.[550]

"Giving information to the enemy makes you a legitimate military target," Felipe Torres emphasized in an interview with Human Rights Watch.[551]

"Three families were told by the local ELN commander that they were under 'investigation' for suspected paramilitary ties," one humanitarian aid worker

---

[549]Human Rights Watch interview with Francisco Galán and Felipe Torres, Itagüí Prison, Antioquia, July 3, 1996.

[550]Translation by Human Rights Watch. "Contra el falso gobierno y la delincuencia unámonos todos," Ramón Emilio Arcila Front, no date.

[551]Human Rights Watch interview with Francisco Galán and Felipe Torres, Itagüí Prison, Antioquia, November 11, 1995.

from the Middle Magdalena region told us. "They left rather than risk a guilty verdict, which would have meant an execution."[552]

Some UC-ELN fronts have a reputation for particular types of abuses. For instance, the Domingo Laín Front executes girls known as *polacheras* or *tomberas*, who flirt with or date local soldiers and police officers.[553] In May 1995, the UC-ELN seized three children and a woman, apparently accused of "being close to members of the army and police." The girls – fourteen and fifteen-year-old sisters and a fourteen-year-old friend – and the woman were tortured before being killed with shots to the head. The Domingo Laín Front and the Simacota Company later took responsibility for the massacre and announced that they would continue to kill girls and women who "put the historical revolutionary process in danger."[554]

Such killings are not only abhorrent because they are carried out against children, but are glaring violations of the laws of war, since they punish an every day part of civilian life.

In the first seven months of 1998 alone, the UC-ELN reportedly bombed the 770-kilometers long pipeline linking Colombia's eastern oil fields with the Caribbean port of Coveñas forty-three times.[555] The UC-ELN targets the pipeline not to contribute directly to military action or to gain a specific military advantage in the circumstances ruling at the time, as is required by the laws of war, but to make a political point about its opposition to the way Colombia deals with the multinational corporations. In their words, these attacks "sabotage... those who

---

[552]Human Rights Watch interview with humanitarian aid worker, Barrancabermeja, Santander, June 28, 1996.

[553]Human Rights Watch interview with Arauca municipal official, Santafé de Bogotá, January 31, 1997.

[554]Human Rights Watch has repeatedly requested from the UC-ELN results on the internal investigation they claim to have carried out on these killings, but to date the UC-ELN has not provided them. The Attorney General's Human Rights Unit is investigating the case and has issued arrest warrants. Human Rights Watch interviews with human rights defenders, Arauca and Saravena, Arauca, January 31, 1997; "Boletín informativo," Comisión Intercongregacional de Justica y Paz, Vol. 8, No. 2. April-June, 1995, p. 66; "Hallan muertas a dos niñas secuestradas en Saravena," *El Tiempo*, May 12, 1995; and Human Rights Watch interview with Francisco Galán and Felipe Torres, Itagüí Prison, Antioquia, November 11, 1995.

[555]Electronic communication with John O'Reilly, British Petroleum-Colombia, July 26, 1998.

support the [neoliberal] opening and the financing of paramilitary groups."[556] In an interview with Radio Caracol, COCE spokesman Pablo Beltrán said that the UC-ELN targets the pipeline "so that all know that we must be more dignified and nationalistic in matters pertaining to petroleum."[557] In addition, the UC-ELN has bombed the pipeline to extort money. Although analysis is necessary to determine the circumstances of each case, when these attacks serve no military purpose and are instead meant to push a political point or threaten the civilian employees of oil companies, they are a violation.

Massacres
Highway robbers: A UC-ELN unit assassinated five people accused of belonging to a gang of highway thieves and posing as UC-ELN members on October 12, 1997, near Ricaurte, Nariño. Family members reportedly buried the victims without making formal complaints, out of fear of guerrilla reprisals. Afterwards, guerrillas stopped cars and trucks at roadblocks to inform travelers that they would continue to "bring justice to" (*ajusticiar*) those who "abused their good name."[558]

Murder and Torture
Edgar Horacio Albarracín Camargo: Representing Chitagá, Norte de Santander, Albarracín was the first mayor killed in Colombia in 1996. Three men fired on the mayor outside his home on January 14. Previously, Albarracín had been accused by the UC-ELN of corruption. The act was later claimed by the UC-ELN's Efraín Pabón Front in a communiqué sent to the army's García Rovira Battalion in Pamplona, which accused the mayor of "[authorizing] payments to his political allies, without consulting with the public, creating division within the political war

---

[556]*III Congreso "Comandante Édgar Amilcar Grimaldos Barón"* (Montañas de Colombia: Ediciones Nueva Colombia, June 1996), p. 74.

[557]Radio Caracol interview with Pablo Beltrán, COCE member, June 30, 1998.

[558]Translation by Human Rights Watch. CINEP and Justice and Peace, *Noche y Niebla,* No. 6, October-December 1997, p. 85; and "El Eln asesinó a cinco personas en Nariño," *El Tiempo,* October 15, 1997.

that the Chitagá region is going through."[559] None of these acts, if true, made Albarracín into a combatant and therefore a legitimate military target.

Rodolfo Antonio Alonso Monsalve: The UC-ELN routinely threatens and kills civilians who refuse to honor an armed work stoppage, or *paro armado*. During such a stoppage in April 1996, Rodolfo Antonio Alonso Monsalve, a retired oil worker, was reportedly assassinated by the UC-ELN when he failed to stop at a road block outside Barrancabermeja, Santander.[560]

Manuel Clavijo: This director of a government-run humanitarian aid group was killed by the UC-ELN on April 2, 1996, as he arrived at a family farm near the city of Arauca.[561] Family members who witnessed the killing told reporters that a guerrilla called "Hilario" killed Clavijo, apparently because he was identified as a supporter of increased army presence in Arauca. The family later received information indicating that "Hilario" and another guerrilla may have been paid to commit the murder by a third party, who remains unknown. After Clavijo's death, other family members continued to receive telephone death threats from the UC-ELN. One reported that an anonymous caller said, "the same thing that happened [to Clavijo] will happen to you."[562] Support for an increased presence of one or another party to the conflict would not, if true, make Clavijo into a combatant and therefore a legitimate military target.

César Espejos Perdomo and Lázaro Barrera: These recruits were with the Counterguerrilla Battalion No. 49 near Arauquita, Arauca when they were attacked by the UC-ELN on April 14, 1996. The army reported that Espejos and Perdomo

---

[559]Translation by Human Rights Watch. CCJ, *Colombia, Derechos Humanos y Derecho Humanitario: 1996*, p. 61; and "Violencia se ensaña contra los políticos," *El Tiempo*, August 10, 1997.

[560]Justice and Peace, *Boletín*, April-June, 1996, p. 10; and "El campanazo,"*Semana*, April 16, 1996.

[561]Justice and Peace, *Boletín*, April-June 1996, p. 15.

[562]Human Rights Watch interview with family members, Arauca, February 2, 1997.

had been captured. Subsequently, the army found their bodies, and reported that they had been tortured and executed.[563]

Marco Díaz Figueroa and Robin Ríos Galindo: On leave from the Counterguerrilla Battalion No. 23, these soldiers were forced to leave a public bus by members of the Domingo Laín Front of the UC-ELN who had mounted a roadblock on a road near Hato Corozal on December 2, 1996. The army reported that the men were tortured before being executed.[564]

Luis Alfonso Ramírez: Two gunmen identified by residents as UC-ELN members shot this municipal personero in his office in Salazar de las Palmas, Norte de Santander, on April 16, 1997. In the same attack, town council member Pedro Julio Rodríguez was wounded. The UC-ELN left pamphlets rejecting the creation of local CONVIVIR groups, which they apparently blamed Ramírez for supporting.[565]

Oil workers: In May 1997, the José David Suárez Front of the UC-ELN announced over a Casanare radio station that it would consider the 1,300 workers at facilities belonging to British Petroleum "military objectives."[566] On May 15, approximately ten guerrillas stopped six buses carrying Colombians who worked for Techint, Petrocas, and Megaservicios, British Petroleum contractors. Four employees were wounded when guerrillas burned the buses. Techint employee Fredy Ariel Sierra

---

[563]Justice and Peace, *Boletín Informativo*, Vol. 9, No. 2, April-June 1996, p. 10-11; and "Infracciones al Derecho Internacional Humanitario cometidas por los grupos subversivos," Inspección General, Oficina de Derechos Humanos, Fuerzas Militares de Colombia, 1997, p. 29.

[564]CINEP and Justice and Peace, *Noche y Niebla*, No. 2, October-December 1996, p. 108; and "Infracciones al Derecho Internacional Humanitario cometidas por los grupos subversivos," Inspección General, Oficina de Derechos Humanos, Fuerzas Militares de Colombia, 1997, p. 46.

[565]Human Rights Watch interviews in Ocaña and Hacarí, Norte de Santander, April 1995; "ELN asesinó a cuatro policías en Norte de Santander," *El Tiempo*, April 17, 1997; and "'Estamos desesperados'" *La Opinión* (Ocaña), April 23, 1997.

[566]CINEP and Justice and Peace, *Noche y Niebla*, No. 4, April-June 1997, p. 115.

Alfonso was killed as he tried to evade the roadblock.[567] Oil workers are civilians even though they may take part in an enterprise that contributes to the state's ability to wage war through the use of oil or the revenues from its sale. This employment does not qualify as taking a direct part in hostilities.

Rigoberto Contreras Restrepo: According to police and witnesses interviewed by a credible source, members of the UC-ELN's Carlos Alirio Buitrago Front forced this police officer from a public bus near Cocorná, Antioquia, on August 6, 1997. Obesity prevented Contreras from wearing a uniform. After his capture was reported, both the Medellín personero and the ICRC attempted to intervene on his behalf, and the UC-ELN informed his family that he was alive. However, on August 22, his badly decomposed body was found near the spot where he had been taken captive. According to police, he had been executed with two shots to the head and his body showed signs of torture.[568]

Jorge Cristo Sahuin and Pedro Cogaria Reyes: Sahuin, a Norte de Santander senator, and Cogaria, his bodyguard, were killed by the UC-ELN's Carlos Germán Velasco Villamizar Front on August 8, 1997, while in Cúcuta. A guerrilla shot both at point-blank range. In a press statement, the UC-ELN took responsibility for the killings and promised to consider candidates belonging to Colombia's traditional political parties as military targets.[569] In September 1998, the Attorney General's Office announced that it had issued indictments against five presumed members of the UC-ELN for their role in the killings.[570]

César Tulio Bonilla: This former president of the Antioquia Mining Union was a candidate for the mayor's office of El Bagre when UC-ELN guerrillas appeared in

---

[567]Electronic communication with John O'Reilly, British Petroleum-Colombia, August 27, 1998.

[568]Letter to Human Rights Watch from Antioquia Gov. Álvaro Uribe Vélez, Medellín, Antioquia, October 1, 1997; and "Hallan muerto a policía secuestrado," El Tiempo, August 25, 1997.

[569]Editson Chacón, "Se recrudece violencia política," El Tiempo, August 9, 1997; and "ELN se atribuye asesinato de senador Jorge Cristo," El Tiempo, August 19, 1997.

[570]"Acusados por la Fiscalía cinco miembros del Eln," El Colombiano, September 2, 1998.

front of his home on October 11, 1997. After calling him to the door, guerrillas killed him in front of his wife, Gloria Tobón, who was injured.[571]

Martín Emilio Ortiz Higuita: An army recruit, Ortiz began serving his obligatory two years in 1997 and was assigned to the Ayacucho Battalion in Manizales, Caldas. On October 19, he was given leave for family reasons. Out of uniform and unarmed, he boarded a public bus that was later stopped at a UC-ELN roadblock near Mistrato, Caldas. Guerrillas were reportedly exhorting passengers not to take part in municipal elections. Ortiz and two other passengers were forced to leave the bus and were summarily killed.[572]

Taking of hostages

Luz Adriana Jaramillo Rendón: On March 10, UC-ELN guerrillas seized the mayor of Guadalupe, Antioquia. The kidnapping was claimed by the Heroes de Anori Front. In a statement later republished in a weekly UC-ELN newsletter, the group said that the kidnapping was carried out to protest the creation of CONVIVIRs. Jaramillo was later released.[573]

Organization of American States (OAS) observers: Chilean Raúl Martínez, Guatemalan Manfredo Marroquín, and Colombian Juan Diego Ardila were kidnapped by the UC-ELN near San Carlos, Antioquia, prior to October 1997 municipal elections and held for nine days. At the time, both Marroquín and Martínez were wearing shirts that clearly identified them as OAS observers.[574] The UC-ELN took responsibility for this kidnapping both within Colombia and through its international newsletter, claiming that the OAS was being punished for "forfeiting" its civilian status by sending observers to Colombia only to "[legitimate] the Samper regime. The kidnapping, they acknowledged, was meant

---

[571]Letter pending to union; and CINEP and Justice and Peace, *Noche y Niebla,* No. 6, October-December 1997, p. 85.

[572]Letter to Human Rights Watch from Volmar Pérez Ortiz, national director, Office of Complaints, Public Advocate's Office, December 12, 1997; and "Guerrilla ajustició a dos civiles en Risaralda," *El Colombiano*, October 22, 1997.

[573]*Correo Del Magdalena: Resúmen informativo de noticias de Colombia*, II Época, No. 26, March 16-22, 1997.

[574]"Guerrilla secuestró a dos observadores de la OEA," *El Tiempo*, October 24, 1997.

to exert political pressure on Colombia and the OAS and gain a forum for their views.[575] The three were released on November 1.[576] This a violation of the ban on hostage-taking, since the definition relies on the hostage's disempowerment in the hands of a party to the conflict and the possibility that the hostage will be exchanged for some concession made by a third party.

Bishop José de Jesús Quintero Díaz: The UC-ELN's Armando Cacua Guerrero Front took responsibility for the November 24, 1997 kidnapping of this Tibú, Norte de Santander bishop. The kidnapping, they claimed, was to exert political pressure and bring attention to political violence in the Catatumbo region, on the Colombia-Venezuela border. In a response to a protest by Pope John Paul II, UC-ELN spokesperson Francisco Galán claimed that Bishop Quintero had also been targeted for being "complacent" with abuses in his diocese. Quintero was released on December 10.[577]

October 26 municipal elections: In the months preceding Colombia's 1997 elections, the UC-ELN kidnapped dozens of mayors, town council members, municipal workers, and candidates from the departments of Antioquia, Bolívar, Casanare, Cesar, Nariño, Norte de Santander, and Santander.[578] Although the UC-ELN described some kidnapping as ways to "evaluate what has been achieved by the authorities and express the population's desires to candidates," the captives were warned that they would be considered "military objectives" if they were perceived to support paramilitaries and would be subject to a "popular trial" and

---

[575]*Correo Del Magdalena: Resúmen informativo de noticias de Colombia*, II Época , No. 55, October 19-25, 1997.

[576] Marisol Gómez, "Libres, delegados de la OEA," *El Tiempo*, November 2, 1997.

[577]Human Rights Watch interview with Francisco Galán and Felipe Torres, UC-ELN spokespersons, Itagüí Prison, Antioquia, December 8, 1997; Human Rights Watch telephone interview with Antonio Leyva, chief, Statistics Department, Centro Nacional de Datos del Programa Presidencial para la Defensa de Libertad Personal, July 9, 1998; and "En carta al Papa. UC-ELN busca justificar secuestro," *El Tiempo*, December 3, 1997.

[578]For instance, see "Secuestran a candidato a alcaldía en Bolívar," *El Tiempo*, June 4, 1997; "Secuestrado alcalde de Yalí, Antioquia," *El Tiempo*, June 16, 1997; "Secuestrados cuatro alcaldes en Nariño," *El Tiempo*, August 6, 1997; "Secuestran a dos candidatos al concejo y a un ex-alcalde," *El Tiempo*, August 25, 1997.

possible execution.[579] After kidnapping four mayors in the department of Nariño, the Comuneros del Sur Front announced that the group "will not respect the presence of candidates from groups linked to political bosses of the traditional parties, the dirty war, paramilitaries, or those supported by CONVIVIR."[580] In a similar communiqué, groups in Antioquia told the newspaper *El Colombiano* that any politician who failed to denounce CONVIVIR associations publicly would be considered a "military target."[581] But as one Antioquia councilman told journalists, "If I speak publicly against paramilitaries and CONVIVIR, what I am actually doing is dictating the color and size of my own coffin, since others will then mark be as a guerrilla supporter."[582]After elections took place, the UC-ELN announced that those mayors inaugurated on the strength of a small number of votes would not be "permitted" to govern.[583] This announcement was followed by continued kidnapping and summary proceedings, prolonging the threat to elected officials into 1998.[584]

Attacks on medical workers, installations, and ambulances

Sarare Regional Hospital: On at least four occasions in 1996 and 1997, the UC-ELN has violated the special protection given to medical units in Article 12 of Protocol II by entering this hospital in Saravena, Arauca, executing civilians protected by the laws of war or setting off explosives. On May 1, 1996, Octavio Giraldo Alzate, a farmer, was being treated for appendicitis when he was killed in his hospital bed by members of a UC-ELN militia. Apparently, the militia members had intended to kill another patient who had survived an assassination attempt

---

[579]Translation by Human Rights Watch. *Correo Del Magdalena: Resúmen informativo de noticias de Colombia*, II Época, No. 4, August 17-23, 1997.

[580] *Correo Del Magdalena: Resúmen informativo de noticias de Colombia*, II Época, No. 45-46, August 3-16, 1997.

[581] "ELN no permitirá proselitismo político," *El Colombiano*, July 18, 1997.

[582] Jorge Iván García, "Elecciones huelen a plomo," *El Tiempo*, June 29, 1997.

[583]"El Laín dice que no hay división del ELN," *El Tiempo*, November 26, 1997.

[584]In 1998, we received reports of the UC-ELN kidnapping mayors in Nariño and Bolívar. "Liberado alcalde," *El Tiempo*, January 4, 1998; "Eln secuestra a alcalde de San Pablo," *El Espectador*, January 9, 1998; and "Confirman desaparición de cinco alcaldes de Nariño," *El Colombiano*, January 27, 1998.

earlier that day and mistook Giraldo for him.[585] The following August, guerrillas reportedly seized a man who had attempted suicide after killing his wife and children and had been rushed to the hospital. Guerrillas dragged him from his bed and executed him nearby, apparently as a punishment for killing his family.[586] On May 19, 1997, UC-ELN guerrillas attacked and wounded María Isabel Romero Ovalle, who owned a business that sold snacks and drinks in Saravena, apparently because she did business with members of the security forces. Taken to the hospital, Romero was being operated on when two guerrillas broke into the operating room and killed her.[587] On September 27, 1997, police reported that the UC-ELN detonated a bomb at the hospital entrance, apparently an effort to ambush a police unit that was delivering a cadaver to the morgue.[588]

Bagadó, Chocó: While townspeople were engaged in a religious celebration, the UC-ELN attempted to seize this town of 13,000 on January 28, 1997.[589] During the attack, the UC-ELN abducted Mario Hernández, a doctor, and Alejandro Noguera, a nurse, both of whom were engaged in medical duties, and stole medicine from the government medical clinic. They were later released. The UC-ELN took responsibility for this attack, claiming that it had destroyed the police barracks and killed six police officers. The abduction of medical personnel constitutes a violation by the UC-ELN of the special protections in Article 9 of Protocol II for individuals carrying out medical duties.

---

[585]Statement from Arauca residents to Human Rights Watch, June 1997; and Criminal complaint from the Sixteenth Brigade Human Rights office to the Saravena prosecutor, May 6, 1996.

[586]"La guerrilla lo acribilló por asesinar a su familia," *El Corredor*, August 3-16, 1996; and Fuerzas Militares de Colombia, Inspección General, Oficina de Derechos Humanos, "Infracciones al derecho internacional humanitario cometidas por los grupos subversivos," 1997, p. 32.

[587]Human Rights Watch interview, Santafé de Bogotá, December 3, 1998.

[588]National Police, Human Rights Office, "Informe: Ataques Subversivos," 1997, p. 24.

[589]Alirio Bustos, "'Vengan por nosotros, si son tan valientes'," *El Tiempo*, January 30, 1997.

Other acts that violate the laws of war

Regidor: On May 11, 1996, the Navy reported that a unit from the UC-ELN's Héroes y Mártires de Santa Rosa Front attacked the *Alfonso Mantilla*, a vessel traveling the Magdalena River with ten navy personnel aboard, from positions set up within the hamlet of Regidor, Bolívar. Guerrillas apparently used the homes of civilians as a shield from attack. The navy officer on board ordered the vessel to reverse course; it passed Regidor unharmed later that morning. According to the navy, while attacks on commercial vessels by the UC-ELN are not unusual, the tactic of using a population as a shield was a novelty in this case.[590] An independent source confirmed that in the Middle Magdalena region, the UC-ELN frequently mounts attacks on the security forces from civilian houses, using them as a shield.[591] Using civilian dwellings as a shield violates Article 13 of Protocol II, which protects civilians against the dangers arising from military operations.

Car bombs: On the night of March 17, 1997, two car bombs placed in Cúcuta, Norte de Santander, by the UC-ELN killed four people, among them eighteen-month-old Martha Liliana Riveros Rodríguez, and wounded seventeen. The first car bomb was detonated in the center of the city, damaging several banks and dozens of commercial establishments. The next car bomb exploded in the Juan Atalaya suburb, destroying a hardware store and damaging ten residences.[592] The UC-ELN attacked again in April 19, and its Northeast War Front (Frente de Guerra del Nororiente) claimed responsibility for several car bombs that damaged the Bavaria brewery and the Cattlemen's Bank and wounded four civilians.[593] In Barrancabermeja, Santander, a UC-ELN car bomb detonated on June 8, 1997,

---

[590]The following September and again in April and May 1997, the UC-ELN attacked ships on the Magdalena River. However, in contrast to the Regidor attack detailed here, they did so from the river bank, not the village according to press reports. These attacks are all under investigation by the Attorney General's Office. Human Rights Watch interview with Capt. Angel Conde, Flota Fluvial del Magdalena, Armada Nacional, June 27, 1996; "Oleada guerrillera," *La Prensa*, January 28, 1997; and 'Summary of attack on Navy sailors, 1995-1996,' Colombian navy.

[591]Human Rights Watch interviews in Magdalena Medio, June 27-30, 1997.

[592]"4 heridos y una menor muerta en acción terrorista," *El Espectador*, March 19, 1997.

[593]*Correo Del Magdalena: Resúmen informativo de noticias de Colombia*, II Época, No. 31, April 20-26, 1997; and "Carros bomba serían retaliación por secuestro de parientes de 'Gabino,'" *El Tiempo*, April 22, 1997.

wounded five civilians, including a two-year-old, and damaged dozens of residences.[594] We have received similar, credible reports of car bombs attributed to the UC-ELN in Saravena, Arauca.[595] We oppose these car bombings as a violation of the ban in Protocol II against indiscriminate attacks.

La Unión, Antioquia: For several weeks in June and July 1997, the UC-ELN attacked ranches near the town of La Unión, Antioquia, apparently because their owners were accused of supporting paramilitary groups and refused to pay a "war tax."[596] On July 1, guerrillas targeted the La Ponderosa ranch, owned by Mario López and his wife, Margarita Ortiz. Guerrillas first went to the house of the foreman, who was told to vacate the area with his family. Then guerrillas activated a bomb next to the area where the López's twin twelve-year-old boys, Santiago Andrés and Mario Alejandro, were sleeping, killing them. Guerrillas also fired on Margarita Ortiz, wounding her in the arm.[597] By the time the attacks subsided, ten ranches had been bombed, among them one belonging to the brother of Gov. Álvaro Uribe Vélez.[598] Support for a party to the conflict or failure to pay guerrillas, if true, does not convert a civilian into a combatant unless they personally take direct role in hostilities. Therefore, we consider these attacks serious violations of Protocol II.

Simití, Bolívar: In this June 30, 1997 attack, the UC-ELN destroyed the local Agrarian Bank, robbing its safe, and seriously damaged the municipal building and

---

[594]Letter to Human Rights Watch from Volmar Pérez Ortiz, national director, Office of Complaints, Public Advocate's Office, December 12, 1997; and "S.O.S. por la población civil de Barrancabermeja," CREDHOS, June 19, 1997.

[595]Human Rights Watch interviews with residents of Arauca and Saravena, January 31, 1997; and "Detona carga explosiva en Saravena," El Tiempo, March 26, 1997.

[596] "ELN dinamitó otra finca," El Tiempo, July 13, 1997.

[597]"Ataques en 7 departamentos," El Tiempo, July 2, 1997; and "Muerte y destrucción dejan ataques dinamiteros," El Colombiano, July 2, 1997.

[598]"ELN quemó finca de hermano de Uribe Vélez," El Colombiano, July 8, 1997; and "Guerrilla destruyó campamento maderero," El Tiempo, July 18, 1997.

the town's central plaza.[599] Police reported that guerrillas took family members of the police officers hostage, threatened their lives to try and force the officers to surrender, and used the family members as human shields to fire on the officers defending the police station. Among the family members was a two-year-old boy and two four-year-old girls.[600] Reportedly, guerrillas also used the wife and daughter of one officer as shields to cover their escape after the attack.[601] Days later, guerrillas returned and reportedly looted and burned the offices of the local prosecutor.[602] The use of family members of combatants to try and force a surrender or as human shields is an egregious violation of the ban on putting civilians at risk from military operations. In addition, guerrillas demonstrated a clear lack of discrimination in choosing military targets. Neither the bank, municipal building, or town plaza qualified as military targets at the time of attack. Guerrillas also looted, violating Article 4 (2) (g) of Protocol II. A month later, the UC-ELN kidnapped town council members, a mayoral candidate, and the town treasurer and threatened mayor Ubaldo de Jesús López, who they accused of misusing funds. López fled the area after the June attack, fearing guerrilla reprisals. The effect on the town following the attack was dramatic, particularly for rural families who depend on its stores and the bank for food, supplies, and loans. "Simití is finished, the economy is done for, the Agrarian Bank has no more money for fear of continued attacks," one resident told journalists.[603] The UC-ELN took responsibility for the July attack in its newsletter.[604]

---

[599]Three police officers died in the fighting. "Combatieron solos durante las 11 horas," *El Tiempo*, July 2, 1997.

[600]National Police, Human Rights Office, "Informe: Ataques Subversivos," 1997, pp. 13-14.

[601]CINEP and Justice and Peace, *Noche y Niebla,* No. 4, April-June 1997, p. 129.

[602]René Sierra, "Sur de Bolívar, secuestrado por el miedo," *El Tiempo*, September 2, 1997.

[603]"ELN secuestró a siete dirigentes en Simití," *El Tiempo*, August 17, 1997.

[604]*Correo Del Magdalena: Resúmen informativo de noticias de Colombia*, II Época, No. 41, June 29-July 5, 1997.

Scout bus: Returning from an eight-day jamboree in Medellín, Antioquia, 140 Boy Scouts between the ages of five and seventeen and their thirty adult escorts were stopped by the UC-ELN on July 5, 1997, near Yarumal. Guerrillas forced passengers to disembark, then set fire to their six buses, chartered from the Rápido Ochoa company. Most of their belongings, including clothing, were destroyed. As the flames lit the area, police approached and shots rang out as they engaged the guerrillas.[605] The UC-ELN violated the ban on attacking civilian vehicles, in this case public buses that had no role in the armed conflict. In addition, guerrillas placed civilians in a situation of extreme risk, lighting a fire they could have predicted would alert the authorities and provoke an attack by the security forces.

Land mines: Human Rights Watch continues to receive frequent and consistent reports that the UC-ELN uses land mines in populated areas of Antioquia, Arauca, and Santander, among others, endangering the civilian population and causing casualties among farmers and children.[606] The UC-ELN employs several types of mines, some available on the illegal arms market and others made by guerrillas.[607] In one particularly egregious case, the UC-ELN detonated a mine on July 9, 1997 in Primero de Mayo, a heavily populated Barrancabermeja slum, in effect using the surrounding civilian houses to ambush a military convoy. The explosion forced the driver of one of the military trucks to lose control and smash into two flimsy homes, killing a seven-year-old girl and wounding two other children. We received no reports of military casualties.[608] This attack violates the rule of proportionality, which holds that combatants must take precautions to minimize excessive harm to civilians and suspend an attack if the potential risk outweighs any direct military

---

[605]"ELN quemó buses donde viajaban 140 niños scouts," *El Tiempo*, July 7, 1997.

[606]Human Rights Watch interviews in Magdalena Medio, June 27-30, 1997; Human Rights Watch interview with human rights defenders, Arauca and Saravena, February 2-3, 1997; and "Minas quiebrapatas cobran más víctimas," *El Colombiano*, April 29, 1996.

[607]The UC-ELN uses M18A1 (Claymore) mines, Chinese-made antipersonnel mines (called Chinese or Vietnamese hats, or *sombreros chinos o vietnamitas*), and so-called "footbreaker" and "fool-catcher" (*quiebrapata* and *cazabobo*) mines, generally fabricated in UC-ELN camps. None are "smart" mines, meaning they never self-destruct. Human Rights Watch interview with Francisco Galán and Felipe Torres, Itagüí Prison, Medellín, Antioquia, December 8, 1997.

[608]Diego Waldron, "Ataque del ELN aplastó sueños de una niña," *El Tiempo*, July 10, 1997.

advantage. Here, the risk was glaring. Guerrillas should have concluded that the attack under the circumstances ruling at the time was too risky, since it could be reasonably assumed that the detonation would harm civilian houses or cause the convoy to crash.

Mogotes, Santander: After guerrillas disguised as civilians entered the Mogotes municipal offices and acted in a suspicious manner, Mayor Doriam Rodríguez called police on December 11, 1997. By that time, guerrillas using, among other vehicles, a public bus, had surrounded the central square. In the ensuing firefight within the municipal building and a building housing the electoral registry, three registry employees were killed. Three police officers also died. The attack seriously damaged the municipal building, the telephone office, the electoral registry, the Agrarian Bank, and a credit cooperative, all civilian buildings. During combat, guerrillas seized Mayor Rodríguez and held him hostage under threat of death for several days.[609] Neither the municipal offices nor the electoral registry qualify as legitimate military targets. Human Rights Watch has also received repeated, credible, and consistent reports about the burning of municipal and public vehicles by the UC-ELN in Barrancabermeja, Santander, a busy Magdalena River port. Public buses, road construction equipment, and private cars have been attacked during so-called "armed strikes" enforced by roadblocks and roving bands of guerrillas who attack civilians perceived to disobey the order to paralyze all movement.[610] We received similar reports from Arauca, where in Saravena, rebels periodically burn civilian vehicles that travel during armed strikes.[611] Civilian vehicles do not qualify as military targets unless they are being used in military operations. When they are dedicated to exclusively civilian use, they are protected under the laws of war.

---

[609]CINEP and Justice and Peace, *Noche y Niebla,* No. 6, October-December, 1997, p. 153; and National Police, Human Rights Office, "Informe: Ataques Subversivos," 1997, pp. 5-6.

[610]Human Rights Watch interviews, Barrancabermeja, Santander, June 27-30, 1996.

[611]Human Rights Watch interview with government officials and residents, Arauca and Saravena, February 2-3, 1997; and "ELN armed stoppage paralyzes transportation in Arauca," Santa Fe de Bogota Inravision, FBIS, Latin America, January 11, 1996.

EPL

> *The force and the pressure of the dissident group led by Francisco Caraballo is focused on finishing off those who were their comrades in armed struggle and who have now rejoined the country's political life.*
>
> *– Jaime Córdoba Triviño, Colombia's Public Advocate*
> *October 1992*

The Popular Liberation Army (Ejército Popular de Liberación, EPL) began armed insurrection in 1967. First active in northern Colombia, by the mid-1980s the EPL had units in six departments and the region known as Urabá, where it was strongest.[612]

By 1990, army attacks, often in coordination with paramilitaries, and internal divisions had severely weakened the EPL. More than 2,100 members agreed to accept a government amnesty and in 1991 turned in their weapons. Some chose to join a new political party called Hope, Peace and Liberty (Esperanza, Paz y Libertad). Other EPL members refused the amnesty. Although the EPL is sharply reduced in strength with fewer than 1,000 armed militants, it retains a presence in Córdoba and the Urabá and Middle Magdalena regions.[613]

EPL commander Francisco Caraballo is serving a sentence in Itagüí Prison, but continues to maintain radio contact with the remaining EPL members in the field.

---

[612]For a history of the EPL written by its supporters, see Álvaro Villarraga and Nelson R. Plazas, *Para Reconstruir los Sueños: Una historia del EPL* (Santafé de Bogotá: Progresar/Fundación Cultura Democrática, 1994).

[613]The EPL continues to be plagued by desertions and defections. Several groups surrendered to the ACCU while another surrendered to the government in 1996. Human Rights Watch interview with "Commander Jacinto" (Rafael Kerguelen), Montería, Córdoba, October 17, 1992; Comisión de Superación de la Violencia, *Pacificar la paz* (Santafé de Bogotá: IEPRI, 1992), pp. 24-28; and "Se entregan 75 guerrilleros en Antioquia," *El Tiempo*, October 1, 1996.

EPL and International Humanitarian Law

The EPL told Human Rights Watch that it respects international humanitarian law, with certain exceptions. For instance, the EPL allows its forces to execute people for certain acts, like participation in paramilitary groups. Although Caraballo did not describe any investigative or trial procedure, he confirmed that guerrillas under his command are also allowed to kill for more vaguely defined infractions, like "doing harm to others."[614]

In a letter to the non-governmental National Reconciliation Commission in 1995, the EPL noted that it "adopts the humanitarian measures promulgated by the Colombian guerrilla movement, which protect the non-combatant population, enemies disarmed in combat, the sick, the wounded, and those whose duty it is to assist them." The document also states that the EPL has "codified as crimes and misdemeanors transgression of these humanitarian concepts by our army."[615]

In an interview with Human Rights Watch, EPL commander Francisco Caraballo said that the EPL had taken several measures to conform to international humanitarian law. Among them, he noted, all militants receive training on the group's rules of engagement. Citing examples, Caraballo said that if an EPL member is accused of a crime, the village where the guerrilla operates is called on to hear the allegations and reach a verdict. If a militant is caught *in flagrante*, he is given a summary military trial.[616] Despite repeated requests, the EPL did not provide Human Rights Watch with a copy of its rules of engagement.

However, Human Rights Watch has received abundant information showing that the EPL engages in persistent and egregious violations of international humanitarian law. Among the most evident was the campaign, begun in 1991, to murder former comrades now in the Esperanza party. An EPL circular

---

[614]Human Rights Watch interview with Francisco Caraballo, EPL leader, Itagüí, Antioquia, December 8, 1997.

[615]Translation by Human Rights Watch. Letter to the National Reconciliation Commission from EPL commanders José Manuel Robledo and Sebastian Arboleda, September 30, 1995.

[616]Human Rights Watch interviews with Francisco Caraballo, EPL leader, Itagüí, Antioquia, July 3, 1996 and December 8, 1997.

signed by Caraballo stated that Esperanza was targeted because it was a "paramilitary group."[617]

While some Esperanza members did command or take part in "popular commands" to attack the EPL and individuals suspected of supporting the FARC, the group is a legal political party. While party leaders acknowledge that some former EPL guerrillas and Esperanza members may have joined paramilitary groups, the party claims that it does not support paramilitaries. According to Esperanza, 348 of its members and amnestied EPL guerrillas were murdered between 1991 and the end of 1995. Of that number, they believe sixty-one were killed by the EPL under Caraballo's command.[618]

In one particularly brutal case, the EPL reportedly executed five Esperanza members — Jaime Betin, Jorge Calle, Gregorio Flórez, Jorge San Martín, and Martha Cecilia Restrepo — near Turbo, Antioquia, on January 10, 1995.[619]

"The force and the pressure of the dissident group led by Francisco Caraballo," reported Colombia's public advocate in 1992, "is focused on finishing off those who were their comrades in armed struggle and who have now rejoined the country's political life."[620]

In 1998, former EPL commander David Mesa Peña, known as "Gonzalo," was arrested in connection with the murders of Esperanza members and others.[621] Drastically reduced in size since 1991, the group currently operates only

---

[617]Human Rights Watch interview with Mayor Gloria Cuartas, Apartadó, Antioquia, July 5, 1996; and "Esperanza, Paz y Libertad: Grupo Paramilitar," signed by Francisco Caraballo, March 1993.

[618]The FARC and its urban militias were believed responsible for 204 murders. "Listado de personas asesinadas pertenecientes a Esperanza Paz y Libertad," Fundación Progresar, February 1996.

[619] Listado de personas asesinadas pertenecientes a Esperanza, Paz y Libertad, Fundación Progresar, February 1996.

[620]The EPL and the FARC have also clashed in the field. Public Advocate, "Informe para el Congreso, El Gobierno, y el Procurador General de la Nación: Estudio de caso de homicidio de miembros de la Unión Patriótica y Esperanza, Paz y Libertad," October 1992, pp. 53-54.

[621]"En peligro, reinserción de la disidencia del EPL," *El Colombiano*, January 20, 1998.

sporadically in northern Colombia. In 1997, the EPL was linked to at least six political killings.[622]

Like the FARC and UC-ELN, the EPL also depends on hostage-taking to raise money and exert political influence. In 1997, the EPL was believed to have kidnapped at least thirty-two people.[623]

Murder

Rafael Angel Restrepo: This rancher was assassinated by members of the EPL's Bernardo Franco Front on January 5, 1996, near Turbo, Antioquia. Guerrillas also set his ranch on fire, apparently in retaliation for his refusal to pay "war taxes."[624] We have no evidence suggesting that Restrepo was a combatant. Instead, he was apparently targeted for refusing to give guerrillas money.

José Tarciso, Juan Climaco, and Moisés Emiro Bacca Bacca: According to human rights groups, members of the EPL's Libardo Mora Toro Front seized these brothers on March 2, 1996 on the Santa Rita farm near Ocaña, Norte de Santander. After binding them, guerrillas took them away. Residents found their bodies the next day, with a sign that read Heroes of America Campaign, considered part of the EPL. Their mother later told investigators that she believed they had been killed because the night before they were taken, they had given shelter to army soldiers.[625] As we noted at the beginning of this report, merely feeding a combatant, serving as a messenger, providing information, disseminating propaganda, or engaging in political activities in support of an armed group does not convert a civilian into a combatant.

Germán Ramírez Mejía and Heriberto Orejarena Olago. These men were part of a group accompanying candidates and siblings María Constanza and Juan Carlos Morales Ballesteros during a campaign tour prior to October elections when they were seized by the EPL at a roadblock in Santander on May 19, 1997. Guerrillas took the Morales Ballesteros siblings and six others hostage. Ramírez was executed

---

[622]CINEP and Justice and Peace, *Noche y Niebla: Balance Sheet 1997*, p. 6.

[623]Letter to Human Rights Watch from Francisco Santos, País Libre, July 3, 1998.

[624]Justice and Peace, *Boletín*, January-March 1996, p. 8.

[625]Ibid., p. 60.

hours later.[626] Orejarena, a student and friend of Juan Carlos, was found on May 22, executed with a single shot to the head.[627] The executions were later claimed by a spokesperson for the EPL's Ramón Gilberto Barbosa Front. In an interview with Human Rights Watch, EPL leader Francisco Caraballo took responsibility for the double execution and claimed that the men were paramilitaries.[628] The Morales family denied that the men were paramilitaries. Even if they had been, as combatants *hors de combat*, they were protected by the laws of war and should not have been summarily killed.

Three soldiers: Jorge López Cárdenas, Germán Granados Gutiérrez, and Carlos Julio Acevedo, army soldiers assigned to the Fifth Brigade, were traveling from Aguachica, Cesar, to Bucaramanga, Santander, when they were stopped at an EPL roadblock on August 3, 1997. As passengers on an interdepartmental bus, the three were forced to disembark and taken by guerrillas into the weeds, where they were killed near El Playón, Santander. Authorities believe that EPL commander Ramón Gilberto Barbosa ordered the execution.[629]

Purificación Lugo: Purificación Lugo was the mother of a former EPL guerrilla nicknamed "El Chonto." El Chonto helped hostages María Constanza and Juan Carlos Morales Ballesteros escape the EPL, then deserted. In apparent retaliation, the EPL seized Lugo and her two other sons on November 18, 1997 in their Barrancabermeja, Santander home. After forcing them to the street, guerrillas executed Lugo and her fourteen-year-old, Orlando. Lugo's other son, Miguel, was

---

[626]"EPL también pide despeje," *El Tiempo*, May 27, 1997.

[627]"EPL sentenció a otro de los secuestrados," *El Tiempo*, May 23, 1997.

[628]Human Rights Watch interview with Francisco Caraballo, Itagüí prison, Antioquia, December 8, 1997.

[629]Human Rights Watch interview with Human Rights Unit, Attorney General's Office, Santafé de Bogotá, December 4, 1997; Report 0707/BR5-FT27-S6-723, from Maj. Luis Rivera Alvarado, commander, Rogelio Correa Campos Battalion, to Regional Prosecutor, August 12, 1997; and "ELN y EPL asesinan a 3 soldados en Santander," *El Tiempo*, August 7, 1997.

seriously wounded, but survived.[630] Francisco Caraballo claimed that the EPL was investigating the killing, but has not provided Human Rights Watch with any results as of this writing.[631] Simply being a family member of a combatant does not covert a civilian into a combatant. Similarly, civilian family members cannot be made to suffer the consequences for the actions of relatives.

Taking of hostages

Adolfo Bula: This parliamentarian was kidnapped by the EPL near Hacarí, Norte de Santander, on April 25, 1997. With him was Aníbal López, a local political leader. Bula is a member of a political party known as the Socialist Renovation Current (Corriente de Renovación Socialista, CRS), made up in part of amnestied UC-ELN guerrillas.[632] In an interview with Human Rights Watch, Francisco Caraballo took responsibility for the kidnapping, and claimed that Bula had been investigated for alleged crimes and obligated to pay an "economic imposition," or ransom. He was later released.[633]

María Constanza and Juan Carlos Morales Ballesteros: This sister and brother were campaigning as mayoral candidates in the department of Santander when they were kidnapped by the EPL on May 19, 1997. Six others were taken at the same time and were released within a month.[634] During their captivity, their father, parliamentarian Norberto Morales Ballesteros, negotiated directly with Francisco Caraballo in Itagüí Prison. Morales himself had been kidnapped by the EPL in 1992.[635] María Constanza and Juan Carlos managed to escape after six months in

---

[630]CINEP and Justice and Peace, *Noche y Niebla*, October-December 1997, p. 111; and "Asesinan a familia del cómplice de la fuga de los Morales B.," *El Tiempo*, November 19, 1997.

[631]Human Rights Watch interview with Francisco Caraballo, EPL leader, Itagüí, Antioquia, December 8, 1997.

[632]"Secuestran a representante a la Cámara," *El Tiempo*, April 27, 1997.

[633]Human Rights Watch interview with Francisco Caraballo, Itagüí Prison, Antioquia, December 8, 1997.

[634]"Liberados a dos," *El Tiempo*, June 12, 1997; and "De regreso a casa," *Semana*, November 24-December 1, 1997.

[635]"EPL secuestró a 2 hijos de Morales B.," *El Tiempo*, May 20, 1997.

captivity and confirmed that they had been held by the EPL's Ramón Gilberto Barbosa Front for U.S. $2 million.[636] On one occasion, guerrillas forced María Constanza to write a letter to her family announcing that she and her brother would be killed if the family failed to pay.[637]

Sardinata, Norte de Santander: On June 8, 1997, the EPL seized three police officers — Jairo Ortiz Molina, Baronio Hormiga Méndez, and Víctor Manuel Gelves Cuervo — and two civilians near Sardinata, Norte de Santander. The kidnapping was claimed by the EPL's Libardo Mora Toro Front.[638] In return for releasing the officers, the EPL demanded the transfer of EPL commander Francisco Caraballo from Antioquia's Itagüí prison to the capital, a press conference, and a portable radio for him.[639] All five hostages were released. In an interview with Human Rights Watch, Francisco Caraballo took responsibility for the kidnapping.[640] The EPL's conduct is a violation of the ban on hostage-taking, since the case clearly satisfies the definition of hostages as persons "who find themselves, willingly or unwillingly, in the power of the enemy and who answer with their freedom or their life for compliance with [the enemy's] orders."

Other acts that violate the laws of war
Barrancabermeja: On December 17, the EPL burned several vehicles and set off explosives in this port town to commemorate the anniversary of its founding as a political movement. One of the explosives was placed in front of a neighborhood association on the city's northwest side. Among the vehicles destroyed were two public buses belonging to the Copetrán and Omega Companies.[641] Civilian vehicles and offices do not qualify as military targets unless they are being used in military

---

[636]"Los hermanos Morales se le fugaron al EPL," *El Tiempo*, November 16, 1997.

[637]Luis Fernando Ospina, "Confesiones de una liberación," *El Espectador*, November 24, 1997.

[638]"Cinco personas más en poder del EPL," *El Tiempo*, June 9,

[639]"EPL exige traslado de F. Caraballo," *El Tiempo*, June 10, 1997.

[640]Human Rights Watch interview with Francisco Caraballo, Itagüí Prison, Antioquia, December 8, 1997.

[641] "Saboteo del EPL a Barranca," *El Tiempo*, December 18, 1997.

operations, which they were not in this case. When they are dedicated to exclusively civilian use, they are protected under the laws of war.

VI. LITTLE BELLS AND LITTLE BEES: THE FORCED RECRUITMENT OF CHILDREN

Gunpowder gives you more energy, like with the desire to kill the troops passing in front of you. You say to yourself: I hope they come my way, and then you load up and shoot off a round and feel more capable, with better morale.

– Colombian child guerrilla
1996

Guerrillas call child combatants "little bees" (*abejitas*), able to sting before their targets realize they are under attack.[642] Paramilitaries call them "little bells" (*campanitas*), referring to their use as an early-alarm system.[643] Guerrillas, paramilitaries, and the security forces all routinely recruit children for combat.

Article 4 (3) (c) of Protocol II prohibits combatants from recruiting children under the age of fifteen or allowing them to take part in hostilities. In addition to domestic legislation protecting the rights of children, Colombia has ratified the Convention on the Rights of the Child, which fixes a minimum recruitment age of fifteen.

Human Rights Watch supports the adoption of an optional protocol to the United Nations Convention on the Rights of the Child to raise the minimum age for recruitment and participation in hostilities from fifteen to eighteen and calls on the combatants in Colombia to adopt a minimum recruitment age of eighteen. Persons under the age of eighteen have not reached physical or psychological maturity and are ill-prepared to face the harsh conditions of warfare. Many who have volunteered or who have been forced to serve emerge at the end of hostilities physically and psychologically scarred, unprepared to live in and contribute to a peaceful society.

The Convention on the Rights of the Child defines a child as any human being under the age of eighteen, unless under the law applicable to the child,

---

[642]Human Rights Watch interview with Colombian Family Welfare Institute (Instituto Colombiano de Bienestar Familiar, ICBF) specialist, Medellín, Antioquia, December 9, 1997.

[643]While all three guerrilla groups admitted in interviews that there are children in their ranks, the ACCU specifically denied that it recruits children. Letter to Human Rights Watch from the ACCU, July 27, 1997.

majority is attained earlier. Eighteen is also the voting age in the vast majority of countries in all regions of the world. Establishing eighteen as a minimum age would be consistent with existing international norms and offer greater protection for children in situations of particularly grave risk.

Human Rights Watch also notes the growing consensus among independent, non-governmental, and inter-governmental sources for setting the minimum age for participation in hostilities at eighteen, including the recommendations made by Graca Machel, the U.N. secretary general's expert on the impact of armed conflict on children, in her 1996 report; the position taken by the 26th International Conference of the Red Cross and Red Crescent in December 1995; and positions taken by agencies such as UNICEF and the U.N. High Commissioner for Refugees (UNHCR).

Human Rights Watch believes that the prohibition on children's participation in hostilities should not be narrowly focused on "direct" participation. Children who serve in armed groups in support functions are often subsequently drawn into direct participation. This is particularly true in the case of conflicts like Colombia's. It is worth noting that Protocol II does not limit its restrictions to "direct" participation, but calls on combatants to refrain from allowing children to participate in any way in hostilities.

Once drawn into a support activities, persons under the age of eighteen may be easily drawn into a direct role. In combat situations, military commanders may be tempted to make use of all resources at their disposal, including under-age troops. As military personnel, those under eighteen are considered combatants and may be the objects of attack, even without being placed in combat situations.

Guerrillas

According to a 1996 report by Colombia's public advocate, up to 30 percent of some guerrilla units are made up of children.[644] The number of children in militias, considered a training ground for future fighters, can be much higher. In an interview with Human Rights Watch, one specialist who works with a government child welfare agency in Medellín, Antioquia estimated that 85 percent of the members of the guerrilla militias he works with are children.[645]

---

[644]Public Advocate's Office, "El Conflicto Armado en Colombia y los menores de edad," Boletín No. 2, Santafé de Bogotá, May 1996.

[645]Human Rights Watch interview with ICBF specialist, Medellín, Antioquia, December 9, 1997.

The UC-ELN is believed to have the most children in its ranks in relation to its total strength. Human Rights Watch received numerous testimonies from people familiar with the UC-ELN about child combatants. One told us that it is common to see a unit with fifteen adult commanders leading up to sixty-five child soldiers.[646]

The FARC and EPL also include children in their ranks. Although the FARC's official recruitment age is fifteen, as one spokesperson noted in a published interview, there are exceptions:

> There are areas where children beg insistently to join the guerrillas, but there are also situations in which their very own mothers, who are desperate, take their children to the guerrillas because their families live in misery... It's very difficult to tell them no.[647]

In a similar vein, the EPL denies that it recruits children under sixteen. However, leader Francisco Caraballo noted that the group accepts children into its ranks if they are family members of militants. These children, Caraballo told us, are not permitted to take part in military actions. However, their activities may be just as dangerous. In April 1996, police reported capturing a fifteen-year-old girl apparently used to collect money extorted by the EPL from merchants in Anserma, Caldas.[648]

Despite their denials and qualifications, Human Rights Watch has received abundant information indicating that all three guerrilla groups continue to recruit children and use them as combatants. The FARC, for instance, has even carried out recruitment campaigns in elementary schools and children's homes, promising to send families a regular salary. According to the Public advocate in Cali, Valle del Cauca, "[Guerrillas] have presented themselves in schools and the homes of

---

[646]Human Rights Watch interview with humanitarian aid worker, December 1997.

[647]Dick Emanuelson, "Interview with Olga, comandante guerrillera de las Fuerzas Armadas Revolucionarias de Colombia, Ejército del Pueblo (FARC-EP)," *Rebelión*, October 14, 1996.

[648]It is important to point out that even when a child may seek to join the guerrillas, they are obligated to prevent that child from taking part in hostilities according to Article 4 (3) (c) of Protocol II. Human Rights Watch interview with Francisco Caraballo, Itagüí Prison, Antioquia, July 3, 1996; and "Menor del EPL," *La Patria*, April 19, 1996.

children offering to take the children to war, enticing them with stories about fighting and offering to sign them up, as a kind of adventure. They have offered their families money and guarantees of security in exchange for allowing their children to join the guerrillas."[649]

While some children may join the guerrillas by choice, others are forcibly recruited. We consider forcible recruitment an additional violation of the laws of war, since it depends on threats of violence made by combatants against civilians, explicitly outlawed in Article 4 (2) (h) of Protocol II. According to a 1996 report by the office of the Public Advocate, 14 percent of the child guerrillas they interviewed for their study said they had been forcibly recruited.[650]

In regions dominated by the FARC, like the department of Guaviare, we have received credible reports that the guerrillas forcibly recruit children as young as twelve. Often, families do not report the forced recruitment of children for fear of reprisals.[651]

Other children are virtually born into guerrilla movements because their parents are members. Kept by others as infants, some are then forced to join their parents' units. One fourteen-year-old told the Public Advocate's Office that she joined the guerrillas at age twelve, brought by her mother. There, she was forced to cook and carry a shotgun (*escopeta*). After refusing to work, she was imprisoned, but managed to escape.[652]

Regardless of how a child comes to guerrillas, however, they are obligated to keep children from combat. Clearly, guerrillas recruit them in part because they consider children valuable assets. "Children are more intrepid, they have more bravery for war," a guerrilla commander told investigators from the Public

---

[649]Translation by Human Rights Watch. Internal communication from Cali Public advocate, May 8, 1996, quoted in Public Advocate's Office, "El Conflicto Armado en Colombia y los menores de edad," Boletín No. 2, Santafé de Bogotá, p. 8.

[650]Ibid.

[651]Human Rights Watch interview with government investigator, San José del Guaviare, Guaviare, May 5, 1997.

[652]Public Advocate's Office, "El Conflicto Armado en Colombia y los menores de edad," Boletín No. 2, p. 11.

Advocate's Office. "And although children are usually given no command responsibilities, they carry out their duties much better than an adult would."[653]

Often, children are given the task of collecting intelligence, making and deploying mines, and serving as an advance shock force, to ambush the paramilitaries, soldiers, or police officers serving on point during patrols. To control his fear, one child guerrilla told the Public Advocate's Office investigators, he and other children drank milk mixed with gunpowder. "Gunpowder gives you more energy, like with the desire to kill the troops passing in front of you. You say to yourself: I hope they come my way, and then you load up and shoot off a round and feel more capable, with better morale."[654]

For these tasks, children are fully armed. One former child guerrilla, recruited at thirteen, told Public Advocate investigators that she had used pistols, AK-47s, Galils, M-16s, R-15s, Uzi submachine guns, Ingrams, and a 357 Magnum. "In the organization, you understand that your life is your weapon, it is your mother, it watches out for you day and night."[655]

The FARC uses children to kidnap and guard hostages. One former FARC hostage told us that during her captivity at the hands of the FARC's Thirty-Sixth Front, she had been guarded by a girl of fifteen. Many of the guerrillas she saw over a period of three months were children, she reported.[656]

Child combatants who manage to escape are considered deserters and can be subjected to on-the-spot execution. If guerrillas believe the child has given the Colombian security forces information, the punishment is death. One mother of a girl who escaped tried to get her former commanders to sign a "certificate of liberty" that would be distributed to other area units, to insure that her daughter would not be killed.[657]

Even children who have been captured by the authorities, convicted, and placed in juvenile detention centers are at risk of being killed. Between 1994 and

[653]Ibid.

[654]Ibid., p. 27

[655]Ibid., p. 30.

[656]Human Rights Watch telephone interviews with former hostage, November 8, 1996 and January 5, 1997.

[657]Public Advocate's Office, "El Conflicto Armado en Colombia y los menores de edad," Boletín No. 2, pp. 12-13.

1996, the Public Advocate's Office found, 13 percent of the children convicted of belonging to guerrilla groups and imprisoned were killed while in custody, apparently by other child guerrillas in the same facilities. One government authority told investigators that he preferred to let these child guerrillas in custody "escape," thus giving them a better chance of protecting themselves. "It is better to know that this girl or boy is alive some place than knowing that because of something we did, they were murdered."[658]

In January 1998, the UC-ELN orchestrated a public release of children they said had given the army information used to mount the joint army-paramilitary attack on Media Luna, Cesar mentioned in this report. During negotiations, the UC-ELN released a statement expressing their "interest" in "taking minors out of the war" and added that a ban on their future involvement would be an important step in an eventual humanitarian accord between the Colombian government and insurgents.[659]

As we have pointed out repeatedly in this report, it is not necessary to have any accord for the laws of war to apply to any of the parties; their application is automatic and is meant to protect the civilian population, not serve the political interests of the parties in conflict.

Security Forces

As we noted above, Colombia ratified the Convention on the Rights of the Child in 1991. At the time, Colombia made a declaration regarding Article 38 and voluntarily chose to accept a minimum age of eighteen for boys to define their military situation by either stating why they were unable to serve the obligatory twelve- to twenty-four-month term or begin their service.

However, Law 48, passed two years later, required all Colombian males who have either reached eighteen years of age or have completed secondary school (*bachillerato*) to define their military status, in effect invalidating Colombia's international commitment. Boys who graduated before reaching eighteen were

---

[658]Ibid., p. 13.

[659] The AUC denied that it had recruited these children. Human Rights Watch interview with Francisco Galán and Felipe Torres, Itagüí Prison, Medellín, Antioquia, December 8, 1997; Paul Bolaño Saurith, "Dramática liberación de los cinco menores de edad," *El Tiempo*, January 31, 1998; "Menores liberados por el ELN no tienen relación con las ACU," *El Tiempo*, February 6, 1998; and "Liberación de menores es un caso puntual, dice el Eln," *El Tiempo*, November 19, 1997.

required to either state why they were ineligible for service or present themselves
for induction into active service. Indeed, children were openly encouraged to serve

The UC-ELN released children they detained under suspicion of helping the army and paramilitaries mount the joint attack on Media Luna mentioned in this report. © Rafael Guerrero/El Tiempo

since the mandatory term for those under eighteen was up to twelve months less than the mandatory term for adult males.[660]

After the Public Advocate's Office drew attention to this contradiction, instead of honoring its international commitment, Colombia withdrew the declaration and continued to recruit children, an apparent attempt to boost the number of males available for service. After widespread protest from the parents of child soldiers, however, Congress passed Law 418 in 1997, exempting boys from obligatory military service until their eighteenth birthdays.

Nevertheless, boys under eighteen who choose to serve may still do so with parental permission. Law 418 and a 1997 Constitutional Court decision

---

[660]Article 13 of Law 48 establishes an eighteen- to twenty-four month obligatory term for regular recruits; a twelve-month term for child soldiers; a twelve-month term for child police officers; and a twelve- to eighteen-month term for soldiers from farm families.

prohibit recruits under eighteen from serving in a "theater of war" or in combat.[661] However, this is a deceptive argument since much of Colombia can be considered a potential battleground and child recruits are often assigned to bases in areas where combat is a frequent occurrence. When a Public Advocate's Office investigators visited a military base in Arauca in 1997, for instance, the investigator reported that soldiers were defusing a truck bomb with two child soldiers nearby.[662]

According to the armed forces, 7,685 children currently serve in the National Police, 7,551 in the army, 338 in the air force, and eighty-three in the navy, a total of 15,657. Of those, 22 percent, or 3,445 children, are fifteen and sixteen years of age.[663]

Both the army and police have also recruited children for civic outreach, then have put them in uniform in war zones, placing them at serious risk of attack. The police recruit children as young as seven years of age as "little patrollers" to take part in police-related activities. Although the approximately 14,000 Juvenile Civic Police and 15,000 Student Police are unarmed and take part primarily in directing traffic or other public safety activities, they are uniformed and work in war zones and are at risk of attack.[664]

On June 13, 1998, the UC-ELN abducted fifteen females, among them five children, who belonged to the "Steel Girls" program run by the army's Fourteenth Brigade in Segovia, Antioquia. According to the press reports, the "Steel Girls" taught poor residents how to improve their reading skills, offered medical counseling, and conducted recreational events. However, guerrillas charged that they were armed and uniformed and conducted intelligence for soldiers.[665]

---

[661]Articles 13, 14, and 15 of Law 418; and SU-200/97, April 17, 1997.

[662]Public Advocate's Office, "Niñas, niños, y jóvenes en el conflicto armado," June, 1998.

[663]"Menores de edad incorporados al servicio militar como soldados bachilleres," Colombian Armed Forces, May 8, 1998.

[664]Human Rights Watch interview with Col. Julio Moreno Llanos, Human Rights Office, National Police, Santafé de Bogotá, May 8, 1997; and National Police, *1995: un año de realizaciones* (Santafé de Bogotá: Policía Nacional, 1995), pp 32-33, 79.

[665]All fifteen were released unharmed on July 3, 1998. Serge Kovaleski, "Young Women Held Hostage In Colombia, Rebel Action Touches A Nerve in Weary Nation," *Washington Post*, July 1, 1998.

Clearly, the army has the power to conduct civic outreach programs; however, by placing children in uniform in a sharply contested war zone, they unnecessarily put them at risk and blurred the line dividing civilians from combatants.

Another way children serve in the security forces is by switching sides, from guerrilla to army ranks. According to the Public Advocate's Office, the army has captured or accepted the surrender of children suspected of being guerrillas, then used them as guides and informants. This violates the children's rights in several ways. Children face serious reprisals from their former comrades for working as informants. Also, they are coerced or threatened into serving the army, a kind of forced recruitment. Often, security force officers, in particular the army, simply fail to ever deliver children to the proper judicial authorities, keeping them in military barracks. In its report, the Public Advocate's Office interviewed children who had been forced to patrol with troops, take part in combat, collect intelligence, and deactivate land mines.[666]

In 1997, CREDHOS reported that a fourteen- and sixteen-year- old detained by Los Guanes Battalion soldiers on May 5 were forced to don uniforms and hoods. They were used as informants during house searches. The two were later released to the proper authorities.[667]

Other child guerrillas remain in military barracks under Law 81, which allows the army to keep individuals convicted of terrorism in barracks confinement if they work as informants and guides. During a Human Rights Watch mission to Colombia in 1996, we were introduced to four children who lived in the Nueva Granada Base.[668] This is illegal, since children are not considered responsible for their actions before the law in Colombia and therefore cannot be prosecuted or jailed. Instead, children twelve and older are required to be delivered to a juvenile judge (juez de menores), who can either release them to family or require that they be housed for a period of time in a government facility for children. Younger children are treated by Colombia's Institute of Family Well-Being (Instituto

---

[666]Public Advocate's Office, "El Conflicto Armado en Colombia y los menores de edad," p. 14.

[667]CREDHOS Urgent Action, May 7, 1997.

[668]Human Rights Watch interviews with former child guerrillas, Barrancabermeja, Santander, June 28, 1996.

Colombiano de Bienestar Familiar, ICBF), a child welfare department of the government.[669]

The army has also forced former child guerrillas to appear before the press and recite testimony prepared by the army and designed to discredit guerrillas. In the Public Advocate's report, a fifteen-year-old who had surrendered to soldiers told investigators that it was necessary to collaborate in order to eventually be freed. "The next day, they presented me to the press, they told me that I had to say terrible things, that [the guerrillas] had forced me to join them, that the commanders had forced me to sleep with them... none of that is true, but [the soldiers] said that if I didn't say these things, the devil would take me." In this instance, the report noted, the army also forced the child against her will to speak with journalists, who took her photograph and published her name, seriously endangering her.[670]

Paramilitaries

According to the Office of the Public Advocate, up to 50 percent of some paramilitary units are made up of children. One former child paramilitary interviewed by the Public Advocate's Office said he had been forcibly recruited at nine years of age. During the time he served, he had no communication with his parents. "There were more children like me, about eleven, and my same age. Another five were between ten and fifteen years of age. We were all serving two years."[671]

Children as young as eight years of age have been seen patrolling with paramilitary units in the Middle Magdalena region. There, residents told Public Advocate's Office investigators that paramilitaries consider service obligatory and service can last as long as two years. Families who refuse risk being considered sympathetic to guerrillas and attacked.[672]

---

[669]We documented the failure of Colombia's juvenile facilities to adequately treat and care for juveniles in Human Rights Watch, *Generation Under Fire: Children and Political Violence in Colombia* (New York: Human Rights Watch, 1994), pp. 50-57.

[670]Public Advocate's Office, "El Conflicto Armado en Colombia y los menores de edad," p. 14.

[671]Ibid., p. 16.

[672]Ibid., pp. 15-16.

"Unless they release their children for service, they must leave the area or risk being killed," a social worker from the Chucurí region told Human Rights Watch.[673]

Other children are used as backup troops, to spy and patrol in their home regions. Girls are at particular risk according to the Public Advocate's Office, which collected interview from girls who reported a high level of sexual abuse by adult paramilitaries.[674]

Despite overwhelming evidence to the contrary, paramilitaries organized as members of the AUC deny they recruit children.[675]

---

[673]Human Rights Watch interview with social worker, Barrancabermeja, Santander, April 8, 1995.

[674]Public Advocate's Office, "Niñas, niños, y jóvenes en el conflicto armado," June, 1998.

[675]"'Paras' dicen no a menores en el conflicto'," *El Tiempo*, November 24, 1997.

VII. FORCED DISPLACEMENT

I live without memory.

– Colombian internally displaced woman
December 11, 1997

When ACCU members found Doris María Torres, a teacher, and the five farmers named on their list for the town of El Salado, Bolívar, they forced them to the town square. Torres's mother later told an investigator that the six were made to lie face down and were executed with shots to the head. Among those forced to watch were Torres's two children.[676]

Over the following week in March 1997, 320 families abandoned El Salado, leaving behind houses, furniture, fields, and schools. When journalists visited later, they found only "empty streets, lined with mute houses... and traveled only by the wind and an occasional starving dog that seemed to be searching for its masters."[677]

Unlike refugees, who escape political persecution by crossing an international border, displaced people flee their homes but stay within their countries. Forced displacement is expressly prohibited by Article 17 of Protocol II. Unless civilians must move for their own security or a clear military imperative, any displacement "shall not be ordered for reasons related to the conflict. Should such displacements have to be carried out, all possible measures shall be taken in order that the civilian population may be received under satisfactory conditions of shelter, hygiene, medical, safety, and nutrition."[678]

---

[676]CINEP and Justice and Peace, *Noche y Niebla*, January-March 1997, p. 50; and U.S. Committee for Refugees, *Colombia's Silent Crisis: One million displaced by violence* (Washington, D.C.: U.S. Committee for Refugees, 1998), p. 34.

[677]Translation by Human Rights Watch. Carlos Sourdis, "Solo los perros se quedaron en El Salado," *El Tiempo*, April 6, 1997.

[678]In November 1995, the Colombian government adopted a decree that allows civilian and military authorities to evacuate families or whole populations from areas where there are military operations. Decree 2027 was made during a "state of internal commotion" declared after the assassination of conservative politician Álvaro Gómez. However, Decree 2027 was framed broadly and allowed authorities to order displacements in almost any situation and without making specific arrangements for the health and safety of displaced

However, since 1980 displacements provoked by all of the parties to the conflict and undertaken without any regard for the civilian population have become the rule and now take place throughout Colombia. According to the Displaced Support Group (Grupo de Apoyo a Desplazados, GAD), an alliance of human rights, church, and humanitarian aid groups, over one million Colombians have been displaced by violence.[679]

The number displaced annually has increased markedly since 1995, according to a 1997 study by the Consultancy for Human Rights and the Displaced (Consultoría para los Derechos Humanos y el Desplazamiento, CODHES), a research and humanitarian aid group. CODHES found that since 1995, forced displacement has almost tripled, reaching its highest ever number in 1997 with at least 257,000 Colombians newly forced to flee.[680] Colombia has the fourth largest displaced population in the world according to the U.S. Committee for Refugees, after the Sudan, Angola, and Afghanistan.[681]

Chief among the causes of forced displacement are human rights and laws of war violations. Displacement is also linked to powerful business interests, who ally with paramilitaries to force poor farmers from their land, then occupy it or buy it for paltry sums.[682]

Forced displacement often results from indiscriminate attacks, the terror caused by massacres, selective killings, torture, and threats. In some cases, Human Rights Watch found that a party to the conflict forced civilians to flee their homes as part of a planned military maneuver. This forced displacement clearly violated

---

families. After Human Rights Watch expressed its concern over this measure as a possible violation of the laws of war, then-Interior Minister Horacio Serpa said that there were no plans to implement the decree, and to our knowledge it has never been invoked. Human Rights Watch interview with Interior Minister Horacio Serpa, Santafé de Bogotá, November 7, 1995.

[679]Diego Pérez, "Informe sobre el Desplazamiento Forzado en Colombia, Enero-Octubre 1997," GAD, November 1997, p. 8.

[680]CODHES, "Colombia: Desplazados, Éxodo, Miedo y Pobreza," March 1998.

[681]U.S. Committee for Refugees, *World Refugee Survey* (Washington, D.C.: U.S. Committee for Refugees, 1997), p. 6.

[682]For an in-depth analysis of forced displacement in Colombia, see U.S. Committee for Refugees, *Colombia's Silent Crisis: One million displaced by violence* (Washington, D.C.: U.S. Committee for Refugees, 1998).

Article 12 of Protocol II. Civilians were not only harmed by the military operations, but were forced to be a central element of those operations.[683] For example, when Human Rights Watch visited Tierralta, Córdoba in 1996, humanitarian aid officials had registered the arrival of 567 families, many of whom told us they had been ordered to abandon their homes by the FARC. At the time, the FARC was pressured by the ACCU and apparently believed that a mass displacement of civilians would delay the paramilitary advance and win them better increased access to provisions.[684]

Similarly, pressured by paramilitaries advancing south, the FARC forced the displacement of an estimated 3,000 people from twenty-seven villages around Currulao to Apartadó, Antioquia, in June 1996, in part to gain access to needed supplies. Families arrived with little more than they could carry on their backs. Children suffered from food and water shortages and lack of proper shelter and medical care.[685] While the FARC may argue that the displacement was a military imperative, recognized by Article 17 of Protocol II, it requires that combatants make provisions for the safety or well being of the civilians involved, including providing for their shelter, hygiene, medical, safety, or nutrition, clearly ignored in this case.

Colombians from all walks of life have been displaced. While professionals, elected officials, and businesspeople forced to flee may have resources to set up a new household and continue in their jobs, most displaced are poor farmers who lose nearly everything when they leave their homes and fields. According to a study done for the UNHCR, three-quarters of displaced are women, often single mothers, and children. Most displaced lose their sole place of residence when they flee.[686]

---

[683]The Colombian constitution also forbids the punishment of expulsion (*destierro*) in Article 34.

[684]Human Rights Watch interview with Horacio Arango, Programa por la Paz, Santafé de Bogotá, June 25, 1996.

[685]Human Rights Watch interviews with Currulao residents, Apartadó, Antioquia, July 5, 1996; and Human Rights Watch interview with Mayor Gloria Cuartas, Apartadó, Antioquia, July 5, 1996.

[686]Andrés Franco, "Los Desplazamientos internos en Colombia: una conceptualización política para una solución de largo plazo," prepared for the UNHCR, March 1997.

Among all combatant forces, only the AUC publicly accepts responsibility for forcibly displacing civilians. In an interview with *El Tiempo*, Carlos Castaño acknowledged that his forces had "a lot of responsibility. Armed conflict produces [forced displacement] as it develops."[687]

Although forced displacement has been registered for over a decade, most internally displaced moved as individuals or families prior to 1996. Since, an increasing number of the displaced move as whole villages or towns. According to CODHES, over one-quarter of the people displaced in 1997 fled in large groups, as combatants clashed near their homes, farms, and businesses.[688]

As María Girlesa Villegas, public advocate for the department of Antioquia, told Human Rights Watch, "The movement of masses of people is only the last step in a long process. It starts with one or two families, then a group of people. Again and again, these communities see atrocities. And when they can stand it no longer, that is when they leave."[689]

Although political violence exists throughout Colombia, there were key regions where massacres, fighting, targeted killings, and threats prompted forced displacement: the northern departments of Antioquia, Bolívar, Cesar, and Norte de Santander; the Middle Magdalena region; and the region known as Urabá, bordering Panama and including northern Chocó department.[690] Forced displacement also spread to new areas formerly at the margins of conflict, including the departments of Chocó and Putumayo.[691]

The department of Chocó was at the margins of conflict until 1996, when an ACCU advance reached the northern tip of the department.[692] In the course of three months, paramilitary massacres, selective killings, and threats paired with direct combat and the Colombian army's Operation Genesis caused between

---

[687]"Los que generan el drama," *El Tiempo*, December 31, 1997.

[688]CODHES, "Colombia: Desplazados, Éxodo, Miedo y Pobreza," March 1998.

[689]Human Rights Watch interview with María Girlesa Villegas, regional Public Advocate's Office, Medellín, Antioquia, December 9, 1997.

[690]CINEP and Justice and Peace, *Balance 1997*, pp. 8-9.

[691]Letter from Carlos Rodríguez, CCJ, to John Donaldson, president, Inter-American Commission on Human Rights, Organization of American States, February 24, 1998.

[692]Human Rights Watch interview with CCJ, Santafé de Bogotá, December 3, 1997.

15,000 and 17,000 people to flee. In a public forum, Father Manuel Napoleón García, from the Quibdó diocese, described how dramatically the department had changed by comparing statistics on violent deaths. In 1995, for instance, Father García said the diocese registered fifteen killings. In comparison, there were one hundred registered killings in only the first six months of 1997, most for political reasons.[693]

Another relatively new phenomenon is the targeting of leaders of displaced communities, accused by combatants of either belonging to an enemy side or arranging displacements as a part of military maneuver. In Rioblanco, Tolima, for instance, described in the CONVIVIR section, families who fled in September 1996 and did not return continued to receive threats from the same group related to their efforts to resettle. On September 2, 1997, Heriberto Hernández, president of the Rioblanco Displaced Committee, was taken by armed men believed to be CONVIVIR members and executed on the outskirts of Rioblanco. Other committee members have also been threatened. As a result, ten families, including twenty-seven adults and twenty-five children, traveled to Santafé de Bogotá to ask for government protection in September 1997.[694]

Not just leaders are at risk. A shelter for Middle Magdalena displaced families was the target of repeated attacks in 1996 and 1997, eventually forcing it to close.[695] Associations of the displaced are under constant threat, particularly from paramilitary groups, who have gone to camps and other areas where there are displaced to threaten them.[696]

On December 1, 1997, paramilitaries identifying themselves as ACCU members arrived at a Dabeiba, Antioquia shelter and demanded to speak to several people to "clear up some matters." Herminio Palomeque agreed to accompany

---

[693]"Los desplazados: la cultura del silencio," *El Tiempo*, September 30, 1997.

[694]Human Rights Watch interview with Rioblanco displaced, Santafé de Bogotá, December 5, 1997; and Urgent Action, Fundación Mencoldes, October 16, 1997.

[695]Human Rights Watch interview at the Peasant Shelter, Barrancabermeja, Santander, June 28, 1996.

[696]Human Rights Watch interview with displaced association, Sabana de Torres, Santander, June 29, 1996; and Letter from Justice and Peace to the Inter-American Commission on Human Rights, April 17, 1998.

them and got into their car. His body, with visible signs of torture, was found the next day. He had been executed with one shot to the head.[697]

"It is very difficult to live in the city," one displaced person told a journalist in Medellín. "On the one hand, there is the misery of poverty, and on the other hand the psychosis [of fear]. People from the ACCU threaten that they will come here and even things up once and for all. So, even as you suffer from hunger, you can't even have peace. It gets to the point that when people came to take a census, at first we didn't want to take part, out of fear."[698]

Some Colombians do cross international borders and become refugees. In 1996 and 1997, the UNHCR reported that there were hundreds of Colombian refugees in Ecuador, Panama, and Venezuela, which share borders with Colombia. Costa Rica, Sweden, Spain, and the United States have also sheltered Colombian refugees.

The Samper administration responded to forced displacement by adopting a plan for the displaced in 1995, creating the post of presidential counselor for the displaced (Consejería Presidencial para Desplazados) in April 1997, adopting a revised national plan on displacement the following May, and promulgating Law 387 in July, which deals specifically with assistance, protection, and prevention issues.

Law 387 is Colombia's first attempt to reflect in domestic legislation the protections for displaced people contained in Protocol II, a positive step. However, Law 387 focuses on general requirements for humanitarian aid once the displaced are already fleeing and contains no specific measures designed to prevent or penalize the act of forcing the civilian population to flee.[699] Law 387 outlines the government's policy on emergency aid, but fails to address issues of justice or the causes of the displacement.[700]

Advocates for the displaced and human rights groups point out that government measures have so far fallen prey to lack of funding, insufficient coordination between government agencies, and poor information. In all, the

---

[697]Letter to Human Rights Watch from Father Javier Giraldo, Justice and Peace, December 3, 1997.

[698]Translation by Human Rights Watch. Carlos Alberto Giraldo, "Los desterrados de Dabeiba," *El Colombiano*, April 8, 1998.

[699]Law 387, July 20, 1997.

[700]Ibid.

government has failed to live up to its responsibility to protect the forcibly displaced, as laid out in Protocol II. According to the Displaced Support Group, during 1996 and the first half of 1997, government relief benefited a mere 38,182 displaced persons nationwide.[701]

In the words of the U.S. Committee for Refugees, which reported on Colombia's internally displaced in a March 1998 report, conditions facing the internally displaced range from "Modest to insufferable...of the estimated one million Colombians who have been displaced from their homes, only a few tens of thousands (including those living in the few camps for displaced persons) are currently receiving financial assistance or food aid from the government. NGOs and church groups assist others, but are only able to reach a small minority of the total displaced population."[702]

Government authorities have been slow to implement Law 387 despite the critical nature of mass displacement occurring even as this report went to press. According to the Colombian Commission of Jurists, the government agencies responsible for attending the displaced lacked any coordination and they were unable to get any overall sense of what government funds were allocated for assisting the displaced.[703]

Additionally, Law 387 provides for the delivery of aid, but also imposes a time limit of three months for families to receive aid, which in exceptional circumstances may be extended for another three months. As humanitarian groups have repeatedly pointed out, displaced people are in need of aid for a much longer period, even if they are among the few who manage to relocate to new land. In an interview with Human Rights Watch, one humanitarian aid worker estimated that the minimum time necessary to reestablish a displaced farm family is two years, since that takes into account the work of clearing, planting, and harvesting that makes a family self-sufficient.[704]

---

[701]Diego Pérez, "Informe sobre el Desplazamiento Forzado en Colombia, Enero-Octubre 1997," GAD, November 1997, p. 22.

[702]U.S. Committee for Refugees, *Colombia's Silent Crisis: One million displaced by violence*, pp. 18-19.

[703]Letter from Carlos Rodríguez, CCJ, to John Donaldson, president, Inter-American Commission on Human Rights, Organization of American States, February 24, 1998.

[704]Human Rights Watch interview with Anthony Sánchez, Mennonite Relief Agency (MENCOLDES), Santafé de Bogotá, December 5, 1997.

Increasingly, the international community has been assisting the forcibly displaced in Colombia. The European Union is the largest international contributor to the relief of the displaced. In addition, the UN High Commissioner for Human Rights and ICRC both have programs in Colombia that assist the displaced. The UN High Commissioner for Refugees (UNHCR) is expected to join them soon.[705]

Conditions for Displaced

Most displaced Colombians continue to live in misery and fear. Colombia's cities have absorbed displaced families into their growing slums, and the displaced often live on the margins of these already marginal settlements. According to the Santafé de Bogotá human rights personero, "Government authorities in the capital have not assumed their responsibility to care for the displaced people who come to the city."[706]

Others take shelter in temporary camps. At the end of 1997, at least four camps for the displaced were functioning: more than 4,200 people were housed at Pavarandó, more than 3,000 at the Turbo stadium, and an estimated 3,000 divided between parks in Ituango and Puerto Valdivia, all in Antioquia. As the Office of the U.N. High Commissioner for Human Rights, which visited many displaced communities in 1997, pointed out in its 1998 report, "The situation of the displaced population, both in collective settlements and on the outskirts of cities, is critical in the extreme and takes the form of lack of access to basic health, food, housing, and education services, and serious overcrowding."[707]

The camp at Pavarandó, for instance, had minimal medical care and almost no other services or activities in 1997. The displaced complained that food distribution was erratic. Even when the displaced received rations, they were not sufficient. Displaced families lived in tents made of black plastic tarps, open to air, weather and the baking sun. Families were forced to eat, cook, and sleep in the four square meters where approximately ten people live. "It is very hot in the tents," one

---

[705]U.S. Committee for Refugees, *Colombia's Silent Crisis: One million displaced by violence*, pp. 25-26.

[706]"Falta mas atención a desplazados," *El Espectador*, December 26, 1997.

[707]Commission on Human Rights, "Report by the United Nations High Commissioner for Human Rights," March 1, 1998.

displaced man told Human Rights Watch. "Many children have hepatitis or malaria. Families are disintegrating."[708]

On the day one humanitarian aid worker visited, he told Human Rights Watch, the displaced had gone four days without food.[709]

At Pavarandó, safety was among the main concerns of the displaced. "The paramilitaries continue to be in the town of Pavarandó and they are constantly telling us that they will enter the camp and kill people," one displaced man told

---

[708]Human Rights Watch interview with displaced man living in Pavarandó Grande, Santafé de Bogotá, July 22, 1997.

[709]Letter to Human Rights Watch from humanitarian aid worker, June 1997.

Most forcibly displaced Colombians live in deplorable conditions like these families from the department of Cesar. © Jennifer Bailey

Human Rights Watch in July 1997. "After the camp was set up, the paramilitaries said they would continue to kill anyone they found in the area."[710]

Conditions for the displaced in Turbo were even worse. There, the displaced were housed in a large unventilated sports coliseum where they live "like pigs on the floor," according to one of the residents. He also reported that during one twenty-day period, no food at all arrived at the camp, forcing the families to subsist on bananas.[711]

With no activities or programs available in the camps, many displaced were seriously depressed. A displaced father of two living in Turbo told Human Rights Watch in July: "When I see the bad life I am living, I feel like I want to take poison and kill myself and my family. I sometimes think I should have died as a little child so that I wouldn't have to be living this."[712]

---

[710]Human Rights Watch interview with displaced man living in Pavarandó Grande, Santafé de Bogotá, July 22, 1997.

[711]Human Rights Watch interview with displaced man living in Turbo, Santafé de Bogotá, August 1, 1997.

[712]Ibid.

Children suffer the most serious effects of the minimal and irregular medical care in the camps. Chronic diarrhea, dehydration, and hepatitis are common. In April 1997, one child died of poorly treated diarrhea. The Colombian Red Cross reported to the Public Advocate's Office that on several occasions older people were denied medical care when the army refused to allow them to be taken from the camp to the hospital.[713]

Corruption and mismanagement have also prevented aid from reaching the displaced. In July 1997, displaced families at Pavarandó and Turbo were surprised to receive winter jackets, in-line roller skates, silk stockings, artificial Christmas trees, and rotten food as aid, in a place where the temperature rarely descends below eighty degrees Fahrenheit and there is no pavement.[714]

Given the insufficiency of government aid, most of Colombia's one million displaced people must survive through their own ingenuity and perseverance and the limited assistance of church and humanitarian groups. Many manage only a precarious existence lacking in food, water, and basic medical care. For example, during a site visit to a farm where displaced peasants from the department of Cesar were relocated by the government, displaced farmers told Human Rights Watch that insufficient water laden with agrochemicals had caused their crops to fail. The seventy-nine residents, including forty-three children, expected to receive food donations only for the next two months, when a program funded by an international group was scheduled to end.[715] In a previous visit to the farm, the Public Advocate's Office had reported chronic malnutrition among children and found that no drinking water had been delivered to the farm for over a month.[716]

Forced return

In some cases, the government has impelled the displaced to return to their communities despite its inability to guarantee their security, a violation of Article

---

[713]Report of the Public Advocate's Office, Delegada para los Derechos de la Niñez, La Mujer y los Ancianos, April 12, 1997.

[714]"Insólita 'ayuda' a desplazados en Urabá," *El Tiempo*, March 28, 1998.

[715]Human Rights Watch visit to Hacienda Los Cámbulos, Tolima, August 4, 1997.

[716]Report of the Public Advocate's Office, Delegada Para los Derechos de la Niñez, La Mujer y Los Ancianos, Regional Ibagué, April 9, 1997.

17 of Protocol II, which forbids the forced movement of civilians except for reasons of their security or military imperative.

For example, according to virtually all informed observers and the displaced themselves consulted by the U.S. Committee for Refugees, from the moment that the Riosucio displaced arrived in Pavarandó and Turbo, the government began pressuring them to return home.

While displaced people said that they wanted to return, they insisted that the government guarantee their security. In November 1997, the government announced that the displaced in Pavarandó had agreed to return home and would sign an agreement to that effect. But the displaced people refused to sign, saying that while the agreement promised them financial assistance to rebuild their communities, it did not guarantee their security.[717]

Indeed, as the year ended, there were reports of new ACCU massacres in and around Riosucio, Chocó, where many of the displaced in camps were from. Although government and military authorities at first denied the reports and claimed that the groups that had received them had engaged in "disinformation," a commission from the Attorney General's Office later confirmed that at least twelve people had been killed and another seventeen were unaccounted for in late December, raising serious questions about the long-term safety of any of the displaced who return.[718]

In early 1998, an estimated 500 displaced people from Pavarandó began to leave for resettlement areas, where they had been promised government support. However, even as they began to arrive, the government failed to provide them with promised assistance, including construction materials for homes and food.[719]

According to the Office of the U.N. High Commissioner for Human Rights, return "has been promoted even though minimum conditions of security

---

[717]Letter to Human Rights Watch from Patricia Luna, Interior Ministry, November 20, 1997; Yaned Ramírez,"El drama de la raza," *El Tiempo*, October 12, 1997; and "A fin de mes empezaría el regreso," *El Tiempo*, October 12, 1997.

[718]Attorney General's Office, Press Release, "Informe de la Comisión que viajó a Urabá," Boletín de Prensa No. 012, Santafé de Bogotá, January 22, 1998; Letter to Human Rights Watch from Father Gabriel Izquierdo, CINEP, February 9, 1998; and Press Release No. 001, Seventeenth Brigade, January 2, 1998.

[719]"En Domingodó, nueva comunidad de paz," *El Tiempo*, March 26, 1998.

could not be guaranteed and the causes which gave rise to the displacement had not been eliminated."[720]

Refoulement

In November 1996, 400 farmers from the Unguia, Chocó region fled to Panama. The UNHCR asked the Panamanian government for access to the refugees and the government agreed, but on the day UNHCR representatives arrived, the Panamanian authorities working with the Colombian air force forcibly returned eighty-eight of the refugees to Colombia.[721]

Human Rights Watch considers this a violation of Panama's obligations under Article 33 of the 1951 Convention Relating to the Status of Refugees, which prohibits the return of a refugee "in any manner whatsoever to the frontiers of territories where his life or freedom would be threatened on account of his race, religion, nationality, membership of a particular social group or political opinion." The Convention, which Panama acceded to on August 2, 1978, protects refugees in its territory and prohibits governments from returning them to situations where their lives would be in danger.[722]

The refugees were housed in the Apartadó Children's Home, where conditions were cramped and unsanitary.[723]

In early March 1997, over 300 Colombian refugees from the Riosucio area arrived in Panama after several weeks' walk. The Panamanian government again promised UNHCR access to the refugees, but in conjunction with the Colombian authorities, returned 325 people, among them 177 children, beginning on April 18, once again without permitting UNHCR to meet them.[724] The UNHCR

---

[720]Commission on Human Rights, "Report by the United Nations High Commissioner for Human Rights," March 1, 1998.

[721]U.S. Committee for Refugees, *Colombia's Silent Crisis: One million displaced by violence*, p. 16.

[722]Colombia signed the Refugee Convention on July 28, 1951, and ratified it on October 10, 1961.

[723]Amnesty International Urgent Action 278/96, November 28, 1996.

[724]"Terminó repatriación de colombianos en Panamá," *El Tiempo*, April 21, 1997; and U.S. Committee for Refugees, *Colombia's Silent Crisis: One million displaced by violence*, p. 16.

strongly condemned the Panamanian government for forcibly repatriating the Colombians without allowing the UNHCR to speak directly with them.[725]

Many of the returnees claimed that the Panamanian police rounded them up and told them they had seventy-two hours to board the helicopters being provided "or else." Others said that they were tricked into returning by Colombian government promises to relocate them and give them money and land. One returnee told Human Rights Watch in August 1997 that no one wanted to return, that they felt it better to die in Panama than return to Colombia, but that the families were taken "by force."[726]

These returnees were sent to a run-down camp-like shelter in the town of Bahia Cupica, Chocó where they faced continued threats and violence from paramilitaries. In August, the ICRC evacuated twelve people, whose names were being circulated on a paramilitary death list.[727] An investigation by the Internal Affairs Office of Special Investigations the following September found abundant evidence that the ACCU maintained complete control of the area. The displaced faced "constant danger... not a single judicial, police, military, or government representative has attempted to stop these murders, torture, or forced disappearances that the inhabitants of these places have been subjected to."[728]

---

[725]UNHCR Briefing Notes, April 11, 1997.

[726]After the return, Human Rights Watch wrote a letter to Panamanian President Ernesto Pérez Balladares expressing our concern that Panama had failed to respect its obligations under the Convention on the Status of Refugees, which Panama has ratified, to protect refugees in its territory, refrain from returning them to situations where their lives would be in danger, and failing to allow the oversight and participation of the UNHCR. We never received a response. Human Rights Watch letter to President Ernesto Pérez Balladares, April 29, 1997.

[727]Human Rights Watch electronic mail from Juan Manuel Bustillo, Secretario Operativo del GAD, September 5, 1997.

[728]Translation by Human Rights Watch. Internal Affairs, Office of Special Investigations, September 22, 1997.

VIII. THE ROLE OF THE INTERNATIONAL COMMUNITY

United Nations

April 6, 1997 marked the official opening of the Bogotá office of the U.N. High Commissioner for Human Rights, led by Amb. Almudena Mazarrasa and staffed by five experts and a deputy director. The office continues to press the government on issues of concern to the Commission, including reforms to the military penal code and respect for international humanitarian law. Experts travel throughout the country to document abuses and hold regular meetings with government officials, representatives of human rights groups, and Colombians wishing to deliver complaints.[729]

During the Fifty-Fourth session of the U.N. High Commission for Human Rights, the office submitted its first report, which was considered hard-hitting. The report concluded that there was abundant evidence of continued joint military and paramilitary actions that ended with human rights violations as well as a disregard for the laws of war by all parties to the conflict.[730]

The Commission on Human Rights chose to show its concern about the situation in Colombia by increasing the number of experts in the Bogotá office from six to twelve. In addition, High Commissioner Mary Robinson expressed her profound concern about Colombia, and noted that most reported violations are attributed to paramilitaries often working with the tolerance of the security forces. She also announced her plans to visit Colombia in 1998, a welcome gesture of support for the office and concern over the serious human rights situation.

European Union

Some European embassies and diplomats have taken high-profile roles in attempting to lessen political violence and the suffering it causes. In April 1997, Netherlands Amb. Gysbert Bos made a three-day visit to the Middle Magdalena region, in part to draw attention to a rise in paramilitary activity and displacement. The visit was seen as especially important given that the Netherlands at the time occupied the presidency of the European Union.

For its part, the E.U. continued to pressure Colombia to improve its human rights record by issuing strong statements criticizing impunity and calling for the implementation of the recommendations of the U.N. Commission on Human

---

[729]Human Rights Watch interviews in Colombia, September 8-13, 1997.

[730]Commission on Human Rights, "Report by the United Nations High Commissioner for Human Rights," 54th Session, E/CN.4/1998/16, March 1, 1998.

Rights.[731] After the murders of human rights defenders Jesús María Valle and Eduardo Umaña, the European Parliament passed resolutions condemning the killings and calling on the Colombian authorities to investigate, "take urgent, effective and preventive measures to protect and safeguard the activity of those campaigning for human, social, trade union and peasant rights and political leaders," and dismantle paramilitary groups and CONVIVIRs.[732]

The European Community Humanitarian Office (ECHO) donated U.S. $5 million dollars in emergency aid to international NGOs to assist the thousands of people forcibly displaced earlier in the year in Urabá.

United States

The United States pursues a two-pronged policy in Colombia. On the one hand, the Clinton administration has made human rights an important part of U.S.-Colombia relations and is supporting peace negotiations. At the same time, the war on drugs remains the centerpiece of U.S.-Colombia relations. In fiscal year 1998, Colombia is slated to receive at least $119 million in U.S. counter-drug assistance, including equipment and training.[733]

In 1997, the State Department issued its most detailed and critical human rights report ever, concluding that "the [Colombian] armed forces committed numerous, serious human rights abuses." In addition, the report noted, "the Samper administration has not taken action to curb increased abuses committed by paramilitary groups, verging on a policy of tacit acquiescence."[734]

This report was followed by an April letter from Secretary of State Madeleine Albright to Sen. Patrick Leahy, co-sponsor of an amendment that placed human rights conditions on some antinarcotics aid. Section 570 of the Foreign Operations Appropriations Act, the so-called Leahy amendment, prohibits funds from being provided to any unit of the security forces of a foreign country if the

---

[731]Declaration by E.U. president, September 25, 1997.

[732]Resolution on the murders in Colombia by the European Parliament, May 14, 1998.

[733]This is an estimate. All monies allocated may not ultimately be spent. Adam Isaacson and Joy Olson, *Just the Facts: A civilian's guide to U.S. defense and security assistance to Latin America and the Caribbean* (Washington, D.C.: Latin America Working Group, 1998), pp. 166-168.

[734]U.S. State Department, "Colombia Report on Human Rights Practices for 1997," p. 454.

secretary of state has credible evidence that such unit has committed gross violations of human rights, unless the secretary determines and reports to the congressional Committees on Appropriations that the government involved is taking effective measures to bring the responsible members of the security forces unit to justice.

In her letter, Secretary Albright announced that the spirit of the amendment would be applied to most anti-narcotics aid, including monies suspended after Colombia was "decertified" a second time in a row for failing to meet U.S. goals in fighting drugs.[735] By mid-1998, only one Colombian army unit had been fully cleared to receive aid. U.S. officials asked the Colombian army to transfer out two officers belonging to an additional unit under consideration, the Twelfth Brigade, because they had outstanding human rights allegations against them.[736]

Human Rights Watch and other groups protested the idea that a simple transfer would satisfy the amendment, since it calls for "effective measures" to bring the responsible members of the security forces unit to justice. In general, the way in which the United States vets security force units for human rights violations before they receive aid remains largely secret, precluding full accountability.

While these conditions have played an important role in sending a strong message to the Colombian security forces that the United States considers respect for human rights a key part of bilateral relations, that message needs to be strengthened by aggressive U.S. monitoring of units that receive aid, including ensuring that soldiers accused of committing abuses are fully investigated and, if believed responsible, prosecuted by an independent and competent court. The procedures used to monitor these units must not be kept secret; transparency is a key part of any mechanism meant to monitor the compliance of an institution, like the Colombian military, that has amassed such a horrifying human rights record.

For its stand on the Leahy amendment, the administration was harshly criticized by some Republicans in the U.S. Congress, who argued that human rights concerns hampered the drug war. Led by the International Relations Committee and its chair, Rep. Benjamin Gilman, Republicans attempted to remove the Leahy amendment from the 1998 Foreign Operations bill, an effort that ultimately failed.

Despite the State Department's decision to apply the spirit of the Leahy amendment to most anti-narcotics aid, to date, the U.S. Defense Department continues to train and equip Colombian army units that have not been reviewed for

---

[735]Letter from Sec. Madeleine Albright to Sen. Patrick Leahy, April 21, 1997.

[736]Human Rights Watch interview with U.S. official, May 5, 1998.

human rights abuses. According to the *Washington Post*, U.S. officers continue to train Colombian units in "'shoot and maneuver' techniques, counterterrorism and intelligence-gathering, even though their members have not been vetted."[737] After similar programs in Indonesia and Rwanda were reported, Senator Leahy proposed legislation that would bar the Pentagon from holding joint exercises with human rights abusers unless the secretary of defense finds an extraordinary need to waive the law.[738]

Human Rights Watch believes that U.S. policy must be consistent in its support for human rights and international humanitarian law, and that all U.S. security assistance, including training, should be subject to the full Leahy amendment.

Indeed, the Clinton administration has continued to push hard for aid to the Colombian military to fight drugs, arguing that funds would be channeled to units without bad records. After months of tense negotiations, the Colombian and U.S. governments signed an end-use monitoring agreement on August 1, 1997 freeing $70 million of the $100 million slated to reach Colombia that year, much of it for the army and navy.[739] Among the items sent were communications equipment, night vision scopes, and parts for helicopters and river patrol boats.[740] Police continued to receive aid throughout the year, including munitions and weapons.

After a series of army defeats at the hands of the FARC, U.S. officials began speaking of Colombia as a threat to regional security and in need of direct assistance to the military to combat guerrillas.[741] In testimony before the House International Relations Committee on March 31, 1998, Gen. Charles Wilhelm, head of the U.S. Southern Command, called Colombia "the most threatened country in

---

[737]Douglas Farah, "U.S. Expands Latin American Training Role," *Washington Post*, July 13, 1998.

[738]The bill was pending as of this writing. Tim Weiner, "Military Spending Approved With Curbs on Rights Abuses," *New York Times*, August 1, 1998.

[739]Washington Office on Latin America, *Reluctant Recruits: The US military and the War on Drugs*, Washington, D.C., August 1997, p. 4.

[740]See U.S. State Department, Memorandum of Understanding, August 1, 1997.

[741]Dana Priest, "U.S. May Boost Military Aid to Colombia's Anti-Drug Effort," March 28, 1998.

the United States Southern Command area of responsibility."[742] Rather than discussing the country's serious human rights situation however, after a visit to Colombia that same month, Wilhelm told journalists that criticism of violations by the military was "unfair" and that guerrillas abuse human rights more frequently than the security forces or paramilitaries, an assertion that not only displays a profound misunderstanding of human rights law, but also seriously misrepresents the facts, contradicting even the State Department's grim assessment.[743]

---

[742]Testimony before the House International Relations Committee, March 31, 1998.

[743]Col. Vicente Ogilvy, a U.S. Southern Command spokesperson, confirmed these remarks to Human Rights Watch on May 28, 1998. "Colombia no es alarma: Wilhelm," *El Espectador*, May 9, 1998.

APPENDIX I

Article 3 common to the Geneva Conventions of 12 August 1949

Article 3. In the case of armed conflict not of an international character occurring in the territory of one of the High Contracting Parties, each Party to the conflict shall be bound to apply, as a minimum, the following provisions:

(1) Persons taking no active part in the hostilities, including members of armed forces who have laid down their arms and those placed hors de combat by sickness, wounds, detention, or any other cause, shall in all circumstances be treated humanely, without any adverse distinction founded on race, colour, religion or faith, sex, birth or wealth, or any other similar criteria.

To this end, the following acts are and shall remain prohibited at any time and in any place whatsoever with respect to the above-mentioned persons:

(a) violence to life and person, in particular murder of all kinds, mutilation, cruel treatment and torture;

(b) taking of hostages;

(c) outrages upon personal dignity, in particular humiliating and degrading treatment;

(d) the passing of sentences and the carrying out of executions without previous judgement pronounced by a regularly constituted court, affording all the judicial guarantees which are recognized as indispensable by civilized peoples.

(2) The wounded and sick shall be collected and cared for. An impartial humanitarian body, such as the International Committee of the Red Cross, may offer its services to the Parties to the conflict.

The Parties to the conflict should further endeavour to bring into force, by means of special agreements, all or part of the other provisions of the present Convention.

The application of the preceding provisions shall not affect the legal status of the Parties to the conflict.

Protocol Additional to the Geneva Conventions of 12 August 1949, and relating to the Protection of Victims of Non-International Armed Conflicts (Protocol II), 8 June 1977.

Preamble

The High Contracting Parties, Recalling that the humanitarian principles enshrined in Article 3 common to the Geneva Conventions of 12 August 1949, constitute the foundation of respect for the human person in cases of armed conflict not of an international character, Recalling furthermore that international instruments relating to human rights offer a basic protection to the human person, Emphasizing the need to ensure a better protection for the victims of those armed conflicts, Recalling that, in cases not covered by the law in force, the human person remains under the protection of the principles of humanity and the dictates or the public conscience, Have agreed on the following:

Part I. Scope of this Protocol

Art 1. Material field of application

1. This Protocol, which develops and supplements Article 3 common to the Geneva Conventions of 12 August 1949 without modifying its existing conditions or application, shall apply to all armed conflicts which are not covered by Article 1 of the Protocol Additional to the Geneva Conventions of 12 August 1949, and relating to the Protection of Victims of International Armed Conflicts (Protocol I) and which take place in the territory of a High Contracting Party between its armed forces and dissident armed forces or other organized armed groups which, under responsible command, exercise such control over a part of its territory as to enable them to carry out sustained and concerted military operations and to implement this Protocol.

2. This Protocol shall not apply to situations of internal disturbances and tensions, such as riots, isolated and sporadic acts of violence and other acts of a similar nature, as not being armed conflicts.

Art 2. Personal field of application

1. This Protocol shall be applied without any adverse distinction founded on race, colour, sex, language, religion or belief, political or other opinion, national or social origin, wealth, birth or other status, or on any other similar criteria (hereinafter referred to as "adverse distinction") to all persons affected by an armed conflict as defined in Article 1.

2. At the end of the armed conflict, all the persons who have been deprived of their liberty or whose liberty has been restricted for reasons related to such conflict, as well as those deprived of their liberty or whose liberty is restricted after the conflict for the same reasons, shall enjoy the protection of Articles 5 and 6 until the end of such deprivation or restriction of liberty.

Art 3. Non-intervention

1. Nothing in this Protocol shall be invoked for the purpose of affecting the sovereignty of a State or the responsibility of the government, by all legitimate means, to maintain or re-establish law and order in the State or to defend the national unity and territorial integrity of the State.

2. Nothing in this Protocol shall be invoked as a justification for intervening, directly or indirectly, for any reason whatever, in the armed conflict or in the internal or external affairs of the High Contracting Party in the territory of which that conflict occurs.

Part II. Humane Treatment

Art 4. Fundamental guarantees

1. All persons who do not take a direct part or who have ceased to take part in hostilities, whether or not their liberty has been restricted, are entitled to respect for their person, honour and convictions and religious practices. They shall in all circumstances be treated humanely, without any adverse distinction. It is prohibited to order that there shall be no survivors.

2. Without prejudice to the generality of the foregoing, the following acts against the persons referred to in paragraph I are and shall remain prohibited at any time and in any place whatsoever:
(a) violence to the life, health and physical or mental well-being of persons, in particular murder as well as cruel treatment such as torture, mutilation or any form of corporal punishment;
(b) collective punishments;
(c) taking of hostages;
(d) acts of terrorism;
(e) outrages upon personal dignity, in particular humiliating and degrading treatment, rape, enforced prostitution and any form or indecent assault;
(f) slavery and the slave trade in all their forms;
(g) pillage;

(h) threats to commit any or the foregoing acts.

3. Children shall be provided with the care and aid they require, and in particular:
(a) they shall receive an education, including religious and moral education, in keeping with the wishes of their parents, or in the absence of parents, of those responsible for their care;
(b) all appropriate steps shall be taken to facilitate the reunion of families temporarily separated;
(c) children who have not attained the age of fifteen years shall neither be recruited in the armed forces or groups nor allowed to take part in hostilities;
(d) the special protection provided by this Article to children who have not attained the age of fifteen years shall remain applicable to them if they take a direct part in hostilities despite the provisions of subparagraph (c) and are captured;
(e) measures shall be taken, if necessary, and whenever possible with the consent of their parents or persons who by law or custom are primarily responsible for their care, to remove children temporarily from the area in which hostilities are taking place to a safer area within the country and ensure that they are accompanied by persons responsible for their safety and well-being.

Art 5. Persons whose liberty has been restricted

1. In addition to the provisions of Article 4 the following provisions shall be respected as a minimum with regard to persons deprived of their liberty for reasons related to the armed conflict, whether they are interned or detained;
(a) the wounded and the sick shall be treated in accordance with Article 7;
(b) the persons referred to in this paragraph shall, to the same extent as the local civilian population, be provided with food and drinking water and be afforded safeguards as regards health and hygiene and protection against the rigours of the climate and the dangers of the armed conflict;
(c) they shall be allowed to receive individual or collective relief;
(d) they shall be allowed to practise their religion and, if requested and appropriate, to receive spiritual assistance from persons, such as chaplains, performing religious functions;
(e) they shall, if made to work, have the benefit of working conditions and safeguards similar to those enjoyed by the local civilian population.

2. Those who are responsible for the internment or detention of the persons referred to in paragraph 1 shall also, within the limits of their capabilities, respect the following provisions relating to such persons:
(a) except when men and women of a family are accommodated together, women shall be held in quarters separated from those of men and shall be under the immediate supervision of women;

(b) they shall be allowed to send and receive letters and cards, the number of which may be limited by competent authority if it deems necessary;

(c) places of internment and detention shall not be located close to the combat zone. The persons referred to in paragraph 1 shall be evacuated when the places where they are interned or detained become particularly exposed to danger arising out of the armed conflict, if their evacuation can be carried out under adequate conditions of safety;

(d) they shall have the benefit of medical examinations;

(e) their physical or mental health and integrity shall not be endangered by any unjustified act or omission. Accordingly, it is prohibited to subject the persons described in this Article to any medical procedure which is not indicated by the state of health of the person concerned, and which is not consistent with the generally accepted medical standards applied to free persons under similar medical circumstances.

3. Persons who are not covered by paragraph 1 but whose liberty has been restricted in any way whatsoever for reasons related to the armed conflict shall be treated humanely in accordance with Article 4 and with paragraphs 1 (a), (c) and (d), and 2 (b) of this Article.

4. If it is decided to release persons deprived of their liberty, necessary measures to ensure their safety shall be taken by those so deciding.

Art 6. Penal prosecutions

1. This Article applies to the prosecution and punishment of criminal offences related to the armed conflict.

2. No sentence shall be passed and no penalty shall be executed on a person found guilty of an offence except pursuant to a conviction pronounced by a court offering the essential guarantees of independence and impartiality. In particular:

(a) the procedure shall provide for an accused to be informed without delay of the particulars of the offence alleged against him and shall afford the accused before and during his trial all necessary rights and means of defence;

(b) no one shall be convicted of an offence except on the basis of individual penal responsibility;

(c) no one shall be held guilty of any criminal offence on account of any act or omission which did not constitute a criminal offence, under the law, at the time when it was committed; nor shall a heavier penalty be imposed than that which was applicable at the time when the criminal offence was committed; if, after the commission of the offence, provision is made by law for the imposition of a lighter penalty, the offender shall benefit thereby;

(d) anyone charged with an offence is presumed innocent until proved guilty according to law;

(e) anyone charged with an offence shall have the right to be tried in his presence;

(f) no one shall be compelled to testify against himself or to confess guilt.

3. A convicted person shall be advised on conviction of his judicial and other remedies and of the time-limits within which they may be exercised.

4. The death penalty shall not be pronounced on persons who were under the age of eighteen years at the time of the offence and shall not be carried out on pregnant women or mothers of young children.

5. At the end of hostilities, the authorities in power shall endeavour to grant the broadest possible amnesty to persons who have participated in the armed conflict, or those deprived of their liberty for reasons related to the armed conflict, whether they are interned or detained.

Part III. Wounded, Sick and Shipwrecked

Art 7. Protection and care

1. All the wounded, sick and shipwrecked, whether or not they have taken part in the armed conflict, shall be respected and protected.

2. In all circumstances they shall be treated humanely and shall receive to the fullest extent practicable and with the least possible delay, the medical care and attention required by their condition. There shall be no distinction among them founded on any grounds other than medical ones.

Art 8. Search

Whenever circumstances permit and particularly after an engagement, all possible measures shall be taken, without delay, to search for and collect the wounded, sick and shipwrecked, to protect them against pillage and ill-treatment, to ensure their adequate care, and to search for the dead, prevent their being despoiled, and decently dispose of them.

Art 9. Protection of medical and religious personnel

1. Medical and religious personnel shall be respected and protected and shall be granted all available help for the performance of their duties. They shall not be

compelled to carry out tasks which are not compatible with their humanitarian mission.

2. In the performance of their duties medical personnel may not be required to give priority to any person except on medical grounds.

Art 10. General protection of medical duties

1. Under no circumstances shall any person be punished for having carried out medical activities compatible with medical ethics, regardless of the person benefiting therefrom.

2. Persons engaged in medical activities shall neither be compelled to perform acts or to carry out work contrary to, nor be compelled to refrain from acts required by, the rules of medical ethics or other rules designed for the benefit of the wounded and sick, or this Protocol.

3. The professional obligations of persons engaged in medical activities regarding information which they may acquire concerning the wounded and sick under their care shall, subject to national law, be respected.

4. Subject to national law, no person engaged in medical activities may be penalized in any way for refusing or failing to give information concerning the wounded and sick who are, or who have been, under his care.

Art 11. Protection of medical units and transports

1. Medical units and transports shall be respected and protected at all times and shall not be the object of attack.

2. The protection to which medical units and transports are entitled shall not cease unless they are used to commit hostile acts, outside their humanitarian function. Protection may, however, cease only after a warning has been given, setting, whenever appropriate, a reasonable time-limit, and after such warning has remained unheeded.

Art 12. The distinctive emblem

Under the direction of the competent authority concerned, the distinctive emblem of the red cross, red crescent or red lion and sun on a white ground shall be displayed by medical and religious personnel and medical units, and on medical transports. It shall be respected in all circumstances. It shall not be used improperly.

Part IV. Civilian Population

Art 13. Protection of the civilian population

1. The civilian population and individual civilians shall enjoy general protection against the dangers arising from military operations. To give effect to this protection, the following rules shall be observed in all circumstances.

2. The civilian population as such, as well as individual civilians, shall not be the object of attack. Acts or threats of violence the primary purpose of which is to spread terror among the civilian population are prohibited.

3. Civilians shall enjoy the protection afforded by this part, unless and for such time as they take a direct part in hostilities.

Art 14. Protection of objects indispensable to the survival of the civilian population

Starvation of civilians as a method of combat is prohibited. It is therefore prohibited to attack, destroy, remove or render useless for that purpose, objects indispensable to the survival of the civilian population such as food-stuffs, agricultural areas for the production of food-stuffs, crops, livestock, drinking water installations and supplies and irrigation works.

Art 15. Protection of works and installations containing dangerous forces

Works or installations containing dangerous forces, namely dams, dykes and nuclear electrical generating stations, shall not be made the object of attack, even where these objects are military objectives, if such attack may cause the release of dangerous forces and consequent severe losses among the civilian population.

Art 16. Protection of cultural objects and of places of worship

Without prejudice to the provisions of the Hague Convention for the Protection of Cultural Property in the Event of Armed Conflict of 14 May 1954, it is prohibited to commit any acts of hostility directed against historic monuments, works of art or places of worship which constitute the cultural or spiritual heritage of peoples, and to use them in support of the military effort.

Art 17. Prohibition of forced movement of civilians

1. The displacement of the civilian population shall not be ordered for reasons related to the conflict unless the security of the civilians involved or imperative military reasons so demand. Should such displacements have to be carried out, all possible measures shall be taken in order that the civilian population may be received under satisfactory conditions of shelter, hygiene, health, safety and nutrition.

2. Civilians shall not be compelled to leave their own territory for reasons connected with the conflict.

Art 18. Relief societies and relief actions

1. Relief societies located in the territory of the High Contracting Party, such as Red Cross (Red Crescent, Red Lion and Sun) organizations may offer their services for the performance of their traditional functions in relation to the victims of the armed conflict. The civilian population may, even on its own initiative, offer to collect and care for the wounded, sick and shipwrecked.

2. If the civilian population is suffering undue hardship owing to a lack of the supplies essential for its survival, such as food-stuffs and medical supplies, relief actions for the civilian population which are of an exclusively humanitarian and impartial nature and which are conducted without any adverse distinction shall be undertaken subject to the consent of the High Contracting Party concerned.

Part V. Final Provisions

Art 19. Dissemination

This Protocol shall be disseminated as widely as possible.

Art 20. Signature

This Protocol shall be open for signature by the Parties to the Conventions six months after the signing of the Final Act and will remain open for a period of twelve months.

Art 21. Ratification

This Protocol shall be ratified as soon as possible. The instruments of ratification shall be deposited with the Swiss Federal Council, depositary of the Conventions.

Art 22. Accession

This Protocol shall be open for accession by any Party to the Conventions which has not signed it. The instruments of accession shall be deposited with the depositary.

Art 23. Entry into force

1. This Protocol shall enter into force six months after two instruments of ratification or accession have been deposited.

2. For each Party to the Conventions thereafter ratifying or acceding to this Protocol, it shall enter into force six months after the deposit by such Party of its instrument of ratification or accession.

Art 24. Amendment

1. Any High Contracting Party may propose amendments to this Protocol. The text of any proposed amendment shall be communicated to the depositary which shall decide, after consultation with all the High Contracting Parties and the International Committee of the Red Cross, whether a conference should be convened to consider the proposed amendment.

2. The depositary shall invite to that conference all the High Contracting Parties as well as the Parties to the Conventions, whether or not they are signatories of this Protocol.

Art 25. Denunciation

1. In case a High Contracting Party should denounce this Protocol, the denunciation shall only take effect six months after receipt of the instrument of denunciation. If, however, on the expiry of six months, the denouncing Party is engaged in the situation referred to in Article 1, the denunciation shall not take effect before the end of the armed conflict. Persons who have been deprived of liberty, or whose liberty has been restricted, for reasons related to the conflict shall nevertheless continue to benefit from the provisions of this Protocol until their final release.

2. The denunciation shall be notified in writing to the depositary, which shall transmit it to all the High Contracting Parties.

Art 26. Notifications

The depositary shall inform the High Contracting Parties as well as the Parties to the Conventions, whether or not they are signatories of this Protocol, of:
(a) signatures affixed to this Protocol and the deposit of instruments of ratification and accession under Articles 21 and 22;
(b) the date of entry into force of this Protocol under Article 23; and
(c) communications and declarations received under Article 24.

Art 27. Registration

1. After its entry into force, this Protocol shall be transmitted by the depositary to the Secretariat of the United Nations for registration and publication, in accordance with Article 102 of the Charter of the United Nations.
2. The depositary shall also inform the Secretariat of the United Nations of all ratifications, accessions and denunciations received by it with respect to this Protocol.

Art 28. - Authentic texts

The original of this Protocol, of which the Arabic, Chinese, English, French, Russian and Spanish texts are equally authentic shall be deposited with the depositary, which shall transmit certified true copies thereof to all the Parties to the Conventions.